Praise for *A Future without Walls*

"This Christian theologian and ethicist—renowned for his analysis of our criminal justice system and those behind prison walls, and author of *The Protestant Ethic and the Spirit of Punishment*—now has turned his attention to broader issues that impact so many 'others' in US society who are cruelly assigned to social spaces within ever-newly built walls that confine. *A Future without Walls* is an essential contribution to public theology today and needs to be read amid the current crises pertaining to borders, hate, and social division. It is a theoretically astute reflection on the themes of difference and othering. This is not an abstract postmodern praise song to, or theoretical treatise on, 'otherness' and 'alterity.' Rather, it is a very reflective but practical set of exercises looking at the way division and othering are reigning problems in the United States today. Snyder is especially adept at offering an abundance of examples and concrete references, drawn from his own rich experience as activist, churchman, theologian, and ethicist. He has developed a template and mode of analysis that gives this book real staying power, too, in Christian theology and ethics for those grappling with the perennial problems of American public life. *A Future without Walls* is especially pertinent to the present moment."

—**Mark Lewis Taylor**, Maxwell M. Upson Professor of Theology and Culture, Princeton Theological Seminary

"This is a courageous, passionate, and timely book. It challenges the assumptions behind the production of inequalities and the nation-state, and passionately presents the future of humanity without walls."

—**Ali Abdullatif Ahmida**, professor of political science, University of New England

"This is a compelling and far-reaching examination of social divisions and of possibilities for new moral imaginings about life together. It is written with the passion and poignancy of someone who has lived deeply into these issues. Its timely insights will resonate with many and deserve a wide audience."
—**R. Drew Smith**, professor, Pittsburgh Theological Seminary, and coconvener of the Transatlantic Roundtable on Religion and Race

"Responding to today's deeply divided world might seem to require hunkering down into our factions or returning to a simpler way of life. Snyder presents a historically rooted and richly argued alternative: that we need a radical transformation that requires all of us to come up out of ourselves as individuals and embrace relationships, connections, and hope as the only foundation for our future existence. This is a nourishing and restorative read."
—**Katherine Cramer**, Natalie C. Holton Chair of Letters and Science, and professor of political science, University of Wisconsin–Madison, and the author of *The Politics of Resentment: Rural Consciousness in Wisconsin and the Rise of Scott Walker*

"Into a world of asymmetrical, conflicting, and competitive ways of knowing, being, and doing, T. Richard Snyder brings a book that is as unpretentious as it is profound, as inviting as well as challenging. Snyder offers a map and a compass for navigating what he calls 'Othering' an all-embracing metaphor for those tragic human practices throughout history that deploy 'differences as a basis for disrespect, dismissal, and even death.'

This is a book that may well infuriate the constructor of walls, embarrass the complicit, and surprise the arrogant even as it awakens human creativity, imagination, and courage. This is a guide that, rightly understood—particularly from the experience and perspective of those living in the interstices and the intersectionalities of this globalized pandemic called 'Othering'—can help (re)build connections, re(create) human dwelling, (re)learn teaching, and (re)store humility. Read alongside an intentional participation with one's personal, professional, and institutional contextualities, it can empower those who would gracefully and lovingly dare to engage with self, other, and world in their shared transformation.

A Future Without Walls is an important and timely companion for the weary, the questioner, the explorer, the activist, the intellectual, the lover of friendlier tomorrows, and the repairers of our broken world."

—**Lester Edwin J. Ruiz**, director of accreditation and global engagement, The Association of Theological Schools in the US and Canada

"Elegantly written, *A Future Without Walls* surveys the remnants of dysfunctional democracies to encourage collective struggle against phobias, persecution, and violence. For centuries, the impoverished and enslaved stitched fragments together to form quilts for utility and beauty, and in memory of our loves and losses. Snyder writes as a quilter—calling all to mindfulness and accountability in shared labor to bind against the dangers that rip us apart."

—**Joy James**, author of *Seeking the Beloved Community*

A Future without Walls

A FUTURE WITHOUT WALLS
Confronting Our Divisions

T. Richard Snyder

Foreword by George Yancy

FORTRESS PRESS

MINNEAPOLIS

A FUTURE WITHOUT WALLS

Confronting Our Divisions

Print ISBN: 978-1-5064-6603-3
eBook ISBN: 978-1-5064-6604-0

Cover design: Laurie Ingram
Cover image: Broken Wall with graffiti/Germany/Westend61/SuperStock

In memory of Paulo Freire and Toni Morrison

Contents

Acknowledgments

If it takes a village to raise a child, it takes a team to publish a book. *A Future without Walls* would not have been possible without the contributions of many people.

I want to begin by thanking my wife, Cassie, for her ongoing support, encouragement, and painstaking editorial help, without which I doubt this book would have seen the light of day.

The close reading, critical feedback, and encouragement provided by Mark Lewis Taylor, Princeton Seminary's Maxwell M. Upson Professor of Theology and Culture, and Craig McEwen, Daniel B. Fayerweather Professor of Political Economy and Sociology Emeritus at Bowdoin College, helped shape the book.

I am grateful to George Yancy, the Samuel Candler Dobbs Professor of Philosophy at Emory University and a leading voice in the African American community, for writing the foreword. His lifelong commitment in the struggle against racism confirms both his authority and perspective to judge the importance of the book in helping to tear down the walls that separate us.

Patti Marxsen, a good friend, literary critic, researcher, and author of many books, including a biography of Jacques Romaine of Haiti, offered valuable feedback throughout the process.

The significant amount of research undergirding the work was made possible by the Princeton Theological Seminary Library, which provided unlimited access to JSTOR and other online resources; the Bowdoin College Library; and the Camden and Top-sham public libraries, which made it possible to access many important books. Special thanks to Carmen Mattei Greenlee and Karen Jun of Bowdoin College Library, who provided guidance formatting notes and bibliography.

Thanks also to the many students who provided feedback for some of the ideas formulated in the book and to the numerous congregations who welcomed my biblical interpretations in sermons.

Last but not least, I owe special gratitude to Neil Elliott, senior acquisitions editor of Lexington Books; Scott Tunseth, senior acquisitions editor at Fortress Press; Eleanor Beach, developmental editor and retired professor of Religion at Monmouth College, IL; Savannah Frierson, copyeditor; and Marissa Wold Uhrina, project editor, for their steady and timely guidance in bringing the work to fruition. Working with Fortress Press has been stimulating and thoroughly gratifying.

Foreword

Some books are written before their time, when the insights they contain go unappreciated until after a prolonged period of historical gestation. Other books are capable of bringing us face to face with ourselves, freeing us from unjustifiable innocence, refusing to let us placate fictions, and encouraging us to "talk back," as bell hooks would say, to hegemonic powers that are designed to dehumanize, oppress, and subjugate. For hooks, talking back is an act of refusal, a renunciation of silence; it is an act of agency, of laying claim to one's position in the world as a subject, not as an object. Richard Snyder's insightfully probing and truth-telling book—*A Future without Walls*—dares to speak in the moment, to talk back with courage and commitment.

Snyder is unafraid to communicate the social and political gravity of our contemporary moment, unafraid to trace its brokenness and imperfections. Yet, this book provides a social, ontologically robust, relational vision that is designed to motivate and sustain us as we address the question of whether or not the walls, the divisions, and the masks we construct can indeed come tumbling down.

The politically provocative and daring title of Snyder's book speaks to the importance of James Baldwin's ethical fortitude and wisdom in the face of social and political roadblocks, towers of self-deception, and altars of perfunctory practices and mummified beliefs that divide us and create monsters.[1] This title places before us a deep challenge; it forces us to face ourselves and to confront a world we have pushed to the precipice of a possible global catastrophe. The book compels us to realize that none of our hands are clean; we are all complicit in the pain and suffering of someone else, of even the earth itself. Rabbi Abraham Joshua Heschel was keen to remind us that while some are guilty, all are responsible.[2] So, we must all participate in the tumbling down of injustice, racism, classism, homophobia, transphobia, nativism, anti-Semitism, ageism, xenophobia, ableism, and so many more forms of acrimonious divisiveness that result in horrible acts of Othering. The complex and multitudinous processes of Othering, and the problematic forces and practices that are responsible for such Othering, form the *descriptive* and urgent core of this important book. And, yet, Snyder provides us with a powerful vision that is undergirded by an indefatigable hope.

The concept of a tearing down of walls is absolutely necessary as we face, in our contemporary moment, the rise of unabashed white supremacy, the horrors of femicide, and the global geopolitical balkanization of the world according to myths of "purity" and "impurity." This is the painful reality Snyder refuses to avoid. In the spirit of Baldwin, he knows any real change must involve the breakup of the world as one has known it, which is another form of tumbling. This is the loss of all that gave one an identity, especially where that identity is predicated upon mythopoetic assumptions regarding "superiority" and "inferiority," and the end of safety, which means one is required to face the unknown and dream dreams of what is possible, of what is not-yet, to risk failure.

When it comes to facing the reality of our deeply disturbing and discordant contemporary moment, Snyder writes:

> It is clear we are living in a world that is divided. The historic divisions of race, gender, and class continue unabated. But these are not the only divisions. We are awash in nationalism, ageism, homophobia, religious divisions, and tribal politics that cast those considered opponents as evil. Violence has been unleashed at all levels—from grade schools to

nations. Bullying, incarceration, torture, terrorism, rape, and war evidence our ability to treat people as Other.

In his capacity as a truth-teller, Snyder refuses to overlook—and dares to name—the many human beings who have been targeted in the form of violent Othering. Pulling from the weight of history, he reminds us that in the Middle Ages, those labeled "heretics" were marginalized and even killed. He also cites how "Jews and Muslims were viewed as infidels and hence punishable by death," and how "Europeans viewed Indians as uncivilized savages." In essence, Snyder provides us with a panoply of historical and contemporary examples of groups who have suffered the social, political, and phenomenological impact of being Othered—Black people, Jews, Dalit, Roma, undocumented persons, Muslims, women, the rural poor, those who identify as queer, the political left versus the political right, prisoners, the elderly, the disabled, Latinxs, and Native Americans. Yet, he offers a broader framework that reveals family resemblances among forms of Othering. Indeed, his project is to provide:

> A comprehensive and complex analysis of Othering that unveils the interrelatedness of all our divisions and their violent consequences. By dealing with Othering in the aggregate rather than focusing on a single group, we are made aware of both the all-encompassing systemic nature of oppression and what [Snyder calls] the interwoven fabric of Othering.

The richness of Snyder's historical analysis arises from not conflating the various ways in which groups have been Othered. That is, he neither flattens the specific dynamics of their respective forms of being Othered nor does he paint with the same brush the phenomenological ways in which each group experienced the process of being Othered. Yet, there is a dialectical truth that frames Snyder's rich account of Othering. Indeed, existentialist philosopher Simone de Beauvoir captures the core dialectic of Othering when she argues no group or individual that constitutes itself as what she calls "the One" without simultaneously installing "the Other."[3] On this score, as Snyder argues, "The Roma were considered outside the norm of what it meant to be an ethnic and nationalistic Pole." In other words, the Roma were deemed "deviant" vis-à-vis a collective Polish identity marked as "the One." Personally, on my trips to Oslo and France, I have seen this continual reality of marking the Roma, so-called "Gypsies." For example, within this Beauvoirian framework, Black people are Othered as racially "bestial" and "inferior" vis-à-vis white people marked as "the One." In each case, "the One" is deemed "superior," "normal," "pure," "civilized." What is important to note, though, is despite who is the target of the Othering, "the consequence," as Snyder writes, "is inevitably violent," whether intentional or unintentional.

Snyder importantly complicates the ways in which those who are deemed "the One" can also be defined as the Other, depending upon which differentially valued markers are stressed regarding the same person. Hence, *poor* white people are constituted as Other vis-à-vis *wealthy* white people. Of course, this does not mean that poor white people and poor Black people, despite their shared political interests and economic status, suffer the same social ontological standing within a white supremacist structure that constitutes whiteness as "the One." Snyder makes this point clear where he talks about poor Black people suffering "the additional burden of racism."

Snyder not only provides us with a rich and complex set of examples of those who have been egregiously targeted as Other, but he also provides a critically engaging and insightful delineation of both blatant and insidious ways in which human beings have been Othered. Anyone committed to challenging and undoing the deep psychological and material mechanisms deployed in the process of violently Othering human beings, and grasping, though painfully, the magnitude of human violence, will find this section ethically, historically, and theoretically crucial as it lays bare various processes of dehumanization. Snyder argues it is important "to be alert to the ways in which Othering occurs [because of] the malleability of its forms. Just when one form of Othering has been denounced as unethical or socially unacceptable, it can reappear in a different form." Snyder's argument is very important as North America moves between the Scylla of actual and potential horrors of a hyper-white nationalism, and the Charybdis of an empty rhetoric of a post-racial utopia. Hence, in these examples Snyder provides—demonization, animalization, numbering, profiling, instrumentalization, ostracism, ethnic cleansing, militarization, and even within the context of comedy (think here of "Blackface")—what becomes clear is we have found toxic ways of ontologically truncating and violating human beings through procrustean gazes, brutal institutional and material forms of usurpation, and discursive violence.

What also makes Snyder's approach to the political, historical, and philosophical theme of Othering so politically rewarding is his courageous engagement in self-critique and self-disclosure—not pitiable self-confession or self-flagellation—which can function as the rub of so many white confessionals. Snyder shares that his father was a member of the Ku Klux Klan. Snyder also shares how he wore his father's hood and robe during Halloween and how his white neighbors found it humorous. Think here of the function of white-willed ignorance, of how white people construct a world they come to see as normative and safe, how they distort the realities and symbols of white supremacy and white bloodlust into harmless play and amusement. Then again, as evidenced by the numerous photos taken, the flaying and burning of the Black body was a white pastime. Snyder also reflects on how all of his friends were white, which demonstrates the vicious reality and legacy of Jim Crow segregation. In short, through critical autobiographical reflection, Snyder reveals what was and is at stake *for him* as he continues to challenge the racist walls within. This section of the book is especially necessary for white people who have not even begun to reflect on their conscious and unconscious racism, and how they are systemically privileged as white. I see Snyder's autobiographical disclosures as forms of demasking, and therefore as forms of love. It was Baldwin who said, "Love takes off the masks that we fear we cannot live without."[4] Snyder is not imprisoned by such masks, such fear. For this reason, inter alia, I see Snyder as an important coworker for justice, one who is profoundly committed to undoing barriers that separate, walls that divide, forms of what I call *suturing* that avoid vulnerability and the recognition of our intimately braided existence.

A Future without Walls is filled with lament, the sort of affective strength that bears witness to human suffering that allows, as Cornel West would say, human suffering to speak and also refuses to allow despair to have the last word.[5] What becomes clear in Snyder's remarkable journey, whether at the Union Church in Rio de Janeiro, studying theologies of liberation, or while teaching at Sing Sing Correctional Facility, is the fact he underwent an important and necessary epistemic rupture, an un-suturing, a form of kenosis (or emptying) as he became enmeshed within the "view from below," from that space where so many human beings are rendered silent, marginal, and nugatory. To learn from those voices from below, it is important to listen with courage, to place in abeyance one's limited understanding. It is within such a context that growth is possible, where one comes face to face not with an "I–it," but with an "I–thou."[6] And while some of the walls did tumble as Snyder underwent what I would call a damascene moment, which created an opening to reach across artificial divides, he continues to understand the complex work ahead. Reaching across divides, as he writes, "must be accompanied by a dismantling of the systems of oppression." Hence, the elimination of prejudices, fear, hatred, stereotypical images, and racial profiles is only one part of the human liberation project; we must also, according to Snyder, eliminate those structural, systemic, and hierarchical social positionalities that implicate us in each other's lives in ways that perpetuate pain, suffering, and injustice.

From a position of our mutual implication, our ontologically interconnected lives, Snyder envisions a deep and interpersonally committed way to address the divisions that we have created. His position—one that counters a neoliberal, atomic ontology of the self—proposes that we are always already woven into the lives of others, already touching or haptic. Snyder pulls from various conceptual resources to support this view. From the philosophy of Ubuntu, he understands our humanity as interwoven. He holds that each of us can only be what and who we are through the preexisting conditions of a larger humanity. Hence, he adopts the philosophy of "I am because we are." Similarly, Martin Luther King Jr. maintained all of us are caught in a profound and inextricable network of mutuality.[7] Snyder writes, "What makes us human is not our independence from one another but rather our interdependence. It is our connectedness to others that defines our humanity; it is a connectedness that is much deeper than simply treating others fairly—it is a sense of being essentially part of one another."

When juxtaposed to the sheer brutality that we have faced (and continue to face) as a species because our idols separate us, which can result in vicious Othering, Snyder's interconnected ontology—what I term an ontology of no edges and an ethics of no edges—speaks directly to the crisis of our moment. We have forgotten who and how we are to each other. Richard Snyder's indispensable book demands we rejoice in our shared humanity and that we embrace *aletheia*, which means truth in the form of unforgetting. Indeed, Snyder passionately encourages us to remember, to recognize the human seam that holds us together. I would agree. And I think it is then, with greater confidence, we can say with Snyder, "the walls can come tumbling down."

George Yancy, Samuel Candler Dobbs Professor of Philosophy at Emory University

Preface

This book is in the final stages of publication during one of the worst pandemics of modern times. I would be remiss to ignore the tragic reality facing our world. There are several lessons I draw from the onslaught of COVID-19. The first is that while we are being told to "socially isolate," that is perhaps a misdirected message. While we should "physically isolate," of course, we need one another socially more than ever; we need to recognize our connectedness. None of us can live without others. If ever there were a time when we recognize that we are all in this together, that we are all one, that there is no respecter of persons—this is the time. And therein lies a lesson for all times. Despite our differences, we are one, and anything that seeks to divide us is wrong. The stories of people reaching out to others, both virtually and literally, are cause for hope. The communal singing and banging of pots remind me of the psalmist who urged us to "make a joyful noise to the Lord." It is our choice.

The second lesson for me is that while this pandemic is horrible, we should not dismiss the "pandemics" of racism, homophobia, anti-Semitism, religious oppression, classism, and other forms of Othering that have traumatized, sickened, and taken the lives of so many who are considered disposable. These injustices have deformed and destroyed both body and soul.

I invite the reader to explore with me the divisions of our world and to commit to confronting them as dramatically as we have responded to the virus that now threatens us. We must erase all that is destroying us. We must tear down the walls of separation. This is the task of our time.

Introduction

We have a problem . . . a tragedy of enormous proportion. Despite our prayers and marches, our preaching and lobbying, our voting and writing, our boycotts and civil disobedience, it seems that things have not changed very much. . . . Despite all our efforts . . . the world remains mired in death.[1]   *Richard Snyder*

1990s

I wrote those words almost thirty years ago, hoping to unite people for justice. Racism, sexism, and classism were widespread, but many of the privileged had become complacent as they enjoyed a historically long peacetime economy. Denominations were increasingly turning inward, fixated on reorganizing. Many of the gains in the struggle for justice were being challenged and coming unraveled. The Crown Heights riot of 1991 in Brooklyn pitted black people against Orthodox Jews. Also in 1991, Rodney King was brutally beaten by Los Angeles police and the video became well known. When the officers were acquitted in 1992, South Central Los Angeles erupted in violent protest. The glass ceiling for women remained largely intact. The Boy Scouts of America dismissed a gay scout leader on the grounds that homosexuality was immoral. The nation was coming apart and the unrest of the oppressed was undeniable.

But, things are even worse now. Working together for the common good has given way to unfeigned distrust and hatred. Nativism and nationalism are ascendant. The worldwide flood of people seeking refuge from violence tests Western democracies. The way ahead seems far more complex and intractable than it was then. More than ever, I am convinced if the walls of division are to be torn down, everyone who cares about justice must take up the mantle of resistance and healing.

We are living in perilous times. The divisions in our world run so deep, are so pervasive and destructive, that it is impossible not to take sides. Either we are for the oppressed or, consciously or unconsciously, for the oppressor. Those of us whose feet are planted in both the world of privilege and the world of resistance are caught in the contradictions. But that cannot be an excuse for inaction.

It is clear we are living in a divided world. The historic divisions of race, gender, and class continue unabated. But these are not the only divisions. We are awash in nationalism, ageism, homophobia, religious divisions, and tribal politics that cast those considered opponents as evil. Violence has been unleashed at all levels, from grade schools to nations. Bullying, incarceration, torture, terrorism, rape, and war evidence our ability to treat people as Other.

There were no divisions in the beginning, or so it's said. Life was harmonious and peaceful according to the Genesis 2 account of Adam and Eve in the garden, in John Milton's epic *Paradise Lost*, Ovid's Golden Age, the myth of Shangri-La, and the novels of Jacques Poulin. Richard Heinberg's cross-cultural study of various paradise myths confirms a universal portrayal of humans living in harmony with nature and each other, depicting the original state of humanity as a time of concord.[2] The persistence of the paradise myth is testimony to the human dream of a peaceful world. Unfortunately, it is in stark contrast to the reality of then and now.

People who are different are often treated as Other. Gay, lesbian, and transgender persons are routinely bullied and abused. Black people, Latinx people, and other people of color are disproportionately arrested, convicted, and imprisoned. Persons with mental or physical limitations are often avoided. Muslims are increasingly looked upon suspiciously as terrorists if they are dark skinned or dressed in traditional garb. Drug addicts are sent to jails and prisons because they are thought to be guilty of a moral failure rather than suffering from disease. We avert our gazes from the homeless and the destitute. Trump supporters are presumed to be racists. College-educated people are written off as elitist do-gooders. Tattooed and unusually pierced persons are often considered deviants. Women are viewed as sexual objects. The rural poor who live in trailers are deemed "ignorant." Persons who speak broken English are considered second class. To be different from the dominant culture (which, in the US, is white, straight, male, healthy, and financially comfortable) is to risk being misunderstood, rejected, or mistreated—to be treated as Other.

> The problem of the twenty-first century is the problem of "othering." In a world beset by seemingly intractable and overwhelming challenges, virtually every global, national, and regional conflict is wrapped within or organized around one or more dimension of group-based difference. Othering undergirds territorial disputes, sectarian violence, military conflict, the spread of disease, hunger and food insecurity, and even climate change.[3]

I use the terms *Other* or *Othering* to designate the full range of treating persons as "those people"; from denigration to extermination, from casting them as inferior to considering them inhuman beasts. Once we categorize someone as Other, it is possible to ignore them, treat them as instruments, discriminate against them, abuse them, or, in the most hideous circumstances, massacre them. To Other someone is to view them as a different order of being, and in some cases, such as the Holocaust, as not even human. The distinctions are viewed as so essential that they create an unbridgeable gap between oneself and the Other. In every case, there is a dividing wall of hostility, and the result is physical or psychological violence.

It is possible differences among us can be respected, valued, and celebrated. This is not Othering. We all have biases and prejudices, and many of them are harmless. My predilection for certain foods and colors based on my taste and memories does not harm anyone. Many of our differing tastes can be accounted for by our upbringing or by pleasant or unpleasant memory associations. We simply differ. However, a bias in favor of a certain clothing label can sometimes harm. If that manufacturer is exploiting its workers, then I am participating in the exploitation, no matter how indirectly. Some prejudices treat other persons and groups in ways that Other, and I am using the term *Othering* to refer to differences as a basis for disrespect, dismissal, and even death.

This is not a new phenomenon. It has occurred in various cultures throughout history and remains alive today. These divisions are not simply a problem to be solved. They are the fabric of Othering, the warp and woof of our culture, and they demand fundamental transformation.

How can one address the phenomenon of Othering that is embedded in both the social structures of oppression and in each of our personal responses? It is impossible to separate the personal from the political, the systemic from beliefs, attitudes, and values. While recognizing the structural roots of Othering, I want to examine closely how those of us who live in the interstices can respond to a culture that is essentially divided between "us and them."

This book is an attempt to understand some of the ways in which Othering functions: its roots, its forms, and its consequences. In response, we are compelled by a vision of a new possibility that offers paths to address this tragedy.

Many important books have been written about our current divisions or the systemic nature of oppression. They largely focus on how a specific difference—such as race, gender, class, religion, nationality, or migrant status, among others—can be used to denigrate, dismiss, and even exterminate people. In contrast, this book offers a comprehensive and complex analysis of Othering that unveils the interrelatedness of all our divisions and their violent consequences. By dealing with Othering in the aggregate rather than focusing on a single group, we are made aware of both the all-encompassing systemic nature of oppression and of what I call the interwoven fabric of Othering. I am convinced the only way forward is to find ways to overcome the historic divisions of race, class, gender, sexual identity, religion, and nationality, as well as the increasing division between Left and Right in our nation today.

The political manifestations of Othering are especially obvious. Yale University sociology professor Jeffrey Alexander has examined civil society, noting the difference between the "discourses of liberty and repression."[4] His conclusion underscores the pervasiveness of Othering even in democratic societies, making it clear how easy it is for large groups of people to get caught up in negative codes and behavior regardless of the society. He notes the numerous groups in United States history that have been objects of these negative codes, including black people, Asians, and native peoples. "Once this polluting discourse [of repression] is applied," he claims, "it becomes impossible for good people to treat and reason with those on the other side. If one's opponents are beyond reason, deceived by leaders who operate in secret, the only option is to read them out of the human race."[5]

One of the most discouraging developments in the United States is the widening division between Left and Right. People who should be standing together to fight the oppressive powers of alienation are increasingly suspicious of each other and are often at each other's throats. The September 11, 2017, issue of *USA Today* published an article recounting the nation's harmony immediately following the tragedy of September 11, 2001, contrasting it with "the great divide" today.[6] This allows the systems and structures of injustice to remain in place.

For seven years, Katherine J. Cramer, a political science professor at the University of Wisconsin, conducted hundreds of interviews with people from rural areas of the state to understand how people make sense of politics, especially when they seem to be voting against their own self-interest. In her fascinating book, *The Politics of Resentment*, she reveals how people who voted for Scott Walker for governor in 2010 were motivated by identity, not by ideology, seeing themselves as people who had been bypassed by government for the benefit of city folk. One of the consequences of Walker's election was the rise in open animosity and even unwillingness for people on different sides of the issues to talk to one another. She concluded, "In a politics of resentment, we treat differences in our political points of view as fundamental differences in who we are as human beings."[7]

Eight months before the 2016 election of Donald Trump and even before his primary win, *Wall Street Journal* columnist Peggy Noonan predicted his victory based on the fundamental division in our society between the protected and the unprotected. The protected are those in power who make policies from which they benefit. The unprotected don't count. They consider themselves to be forgotten, their lives on a downward trajectory. The remarkable thing about this moment in history is the unprotected are no longer willing to accept their lot in life. "It is the rise of people who don't have all that much against those who've been given many blessings and seem to believe they have them not because they are fortunate but because they're better."[8]

The rise of the Alt Right movement has sometimes led to violent confrontations between the supporters and resisters of President Trump, his policies, and appointments. Gavin McInnes, the leader of Proud Boys, has called for white people to stand up and counter the Left whom he considers violent. "The Right isn't violent. The Left is. By allowing these sociopaths to shut down free speech with violence, you are all but demanding a war. Okay, fine, you got it. It's official. This is a war."[9]

It is not just the Right. Dismissive comments by liberals about those who voted for Trump are also commonplace. Trump voters are considered ignorant, racist, and deluded. In some cases, they have been mockingly portrayed as living on another planet—certainly not one of us. Such categorizing not only creates a barrier, it can fuel abuse and violence. On June 15, 2017, a follower and volunteer for Bernie Sanders shot and wounded four Republican congressmen who were practicing for a baseball game. One of them, Representative Steve Scalise, was seriously injured and placed on the critical list.[10]

The divide in our nation seems to be widening: rural versus

urban, white versus people of color, citizens versus undocumented persons and refugees, Republicans versus Democrats, straight versus LGBTQ+, Christians versus Muslims, and rich versus poor. Whether the divisions and hostilities are worse than at other times, we now face a serious threat to our commonweal. The soul of our nation and each of our own are at stake.

I have seen firsthand both sides of many of these divisions. For a good deal of my early life, I was exposed to others whom I viewed as different, inferior, or not worth my attention. My socialization into Othering was rooted in the larger system of racial oppression, as well as the culture of family, community, and church in which I grew up. Raised in a comfortable suburb of Philadelphia during the forties and fifties, I experienced both subtle and overt divisions. *His father* There were walls. My father was an equal-opportunity bigot. He routinely disparaged black people, women, Jews, Roman Catholics, Poles, Latinx, Asians, Italians, and gay men. Although he made exceptions for some individuals whom he knew personally, he viewed others stereotypically. He considered them inferior, and they were fodder for his humor and vitriol. For a brief time in his early twenties, he was a member of the Ku Klux Klan in our predominantly white, northern suburb.

I've often wondered why he, a working-class white man, considered himself superior to so many others. Was it psychological compensation because his father and stepmother rejected him and shipped him off to his grandmother's care when he was a child? Was it because he felt humiliated when he was forced to wear his sister's lace-up boots to elementary school since his grandmother couldn't afford to buy him "boys'" shoes? Or was it because he felt demeaned and rejected when his mother threw him pennies from the upstairs window of her apartment in the city, rather than spend time with him when he visited her?

He was deeply affected by the Great Depression. He worked for a brief time for the Reading Railroad, but when the Depression came, he opted for the security of a job with the US Postal Service. For the next thirty-three years, he worked at a job he considered beneath him while being managed by persons he considered inferior. To compound his sense of inferiority, the post office watched the employees' every move, including in the bathroom, using an observation walkway with two-way mirrors. He was filled with rage. While I will never know all the reasons why he felt the need to treat some people as Other, I conjecture both his childhood and a working life of humiliation contributed to his need to disparage and demean persons different from himself.

As a high school freshman, I dug out my father's old Ku Klux Klan hood and robe from the attic to wear for Halloween. With no appreciation of the horrendous history symbolized by the robe, I went trick or treating through the streets of our neighborhood. Most people who greeted me at their door found it humorous and didn't suggest it was inappropriate. A few years later, my mother destroyed the robe.

The fundamentalist church I attended from age twelve until my early twenties reinforced the sense that the world was divided by impenetrable walls. Roman Catholics were viewed as a threat to our nation and representatives of the antichrist. Jews were considered to have been bypassed by God because of their rejection of Jesus as the Messiah. Gay and lesbian persons were deemed sexual deviants who, with the right help, could be restored to "normality" if they were "born again." And Communists were seen as the "godless" enemy of western civilization. At the height of the McCarthy hearings, it was difficult to distinguish between the haranguing of the senator and many fundamentalist preachers who visited our church and stayed in our home. In that theology, people were divided into the saved and the lost. Women were second-class worshippers in our thriving church that was dominated by male leadership. And black people were invisible. I bought the whole story.

There were also walls between the white community and the black community. I attended public schools and played sports with both black people and white people. But mixing on the field or track was the limit of our interaction. We lived separate lives. All my friends were white, and I knew nothing about the lives of the black students who were in my classes or with whom I played sports. There was an invisible wall that separated our relationships and our neighborhoods. While our township was relatively well-to-do with homes for white people ranging from comfortable middle-class dwellings to mansions, there was no such range for the black community. Most black people lived in only two neighborhoods, and their homes were notably smaller, less well built, and closer together. The only dirt roads in our township were in the two black communities, and white people seldom, if ever, drove on those roads. Nor was there much interaction between the black and white communities except when hiring menial labor. We lived separate and unequal lives. Black people were Other.

The media, especially movies and TV, also played a major role in fostering the idea there were others of whom we need to be wary. The visual images in the World War II propaganda movies regularly portrayed the Japanese as vicious animals that were out to destroy everything our nation stood for. "Dirty Japs" routinely came from my lips when playing war games with other children. They were Other. And on Saturday mornings, I saw movies depicting cowboys and Indians in superior/inferior roles. The Indians were blood-thirsty savages who cut off the scalps of innocent settlers, and the cowboys wore white hats and rescued those in peril. It did not take long for me to get the message that the Indians were Other who needed to be controlled or eliminated if civilized society was to survive.

Despite being a college graduate with a philosophy major and two years of graduate theological study at Princeton Theological Seminary, I was oblivious to the plight of the poor and the forgotten. My life was comfortable and on a promising trajectory. Like many of my fellow classmates, I was being groomed to pastor a large, white, "steeple" church. I had joined the predominately wealthy, white Presbyterian church in Princeton rather than the smaller predominately black Presbyterian church. I was on the way.

My myopia was shattered when I served as an intern at the English-speaking Union Church in Rio de Janeiro after my second year at seminary. My eyes opened to the people in the favelas of Rio while serving as the assistant minister at the Union Church in Rio de Janeiro. As a perk of my internship, I lived in the luxurious homes and apartments of expatriates who were vacationing, allowing me to enjoy the lavish benefits of servants, swimming pools, and the beach. For five months, I lived in an apartment overlooking Copacabana Beach with a view of the swimming pool and patio of the Copacabana Palace Hotel. The Brazilian president's apartment was directly above. Servants prepared meals and cleaned. Later, I lived in a four-story home cut into the hillside overlooking Ipanema and Leblon beaches and the ocean, complete with its own swimming pool, servants, and chauffeur. But despite the distractions of borrowed wealth, it was impossible to avoid noticing the squalid conditions of people living in the favelas just a few blocks away, in shacks made of tin, cardboard, and wood that lacked running water or sewage facilities.

At first, the favelados (the favela dwellers) were simply an unwelcome presence marring my enjoyment of the incredible beauty of the beaches and the good life that was available to a foreigner living in opulence. In time, however, their presence began to encroach on "my world." An occasional theft, a news report of a murder in a favela, the warnings of friends and acquaintances to be on my guard, and the gated homes and guards at the finer apartment buildings began to paint a picture difficult to ignore.

My awareness changed while dining in the home of a wealthy American expatriate who was an officer of a major US corporation and leader in the church. We were served an exquisite meal prepared by a chef from Bahia, the heartland of Brazilian cuisine. Finishing with French cognac and a Cuban cigar, the conversation turned to the extreme famine in northeastern Brazil. Earlier that week, I had read in the local English-language paper about agrarian reform as a possible resolution to the famine. While I was totally ignorant about agrarian reform, it seemed reasonable that someone with thousands of acres might grant two or three acres to each worker. When I innocently inquired about its possibility as a preventive step in eliminating famine, my host went into a tirade supporting laissez-faire capitalism. When he finished, I asked what he thought should be done for the poor who were starving. He replied coldly, "Let them die." Something inside me changed forever.

That was the beginning of my journey to pay attention to people I had previously ignored. I did my best to learn about the favelados, and I began spending time walking their dirt streets. While my exploration was quite limited and naïve, the exposure to the extreme poverty of the favelas had a profound impact. When I returned to the United States, I saw with new eyes the plight of black Americans, Latinx Americans, gay and lesbian people, innocent women and children in Vietnam, the homeless in our cities, and the physically and mentally disabled. Suddenly, "those people" were everywhere, and the systems that kept them marginalized and oppressed became increasingly evident.

It is impossible for a person of privilege to walk in the shoes of those whose lives are so different. But it was a beginning that led me to become involved in the struggle for racial justice. A few years later, I returned to Princeton Theological Seminary for my PhD studies, with a focus on liberation theology that provided the opportunity to explore ideas I had previously ignored.

When I was called to teach and serve as dean at New York Theological Seminary seven years later, I was thrust into a community that was about 50 percent black, 20 percent Latinx, 20 percent white, and 10 percent Asian. The contrast with my myopically white days at Wheaton College and Princeton Seminary couldn't have been greater.

Suddenly, I was face to face with students, faculty, and staff who represented those I had once considered Other. I thought I had a handle on things—after all, since returning from Brazil I had been marching for civil rights and against the Vietnam War, supporting these issues at the church where I served for several years as assistant minister. I had also organized the Religion and Race office of the local Presbytery and served as its first director. I thought I was ready.

But the air was let out of my balloon one night when I was invited to speak at a black church in Harlem about how the seminaries were engaging white people, black people, Latinx people, and Asians in the struggle for justice. When I finished, an elderly black woman said to me, "Dr. Snyder, you are Madison Avenue slick." My white privilege stuck out like a sore thumb. I remember saying to her, "Wow! I'm trying so hard, please help me." And she did, and so did many students, colleagues, pastors, and community workers.

A critical part of my journey was my introduction to various theologies of liberation that grew out of the experiences of oppression. Latin American theology, black theology, feminist theology, Hispanic theology, Minjung theology (Korean), and Dalit theology (Indian "untouchables") revealed new ways of understanding a tradition I had assumed was owned by white Western males. I came to understand the power of "the view from below" from communities that had been silenced, made invisible, exploited, and considered expendable.

Then, in 1984, I entered a world that had been totally off my radar screen. New York Theological Seminary began a master's program at Sing Sing Correctional Facility where I taught ethics to a class of fourteen long-term prisoners who had obtained undergraduate degrees either before or during their time in prison.

I was frightened. To me, they were Other, and the punitive structure of prison was an alien world. The long walk through the corridors of Sing Sing, where gates slammed shut behind me and razor wire was visible through the barred windows, was a stark contrast to my own freedom. The men had been convicted of heinous crimes and hardened by long prison sentences. They wore prison garb and were identified by assigned numbers, and I was dressed in preppie clothes and called "Doctor." We were different. All but one of the student inmates was black or Latinx. My whiteness, my privilege of being able to leave at the end of the day, and my power as a professor became conspicuously evident. A corrections officer asked why I was wasting my time on these "no-goods."

As we studied and talked together, it became increasingly clear the men were neither ignorant nor unfeeling, nor were they the same persons who had entered prison as many as thirty years before. They were eager to learn, ready to grow, and passionate about justice. It wasn't always easy. Sometimes, their anger would burst forth and heated disagreements would ensue. This was both exciting and exhausting. But to many of the corrections officers and citizens outside the walls, the prisoners were demonic, unredeemable trash to be removed from civilized society, and the system of justice that controlled them was considered by most to be a response to their behaviors rather than a fundamental cornerstone of an oppressive system.

With the rise of the Tea Party and the election of Donald Trump, I have had many of the same feelings toward those with whom I so fundamentally disagree as I had in the past toward those I considered Other. It has led me to ponder how to view and treat people, those with whom I differ and often oppose, as fully human, while at the same time honoring my deepest values and goals. The journey continues, but it is not easy.

All of these experiences and many others have prompted me to ask: Why are we so divided? Why do we treat others as inhuman, as trash, as expendable? I have concluded that the struggle for justice and healing is complex, involving both resistance to the social structures that create Others and finding ways to understand and ally with those who have been made Other. While a major concern in this book is to find ways to reach across the divisions, it will be apparent that this must be accompanied by a dismantling of the systems of oppression. I believe the walls can come tumbling down.

1

The Dividing Walls of Hostility

Those who cannot remember the past are condemned to repeat it.
—George Santayana, *Reason in Common Sense*

The debate over a border wall between the United States and Mexico has exposed the walls that separate us from each other, and our nation from other nations. The treatment of people as Other is not a recent phenomenon. My focus in this chapter is on the walls of hostility that have been built in recent times. It is not intended to be a complete history but rather a series of examples, primarily focusing on the United States. But in order to understand the extent and depth of the problem, it is important to consider a few pre-twentieth-century examples that have influenced the shape of our nation today.

In the remarkable Code of Hammurabi, written in ancient Babylon about 1754 BCE, nobles, commoners, and slaves received different punishments for the same crime. While the Code clearly states its intent to protect the weak from the strong, there are, nonetheless, obvious distinctions based on rank that reveal Othering. The laws of the Hebrew Bible do not make such class distinctions and exhibit an egalitarianism embodied in the admonition to love your neighbor as yourself.[1] However, prophetic oracles demonstrate how often the Torah ideal of egalitarianism was undermined by practices of unequal and abusive power.[2] *Amos 4:1-3*

Moreover, the notion of neighbor was often limited to the people of Israel, and there are numerous passages in which they are commanded to annihilate their enemy. The story of Joshua and the walls of Jericho includes the demand to destroy all that is inside the city except for the silver, gold, bronze, and iron, a ritual practice known as the ban.[3] The narrative tells us all the people and animals were slain except Rahab the harlot and her family who had assisted the Israelite spies. The biblical accounts do not leave such episodes unquestioned. In a humbling mirror image, the Babylonians breach the walls of Jerusalem and take its inhabitants into exile, also by God's intention, to chastise those who once considered themselves the victors.[4]

Remnants of biblical Othering remain in New Testament passages about both Canaanites and Samaritans. The Gospel of Matthew recounts how Jesus first ignored a Canaanite woman's request to heal her daughter, then rebuffed her by saying that he was sent only to the "lost sheep of the house of Israel."[5] Comparing her to a dog, his response indicates a rejection rooted in the deeply ingrained cultural legacy that created a wall between Jews and Canaanites. However, her persistence and faith eventually allowed him to see her as a person in need, overcoming the barrier. A similar response on his part was toward the Samaritans, who shared almost the same scriptures as Jews but worshipped at a sanctuary north of Jerusalem. He is reported to have told his disciples to "enter no town of the Samaritans but go rather to the lost sheep of the house of Israel."[6] But that wall was overcome when he engaged in conversation with a Samaritan woman at the well and when he used the Samaritan as an example of a good neighbor.[7]

The stories of underdog Israelites overcoming Canaanite kings and taking possession of territories have generated parallel narratives beyond the biblical model, as we shall see. One of the interesting questions this raises is, who are the underdogs and who are oppressors? Clearly, Israel later used these narratives to support their role as victims seeking justice and a right to exist. But are the victims to be victims forever? As the history of ancient and contemporary Israel attests, there are times when the oppressed becomes the oppressor. It is always a question of power.

Western cultures have held up Greeks as the originators of democracy. But Greeks drew a stark distinction between themselves and those whom they called barbarians, non-Greek-speaking foreigners. Barbarians were Other. But women were too. Classics professor Page duBois notes the Greek citizen was defined as "Not animal, not barbarian, not female."[8] The reference to women and barbarians in the same category as animals is telling. Clearly, despite some elements of democracy, deep divisions existed; polarity was at the heart of Greek citizenship. Not everyone was included.

In the early Christian era, the Romans accepted Jews as followers of an established religion and allowed Christians to live under the umbrella of Judaism. That changed, however, as Christianity increasingly distinguished itself from Judaism. Eventually, Christians no longer enjoyed the protection afforded them as a branch of Judaism. Christians were now Other, which led to their persecution by Rome.

A short time later, the protection afforded the Jews also eroded in response to the Jewish revolt (66–70 CE). Rome destroyed the Jerusalem temple and now viewed both Jews and Christians as threats. Over the next several hundred years, as Rome sought to maintain its place and power in the face of rising pressure from rulers around the Mediterranean and from northern tribes, a series of emperors arose with goals to bring the empire under a unified religious system. Anyone who refused to worship in the prescribed manner, which increasingly required venerating the emperor, was considered a traitor and subject to persecution. In some situations, the persecution was death. Those who did not bow to the emperor were Other.

The history of Christianity itself is filled with internal divisions, especially after the once-hostile Roman Empire came under the rule of Constantine. Constantine's Edict of Milan in 313 reversed the persecution of Christianity, which had become the official religion of the empire by the end of the century. With state endorsement, however, came the need to define which of several theological streams was the official Christianity. Establishing orthodoxy meant deciding between competing doctrines and eliminating the losers, a process that produced both creeds and heretics. After 381, groups that did not affirm the Nicene Creed's trinitarian doctrine were denied all recognition except as objects of persecution by imperial enforcement. Over the next centuries, thousands of heretics were treated as Other, often facing death. Those who did not identify themselves as Christians were also deemed heretical and were either marginalized or even killed. Major differences between Western and Eastern centers of church and empire continued until a formal split in 1054 resulted in what are now the Roman Catholic and Eastern Orthodox churches.

R. I. Moore's historical investigation of the later Middle Ages (950–1250) substantiates the continuing pervasiveness of the marginalization and death of those labeled heretics.[9] While the persecution of heretics lasted for a thousand years before the twelfth and thirteenth centuries, Moore emphasizes there was a sea change in the culture that led to systemic persecution, likening it to the difference between a society with slaves and a slave society (i.e., one based on slavery).[10] Moore says those in power often used persecution as a means of control.

Heretics, lepers, Jews, and homosexuals, in particular, were singled out for persecution through exclusion, the loss of rights and property, and even the loss of their lives. Moore expands upon Edmund Leach's claim that while it may be difficult for us to change the external environment, we can "play games" with our internalized environment and "carve up the external world into named categories, and then arrange the categories to suit our social convenience."[11] Moore argues each of these groups was the object of stereotypical categorization.

When a person was categorized as a heretic, leper, Jew, homosexual, or enemy, they were considered dangerous and subjected to persecution. Heretics threatened the control of both the government and the church. Lepers threatened the health and life of those who were well. Jews threatened the economic and religious order. And male homosexuals threatened the purity of the church. In each case, the threat was considered sufficient for those in power to marginalize, punish, and sometimes kill those considered Other.

The period of the Crusades was another tragic occasion of Othering. For about two hundred years, beginning in 1095, eight Christian crusades attempted to wrest control of territory, wealth, and religious sites from the Muslim realms of the Middle East. At the request of the eastern Byzantine ruler for aid against Muslim Turkish threats, the Roman Pope Urban II called for western Christians to join the Byzantine efforts and reclaim the Holy Land. European Jewish communities in the path of the march were attacked despite efforts of some local authorities, resulting in the death of thousands. During the capture of Jerusalem in 1099, most Jews there were massacred, along with the Muslim defenders. Ironically, some Crusaders were inspired to imitate Joshua's procession around Jericho, but traditional siege techniques were more successful. The tragedy of the Crusades can be attributed to several factors, among which was the attempt to restore Christian control of Jerusalem from those deemed Christ Killers (the Jews) and those who had conquered the land from Christians centuries before (Muslims). Both Jews and Muslims were viewed as infidels and hence punishable by death. Warfare of the period also had economic benefits for winners, in the form of looted material wealth and ransom of captives.

This disastrous treatment of those labeled heretics, infidels, or demons continued unabated. To name but a few, there was the Spanish Inquisition, John Calvin's support of the burning of Servetus, Martin Luther's letter to the German princes to kill the peasants who were clamoring for their own expression of faith, the English burning of Joan of Arc, and the Salem witch trials. Because they were perceived as a threat to the power, decency, and order of the established church, they were marginalized or eliminated. "Those people" were nonconforming; they were Other.

With the colonizing of the Americas, its indigenous people were treated as Other. With few exceptions, the Europeans viewed Indians as uncivilized savages who needed to be conquered, civilized and converted, removed, or killed. At least, that is the impression left by the disregard for hundreds of treaties with Indian nations that are still on the books, still documenting the responsibilities once pledged in exchange for native cooperation, still being presented as witnesses to unfulfilled promises. The forcible removal of Indians from their homes and territories, and their systematic extermination, are well documented. It is not an overstatement to label our nation's policies and treatment as genocidal. That American colonists thought of themselves as Israelites entering the Promised Land and vanquishing Indians like the Canaanites is documented by Puritan sermons![12]

In the mid-1800s, a cluster of concepts relating to the expansion of US control to the Pacific was signified by the term *Manifest Destiny*: an inexorable movement to settle and make productive the western lands under the special character of the American people and institutions. More a slogan than a formal policy, in practice it raised issues of the expansion of slavery and relations with Mexico.

Today, the US is still dealing with consequences of annexing more than one hundred thousand Mexican citizens and their properties by the Treaty of Guadalupe Hidalgo in 1848 to end the Mexican-American War.[13] They were not immigrants; they were there before the Americans. More Indians were also in the newly annexed lands.

The acquisition of the Pacific coast increased contact with Asians, especially those who came to work: the Chinese during the Gold Rush and construction of the transcontinental railway; then, after the Chinese Exclusion Act of 1882, the Japanese. Beyond the West Coast, expansion of American interests continued to the Pacific islands—Hawaii, Samoa, the Philippines—and with all these territories came the nonwhite people who lived and worked there. In Hawaii, for example, missionaries carried out a systematic program of evangelization for the purpose of civilizing the native population. In time, the indigenous population was reduced, their political organizations were supplanted, and economic and political control was taken over by US corporations, especially for plantation farming.

Often called "America's Original Sin," slavery was the foundation of much of our nation's wealth. Most servitude in the early colonies was indentured, which meant people could work their way out of debt over a period of time. Originally, the indentured slaves were both white and black. But as land grant programs released large tracts for cultivation of raw materials to benefit the English crown, the Southern plantation economy developed and with it the need for more laborers. Enslaved Africans arrived in Virginia as early as 1619, and a new form of slavery arose with black people, first in the Caribbean and then directly from Africa, to serve as slaves for life. This change was accompanied by the dehumanization of black people, which justified their inhumane treatment. They were "pagans" and "uncivilized." They were not like white people.

The treatment of Africans brought to our shores via the Middle Passage was unimaginably inhumane. Ships were dangerously overloaded with human "cargo" that was treated like freight. The enslaved often were shackled together and wedged in such crowded conditions that they were unable to move during the entire journey. Sanitation was ignored. Diseases were rampant and, in some cases, nearly half the "cargo" died before reaching the shores of the colonies. Incredibly, the loss experienced by the slave traders and ship captains was considered lost revenue instead of lost lives. The enslaved were purely profit or loss.

One of the most egregious aspects of slavery was the breaking up of families. Spouses were often separated, and children were frequently separated from their parents. White slaveholders could engage in this economically advantageous but morally destructive practice because they believed there was little or no familial bonding among black people. They were considered fundamentally different from white families.

And yet, from this environment, where the religion of the master was imposed upon the enslaved, came the transformative power of spirituals. "Joshua fit the battle of Jericho, and the walls come tumblin' down." What sounds like conquest becomes praise and hope for the release from oppression.

This brief overview of examples sets the stage for some of the major expressions of Othering of the twentieth and twenty-first centuries.

Black Americans

Racism has been a tenacious form of Othering in the United States. Our nation's history of slavery, Jim Crow laws, and mass incarceration systematically enforced the Othering of black people. Following the "official" end of slavery with passage of the Thirteenth Amendment in 1864 and the period of Reconstruction (1865–1877), one by one Southern states enacted Jim Crow laws mandating the separation of black and white people in public schools, restrooms, transportation, restaurants, parks, swimming pools, and other public facilities. The laws set forth legal limits on the contact of the races, ostensibly to ensure "separate but equal" treatment of both white and black people. The Supreme Court decision of *Plessy v. Ferguson* in 1896 upheld "separate but equal," which then remained the law of the land for the first half of the twentieth century. However, in reality, the law did not guarantee equality, only separation, and it reinforced the underlying racist assumptions that had been the foundation of slavery and the treatment of black people as second class.

Despite having elected the first black president of the United States in 2008, we remain a nation divided. Michael P. Jeffries documents the ongoing disparity between black and white people in four areas: wealth and housing, education, incarceration and policing, and health and health care. In all four, he concludes, "Black Americans live under a system of race-based inequality that is nakedly unjust, thickly woven, and multi-generational."[14] The Black Lives Matter movement, an anguished and angry response to the killing of black people by white police officers, is the most recent in a history of protests by black people over their treatment as invisible, marginal, and expendable—as nonpersons. These killings are modern occurrences of a long and tragic history that has included lynchings, church bombings, and assassinations of leaders.

The early portrayal of black people in film is a painful tale of Othering. D. W. Griffith's 1915 silent film, *The Birth of a Nation*, galvanized white people's fears of uncontrolled black sexual violence toward innocent white women and raised the specter of black people destroying white civilization. The counterpoint to the threatening black image was the portrayal of the black person as a "coon." In his fascinating study of black people in American films, Donald Bogle says, "Before its death, the coon developed into the most blatantly degrading of all black stereotypes. The pure coon emerged as no-account niggers, those unreliable, crazy, lazy subhuman creatures good for nothing more than eating watermelons, stealing chickens, shooting crap, or butchering the English language."[15] Stepin Fetchit was the epitome of the black man as coon, ironically making the actor who portrayed him (Lincoln Theodore Monroe Andrew Perry) the first successful black film actor. Whether as threat or coon, they were Other.

Ralph Ellison captured the essence of racism in his novel *Invisible Man* (1952), which tells of the relationship between a young black man at a black college and Mr. Norton, a white founder and benefactor of the school. Although Mr. Norton speaks caringly to the student, and despite long conversations, he does not bother to discover the student's name. He is simply "boy." When Mr. Norton suffers a mild stroke, a black veterinarian comes to his aid. As Norton recovers, the vet says to him, "To you he [the student] is a mark on the score-card of your achievement, a thing and not a man; a child, or even less—a black amorphous thing."[16]

In spite of *Brown v. Board of Education* (1954), the Civil Rights Act of 1964, and affirmative action, the story has scarcely changed. Approximately forty years after Ellison penned his words, Derrick Bell contended, "Racism is an integral, permanent, and indestructible *Caste* component of this society."[17] He recounts a conversation between himself and a black New York City cab driver named Semple. Bell, a former law professor at Harvard, was defending the importance of the Martin Luther King Jr. holiday established in 1986, but Semple would have none of it. His experience as a working-class black person led him to conclude that all black people ever got were symbols, and this was just one more instance. He believed real change was needed and electing Jesse Jackson to be president in 1988 could bring about that change. He thought Jackson was on the right track, encouraging black people to affirm their essential worth and humanity while also recognizing the enormous barriers that lay ahead. Referring to Jackson, he said, "He was O.K. when he had them repeat 'I am Somebody' with the outside hope that a few of them might believe despite the whole world telling them that they are, have been, and will be—nothing."[18] *1993*

Even black people who have "made it" suffer the ignominy of racist treatment. Ellis Cose, an author and contributing editor of *Newsweek*, related in his book *The Rage of a Privileged Class*, stories of black professionals viewed suspiciously in stores, walking in neighborhoods of the privileged, or "DWB"—"driving while black."[19] In *Race Matters*, Cornel West recounts his experience when he was on his way to deliver a lecture in Manhattan, briefcase in hand and impeccably dressed, waiting vainly while taxi after taxi passed him by, forcing him to take the subway and arrive late for his lecture.[20] In 2009, Harvard professor Henry Louis Gates Jr. was arrested on charges of disorderly conduct when attempting to force open a stuck door at his own home. The charges were dropped and the incident was resolved when Gates and the arresting officer met at the White House, where President Obama used the occasion to speak about the disproportionate number of people of color who have been historically stopped by police. Whether any of those or similar incidents are acknowledged by white people as direct evidence of racism, the reality is black people who have been the object of such treatment experience it as such.

For black people who are not well off or well known, the reality is even starker. In his exposé of deaths resulting from police violence throughout the nation and from political decisions in Flint, Michigan, Marc Lamont Hill details the plight of vulnerable black people. In case after case, from the 2014 killing of Michael Brown in Ferguson, Missouri, to the contamination of the water supply in Flint that resulted in a public health crisis and became a federal state of emergency the same year, he documents the disregard of black lives. Hill concludes to be black is to be "Nobody."[21]

The racist roots and treatment of black people—especially black men—in our criminal justice system is undeniable. Our nation currently incarcerates approximately two million people, which is the highest per capita rate in the so-called developed world. When we add those on parole or probation, the numbers soar to over eight million. Almost 40 percent of those in the clutches of the criminal justice system are black, although they represent only slightly over 13 percent of the population.

Data from The Sentencing Project shows the injustice of this imbalance.[22] While the number of black people arrested is much higher than white people, many of those arrests are related to drug use. Despite drug use being at least as great among white people as among black people, the arrest rate for black people is five times higher. The data also reveal the incarceration rate for black males in the United States is six times higher than for white males, and it is two times higher for Latinx than for white people. It is the same for youth. Although the use of drugs by white youth actually exceeds that of black youth, the arrest rate is similarly disproportionate. A 2012 study by the National Institute on Drug Abuse reported secondary-school white students were more likely to abuse an illegal substance, but black youths were arrested twice as often.[23]

A survey reported in the Bureau of Justice Statistics found, regardless of respondents' race, a vast majority of Americans associate black people with terms such as *dangerous, aggressive, violent,* and *criminal*.[24] However, assuming race solely accounts for the increased number of property and violent crimes by black people fails to recognize the fundamental role of poverty underlying such crimes. Black people are disproportionately poor and live in disadvantaged communities, which are serious factors in fostering crime. Researchers at the University of Ohio found the difference in the number of violent crimes committed by black people and white people can be largely attributed to the differences in the economic disadvantage of black communities.[25]

Michelle Alexander's groundbreaking book, *The New Jim Crow*, documents how the racist views and practices of historic Jim Crow laws are reenacted in new forms today.[26] She underscores the cause is not simply racist attitudes but also the existence of a fundamentally racist criminal justice system with deep roots in the War on Drugs. While the criminal justice system dealt with a relatively small number of persons in the past, we are now caught up in the throes of a racial caste system that takes the form of unprecedented mass incarceration with arrest, sentencing, and post-release experiences of discrimination, marginalization, and oppression. Although officially colorblind, our criminal justice system guarantees the disproportionate number of black people it ensnares will continue to be considered Other.

It is important to underscore Alexander's central claim that our criminal justice system is racist because of its consequences. Millions of black people who have been swept into the criminal justice system experience the same realities as those imposed by Jim Crow laws of the past: disenfranchisement from voting, discrimination in employment and housing, exclusion from certain professions, and ineligibility for certain public benefits (e.g., food stamps). These are the same or similar conditions black people suffered during the era of Jim Crow; but because this system claims to target criminals rather than black people, it is assumed to be colorblind. However, when one realizes the enormous disproportionality of black people trapped in the system, we are confronted with de facto racism.

Chris Hayes argues we actually have two justice systems: one that serves the nation that is essentially white, and the other that serves the colony composed of people of color. This distinction goes deeper than most white people's perceptions that the police are our guardians and black people's perceptions that the police are a threat. Hayes's point is the problem is rooted in the way our society is structured. The nation's justice system protects the dominant economic and political interests while the colony's justice system subdues and marginalizes the "colonized" people of color.[27]

His notion of a colony is reminiscent of an interview I heard many years ago with Anthony Buza, who was the police district commander of the South Bronx in New York City. He spoke sadly of the transformation of police academy graduates, noting within six months after being assigned to the South Bronx, most had lost their initial altruistic concern for those in the community and had become hostile. He lamented he was running an army of occupation similar to Vietnam and was keeping invisible what should be seen and silent what should be heard.

In exposing the roots and consequences of the mass incarceration of black people, Alexander charges the United States has created a new caste system that has systematically denied millions of black people their basic human dignity. This denigration of the humanity and dignity is characteristic of every caste system. Whether one calls the state of black people in the United States a caste system or a colony, the reality is the same—Othered.

Women

The United States is currently undergoing what some consider a long-overdue change in issues of gender. Women have made significant strides obtaining equality and are now granted the same rights as a man to vote, file for divorce, be heard in court, and inherit wealth and property. The #MeToo movement has encouraged women to speak out about their mistreatment by men. The legalization of same-sex marriage has provided a vehicle for lesbian women to openly affirm their love and to build families. The earnings differential between men and women has been slowly closing. But despite these gains, women are still often considered and treated as Other.

For hundreds of years, women in our nation were kept subservient and silenced. During that time, they existed under the sway of coverture, which "held that no female person had a legal identity."[28] Women were required to take their husband's name, could not sign contracts, would lose their children in the case of divorce, owned nothing of their own, and were prohibited from voting. Once married, their bodies belonged to their husbands.

In 1630s Boston, Anne Hutchinson refused to remain in a subjugated status. She was accused of criticizing the male Puritan preachers, holding meetings in her home, and, perhaps most importantly, claiming unmediated access to God. While the Reformation challenge to Rome had set aside the pope, priesthood, and sacraments of the Roman church as the means of access to God, Protestant national churches maintained hierarchical structures for interpreting scripture and theology and governing congregations. Even Puritans reserved this authority to their pastors. Hutchinson's claim to teach, interpret, and receive direct divine guidance, although never in public gatherings, resulted in her banishment and excommunication. Baruch College professor Cheryl C. Smith says in the minds of the Bay Colony magistrates, the crime Hutchinson committed was "having stepped out of her place in a very specific way: by stepping up."[29]

With the advent of the women's suffrage movement, many conditions limiting women's participation were challenged. Even before 1848, activist women organized in temperance leagues and abolitionist groups. The 1848 Seneca Falls Convention was a landmark toward acquiring equal rights. This movement, which became a seventy-year struggle led by Elizabeth Cady Stanton, Lucretia Mott, Susan B. Anthony, and others, culminated in the ratification of the Nineteenth Amendment in 1920, finally granting women the right to vote. Their political identity was now recognized.

But the refusal of men to consider and treat women as equals continued. In 1923, advocates proposed an Equal Rights Amendment guaranteeing full rights to women. It has not yet become the law of the land. Although Congress authorized the Equal Rights

Amendment in 1972 and sent it to the states for ratification, successful approval by the remaining necessary three states is being contested for having come after an extended deadline. Most juries were all-male until the 1960s, and it wasn't until 1993 that marital rape was made a crime in all fifty states. The recent revelations of powerful men abusing women are devastating reminders of how women continued to be treated as sex objects in professional settings. On the economic front, women have encountered glass ceilings that have maintained a disproportionate number of white men in positions of power and leadership in business, government, and religion. Additionally, female workers historically have earned less than men; the current gap is 17 percent.[30] For example, the 2019 world champion US women's soccer team is suing the sport's world governing body, the Fédération Internationale de Football Association (FIFA), for economic equality. Women's team members are paid approximately one-fifth of what the men's team members receive. Despite gains, many women continue to be treated as Other.

Hispanic and Latinx Americans

I use both terms since they are not synonymous. In an attempt to avoid the gendered adjectives Latino or Latina, Latinx now refers to a person from Latin America living in the United States, regardless of the language of their home country—Spanish, Portuguese, English, or French, while Hispanic refers to a Spanish speaker. In either case, they are treated as Other.

In a study of school textbooks and feature films, Greenfield and Cortés conclude Mexicans, and Latin Americans in general, are routinely disparaged and their histories are distorted. There is a consistent pattern that ignores their cultures' intrinsic worth and "for the most part, [in the case of Mexicans particularly] derogates Mexico or deems it worthy of notice only as a peripheral reflection or extension of developments in the United States."[31]

One of the consequences of this socialization is certain persons whose original language is not English are commonly viewed as second class. A Latin-American Spanish accent, for example, is thought by many to be an indication of ignorance, while a French accent is considered a mark of sophistication and cosmopolitan savoir-faire. Moreover, Latinx people are frequently subjected to slurs. The 2015 reference by then presidential candidate Donald Trump to Mexican immigrants as criminals and rapists escalated both the rhetoric and treatment of Latin Americans as Other, a trend that has seen more deadly hate crimes such as the 2019 shooting of Latinx people in El Paso that left twenty-two dead. Furthermore, a real wall is now under construction.

Although they are the largest ethnic minority and the fastest-growing population in the United States, Latin Americans remain among the lowest paid. According to the Pew Research Center, in 2015 their wages were approximately two-thirds the wages of white people and about one in five were living in poverty.[32] They perform much of the labor white people avoid because the work is hard: dishwashing, agricultural work, lawn care, and housekeeping, for example.[33]

When I served on the board of the statewide Rural and Migrant Ministry in New York, we visited a duck farm where a number of migrants from Latin America were employed. As we entered the gigantic barn, we were overcome by the stench. The ducks were jammed into overcrowded pens and were standing in their own dung. We could only tolerate the oppressive conditions for a few minutes, but the workers spent between forty-five to sixty minutes every four hours in those fetid conditions, force-feeding the ducks in order to fatten them for market.

The migrants lived in trailers that housed three shifts of workers. Each shift was permitted to sleep for an allotted time before the next shift arrived to occupy the same bed. There was almost no privacy and, according to one of the workers, some of the wives were sexually abused by supervisors while the workers attended to the ducks. Since there was no public transportation and most stores were located at a considerable distance, workers were forced to buy their groceries and other necessities from the farm store at significantly higher prices. They were doubly exploited.

Rural Poor

A great majority of the rural poor are white,[34] and while poor black people in rural areas suffer the additional burden of racism, poor white people are also labeled Other. Most of them have worked hard all their lives and believed in the promise of upward mobility, but the ravages of capitalism have turned their world upside down. Jobs disappeared when mills and factories closed or moved—many abroad—and small local firms have been bought by larger firms who sold off their assets until there was nothing left and they were forced out of business. Agribusinesses have driven many small farmers from their land and livelihood. Towns have become shells of their former lives. Hospital mergers have left many rural areas without readily accessible medical care. Since the poor have nowhere to go, they stay and vote for candidates they think will fight for them.

Rather than understanding their plight, some of my liberal friends have dismissed poor rural white people. They are seen as ignorant because they voted for Trump or the Tea Party, racist for blaming black urban dwellers for receiving government assistance, intransigent for not getting more education, lazy and stubborn for remaining in their community, narrow-minded for their failure to support a liberal social agenda, unenlightened for not understanding the plight of the oppressed, or conned for thinking less government is the answer. These criticisms are often made by those who have had many privileges from childhood through retirement, including education, jobs, professional careers, and relative wealth.

Ironically, it is not just the left that looks down on the rural poor. So, too, do some conservatives. In an article in *New Republic*, Sarah Jones quotes J. D. Vance, who blames poor whites for their plight. According to him, "We spend our way to the poorhouse. We buy giant TVs and iPads. Our children wear nice clothes thanks to high-interest credit cards and payday loans. We purchase homes we don't need. . . . Thrift is inimical to our being."[35]

My cousin's portrayal of the "hillbillies" in southeastern Kentucky where she served as a missionary reinforced my family's stereotypes of "white trash" and our sense that we were better. When she came north to raise money for her work, she brought stories and photographs of the extreme poverty in the area. The poor in the photographs were all white. They were missing teeth, their faces had vacant stares, their houses were dilapidated shacks, and the children were dressed in tattered rags. At one level, we were thankful that, but for the grace of God, we were not like them. But deep down, we believed there was something about them that caused their impoverishment and something that lifted us above their level.

The idea of "white trash" was popular during the Progressive era of the late nineteenth and early twentieth centuries. Many experts in economics and the social sciences believed the Darwinian notion of the survival of the fittest applied to white laborers also. For them, inherited traits accounted for the difference between those who were successful and those who were paupers, feebleminded, and promiscuous. Thomas C. Leonard traces their condition to class and a deficiency of intelligence and morality rather than to race.[36]

Today, we are again caught up in divisions between the deserving and undeserving, the fit and the unfit, the moral and the immoral, the wise and the ignorant—divisions that could prove to be the groundwork for violent and fascistic Othering.

Indians

In the introduction, I mentioned how movies portrayed Indians as warlike and brutal, conveying a "primitive" and "uncivilized" nature. History reveals a wide-ranging, even genocidal, brutality by our "civilized" government toward them. The Indian Removal Act of 1830 decreed the tribes would be moved from their lands east of the Mississippi to territories in the area of present-day Oklahoma. The Choctaw and Cherokee tribes were forced to leave millions of acres of land in the southeast and walk 1,200 miles to the new territory, a forced migration they call the Trail of Tears. It is estimated as many as seven thousand died from disease, cold, and starvation.

In Virginia, Indians were lumped together with black people as "colored" and treated as second class, at best. According to Dartmouth College professor Colin Galloway, George Washington was "the father of America's tortuous, conflicted and often hypocritical Indian policies. While he aspired . . . to reconcile taking Native land with respecting Native rights, he . . . employed deception and violence to attain his own and his nation's ends."[37] Even those Indians who adopted aspects of white culture, such as the Cherokee, did not escape being dislocated and, like the rest, were eventually driven off their land.

As the population of white settlers moved relentlessly west, Indians were driven out of even the territories assigned to them and moved to reservations. Frequently, they had scarce resources, and they were also in areas that became dangerous for human habitation. James P. Gregory reported a Western Shoshone reservation in Nevada "is situated between a chemical testing ground, bombing range, chemical depository, magnesium plant, uranium-processing plant, a nerve gas storage facility, and a low-level radioactive waste deposit site."[38] As a result, residents have been exposed to massive radioactive fallout and other hazardous materials, with severe health consequences. The reservations have been called sovereign nations, but they are treated as colonies.

The Othering of Indians was reinforced by the Indian boarding schools that were designed to destroy native culture and ensure assimilation. Although there were earlier schools, including ones established by Indians themselves, the industrial school founded in Pennsylvania by Captain Richard M. Pratt in 1879 became a model for government-sponsored boarding schools. Pratt's philosophy was summarized in his approval of a general's comment: "The only good Indian is a dead one. In a sense, I agree with the sentiment, but only in this: that all the Indian there is in the race should be dead. Kill the Indian in him, and save the man."[39]

Sadly, the Othering of Indians continues, both in popular culture and in our legal system. As I observed in the Introduction, the negative portrayal of Indians in contemporary media has influenced many people to think of them as substandard, a threat to civilized society, and, if necessary, expendable. According to noted legal scholar Robert A. Williams Jr., the idea of Indians' inferior primitive condition and white Americans' civilized superiority is an enduring legacy of colonialism that also affects our current legal system. He elaborates how that racial imagination has become part of our legal system today.[40] They were and continue to be Other.

Jews

Anti-Semitism has been a bitter reality throughout much of Western history. However, the genocidal killing of approximately six million Jews by the Nazis was the most horrific incident of Jewish dehumanization ever recorded. When the National Socialist German Workers' Party (Nazi Party) gained power in Germany in 1933, it implemented both anti-Jewish legislation and police terrorism. On November 9 and 10, 1938, the Nazis unleashed the infamous pogrom, Kristallnacht. Thousands of Jewish homes, hospitals, and stores, as well as hundreds of synagogues, were ransacked or destroyed. About one hundred Jews were killed, and thirty thousand more were rounded up and sent to concentration camps. It was the beginning of what was to become The Final Solution—the intended extermination of all Jews in the territories of German conquest. Six million Jews were killed. The images of mass shootings and gas chambers, burning buildings, ghettos, confiscated property, naked bodies stacked in common graves, and emaciated people being marched to their death are burned into our hearts.

In the early 1900s, many European countries, in addition to Germany, shared a strong bias against Jews. However, the rise of the Nazis in the 1920s and 1930s provided the rationale for an increase of anti-Jewish phobia in other European nations. Hostility toward Jews was compounded by widespread economic collapse throughout much of Europe after World War I, by the Bolshevik Revolution in Russia, and by the migration of Jews from Eastern Europe. These factors helped intensify mistrust and hatred of Jews that contributed to the Holocaust.

When I visited Yad Vashem, the Holocaust memorial in Jerusalem, I was overcome with grief and revulsion at the tragedy presented there. The documentation of such horrors was overwhelming. How, I wondered, could anyone treat another human being like that? The harrowing answer is that the Jews were not considered human beings. They were Other.

But the murder and denigration of Jews did not cease with the end of World War II, nor have they been limited to Europe. The Othering continues to this day and in our own nation. Hate speech against Jews fills our social media. At the Charlottesville white supremacist rally in 2017, some wore shirts with swastikas and chanted "Jews will not replace us." Headstones in Jewish cemeteries in numerous states have been vandalized. Neo-Nazi websites have called for the burning of synagogues. Synagogues have been targeted with graffiti and their windows smashed. There have been bomb threats against Jewish institutions on campuses, and memorials grieving for lost lives of victims have been covered with anti-Jewish graffiti. Thrown rocks have damaged plexiglass panels of the New England Holocaust Memorial twice.

As dreadful as signs, chants, threats, warnings, and vandalism are, they are only part of the problem. The hatred of Jews has led to bloodlust. Jewish synagogues and establishments have become vulnerable targets: at the Tree of Life Synagogue in Pittsburgh in 2018, eleven persons were killed and six were wounded; one person was killed and three were wounded at the Poway Synagogue near San Diego in April 2019; six people died at a kosher grocery store and a related shooting in Jersey City, New Jersey, in December 2019; and five Jews were stabbed in their rabbi's home in Monsey, New York, in early 2020. It is too easy to find recent and vicious reminders of the walls of hostility confronting Jews in the United States.

Asian Americans

In 1966, I joined the staff of Metropolitan Associates of Philadelphia. Jitsuo Morikawa, an executive with the American Baptist Churches, was largely instrumental in the formation of this ecumenical project focused on organizational change. He was a creative, dignified, and gentle man who had been confined for eighteen months at a Japanese internment camp in Arizona during World War II. Out of his experience came a fierce commitment to justice.

It was my first realization of the extent and tragedy of President Franklin D. Roosevelt's 1942 Executive Order 9066, which authorized establishing military encampments for enemy aliens (Japanese, Germans, Italians). The forced internment of up to 120,000 persons of Japanese descent (most of whom were US citizens) in ten camps was among the worst civil rights abuses in recent history. Surrounded by barbed-wire walls, they lived in inferior housing, such as former stables, where the majority were kept until the end of the war. In their absence, their properties were confiscated. Racist cartoons, slurs, and comments abounded throughout the nation—all because they were Japanese. Recognizing the horror of what we had done, President Gerald Ford repealed the executive order in 1976 and Congress apologized, authorizing $20,000 each in reparations to more than 80,000 Japanese Americans.[41] (This suggests a precedent for those currently seeking reparations for our nation's slavery.)

Our nation's treatment of the Japanese was preceded by a series of policies directed toward the Chinese, who had come in large numbers to work in the Gold Rush in the 1850s and the railroad in the 1860s. In 1875, Congress passed the Page Act, prohibiting the immigration of Chinese women, who were accused of being prostitutes. This was the first serious ban on immigration and paved the way for the Chinese Exclusion Act of 1882, which banned Chinese immigration for ten years and prohibited naturalization for any who were already in the country. This exclusionary law was extended for an additional ten years by the Geary Act of 1892, and at the end of those ten years, Chinese immigration was made permanently illegal, a ban that remained in effect until it was partially modified in 1943. The Geary Act also required special documentation be carried by all Chinese, an eerie precedent for the passbooks required of black people in South Africa during apartheid. This was followed by the Immigration Act of 1924 that restricted "other 'undesirable' groups such as Middle Easterners, Hindu, East Indians, and Japanese."[42] Once again, the notion of white superiority was the order of the day.

To this day, Asians suffer from both the personal prejudices and social structures as a result of racism. Despite being the "model minority," Asian Americans experience many of the deleterious effects of systemic racism. In addition to slurs such as Gook (Korean and Vietnamese soldiers) and Bananas (yellow on the outside and white on the inside), and the limited acknowledgment of the millions of Asians killed during our wars in Korea and Vietnam, they suffer from lower employment, lower pay than white people for the same work, and almost total invisibility in films and TV.

The 2020 crisis of a novel coronavirus is giving vent to increased anti-Chinese actions and comments. There are reports of signs placed on stores and businesses in several Asian nations, the United Kingdom, and Canada that state "No Chinese." This is dangerously reminiscent of the anti-Jewish signs in 1930s Germany. A British citizen reported "on the bus to work last week, as I sat down, the man next to me immediately scrambled to gather his stuff and stood up to avoid sitting next to me."[43] While these individual responses do not rise to the level of policies, there is a danger they could. It would not be the first time that freedom of movement, access, and speech was curtailed, as noted above.

Muslims

Muslims have long been viewed through Western eyes as "Orientals"—hence, as uncivilized barbarians—despite the fact Muslim scholars preserved and retransmitted Greek and Roman classics back to medieval Europe, works that had been lost after the decline of the Roman Empire. Edward Said has shown how ideas that Arabs and Muslims are essentially different from Westerners are the result of colonization, which has shaped policies and practices. In considering the West's contemporary forms of this prejudice, he writes about the transfer of anti-Semitic animus from the Jews to Arabs with the creation of Israel. "In films and television, the Arab is associated either with lechery or bloodthirsty dishonesty. . . . Lurking behind all these images is the menace of jihad. Consequence: a fear that the Muslims [or Arabs] will take over the world."[44]

Enslaved Africans were among the first Muslims to arrive in the Americas. They were, of course, discouraged from practicing their faith, but several of the US founding generation were more tolerant. The Constitution guarantees religious liberty, and Thomas Jefferson mentions Muslims directly in writing about the freedoms guaranteed by Virginia's legislation.[45] Immigration for economic opportunity brought many Muslims as early as the late 1800s and early 1900s, notably to the Ford Model-T plant and its successors in the Detroit, Michigan, area. Today, Islam is the third-largest religion in the United States, but interestingly, it is also the most diverse. In 2011, the Pew Research Center stated that 30 percent of Muslim Americans report their race as white, 23 percent as black, 21 percent as Asian, 6 percent as Hispanic, and 19 percent as other or mixed race.[46]

The Othering of Muslims has been steadily on the increase in the United States. An article in the *New Republic* recounts how white supremacists in Liberal and Garden City, Kansas, have been influenced by conspiracy theories that portray Muslims, especially those from Somalia, as a dire threat to freedom and safety in the United States. This was reinforced by candidate Trump's warnings that Muslims were seeking to enter the United States to create terror. The Crusaders, as the Kansas group called themselves, developed a plan that included "kidnapping and raping the wives and daughters of refugee workers, setting fire to their mosque during prayer time, and even shooting them with arrows dipped in pig's blood."[47] Patrick Stein told his fellow Crusaders, "The only good Muslim is a dead Muslim. If you're a Muslim, I'm going to enjoy shooting you in the head."[48] Fortunately, the FBI and local police intervened before a massacre could be carried out.

Tragically, the Crusaders' vitriol is not an isolated incident. Hate crimes against Muslims abound. According to a Pew Research Center analysis of new FBI hate crime statistics, physical assaults against Muslims in the United States are higher than during the aftermath of the 2001 attacks on the World Trade Center and Pentagon, as well as the thwarted attack that led to the airplane crash in Stonycreek Township, Pennsylvania. In 2016, there were 127 reported victims of aggravated or simple assault, compared with 91 the year before and 93 in 2001.[49] Mosques are an especially public target. And the assaults are not limited to the United States. Fifty-one people died in one day from attacks on two mosques in Christchurch, New Zealand, in 2019.

It is not unusual to hear Muslims referred to as "those people." President Trump's continuing attempts to impose travel bans on Muslims entering the country has added fuel to the fire. After several court decisions determined the initial ban unconstitutional, the President narrowed the ban to refugees and immigrants from seven to six "mostly Muslim" nations he deemed sources or supporters of terrorists. In June 2018, the Supreme Court upheld a modified ban.[50] While the specifics of his ban are continually changing and expanding into 2020, his fundamental distrust and rejection of Muslims remain constant.

When Trump campaigned in Portland, Maine, on August 4, 2016, he associated the Somali immigrants, most of whom are Muslim, with crime: "We've just seen many, many crimes getting worse all the time, and as Maine knows—a major destination for Somali refugees—right, am I right? Well, they're all talking about it. Maine. Somali refugees."[51] His allegations emboldened many of the state's citizens to engage in anti-Muslim rhetoric and action.

The leadership of the Somali community denounced what it

called stereotyping and lies. Acting police chief, Brian O'Malley of Lewiston, Maine—one of the two largest Somali communities in the state—countered there was no correlation between Somali immigration and increased crime, and the city's crime rate had steadily decreased since Somali immigrants began arriving in Lewiston in the 1990s. Portland is home to the other large Somali community, and its police chief, Michael Sauschuck, said property and violent crime rates also decreased in his city—property crime declined 14 percent and violent crime declined 24 percent from 2015.[52]

Despite confirmations from the two police chiefs and many community members about the substantial contributions of the Somali refugees, stereotyping and hatred continue. In its fall 2017 newsletter, the Maine Council of Churches reported a white woman at a laundromat pulled the clothes belonging to two Somali immigrants from the dryer and threw them on the floor shouting, "Go back where you came from."

President Trump himself encouraged such sentiments in July 2019 tweets against Representative Ilhan Omar of Minnesota, which his campaign rally picked up, chanting, "Send her back!" Omar's response was her 2020 reelection slogan, "Send her back to Congress!"

As one would imagine, this rhetoric and behavior have engendered a pervasive fear in the Muslim community that their lives don't matter. The deaths of thousands of Muslims during the ethnic cleansing in Bosnia from 1992 to 1995 while the West watched silently seems to be an ominous warning, reinforced by the increasing number of negative stereotypes. They are reminded almost constantly they are Other.

LGBTQ+

Although the landmark 1969 Stonewall Inn resistance event was fifty years ago, LGBTQ+ persons remained largely invisible to mainstream American culture in its immediate aftermath. The few who had the courage to "come out" were feared, castigated, maligned, marginalized, and viewed as deviants. Public awareness of AIDS in the early 1980s also called attention to what was called the "gay lifestyle," for which the disease was viewed by many as deserved punishment. My early life was filled with jokes and put-downs of gay people. The fundamentalist religion in which I was raised claimed gay and lesbian people who did not repent and give up their "degenerate" lifestyle were condemned to hell—a belief still maintained by many of the Religious Right.

A few leading contemporary fundamentalist preachers, including Jerry Falwell Sr. (now deceased), Pat Robertson, and Billy Graham's son, Franklin Graham, have bitterly opposed lesbian, gay, bisexual, transgender, and queer or questioning people (LGBTQ+s). Robertson claimed seeing gay people kiss made him want to vomit, and feminism leads to lesbianism. Falwell blamed gay people, feminists, the American Civil Liberties Union (ACLU), and others for the national immorality he said was punished by God in the 9/11 attacks, and Graham notoriously praised Vladimir Putin's antigay laws.[53]

For years, many states had sodomy laws that criminalized certain sexual acts. While these laws sometimes included acts between heterosexual couples, including married couples, their primary intent was to prohibit homosexual acts. In some states, the penalty was life imprisonment. Although the US Supreme Court in 2003 ruled sodomy laws unconstitutional, sixteen states still have these laws on their books in 2020.[54] This legal holdout reflects the tenacity of homophobia in our nation.

In 2015, the Supreme Court legalized same-sex marriage in all states. While many years of cultural and legal struggle preceded this development, when change finally came, its pace seemed breathtaking after the first state's legalization in 2003. But despite the legal acceptance of same-sex marriages, widespread consternation and even revulsion still remain. For many, the idea of same-sex relationships, let alone marriage, is still considered "unnatural," which is another way of saying, "you are not one of us, the 'natural' ones."

The struggle of transgender people (persons whose gender identity is different from their assigned gender at birth) has come to the forefront in the last few years.[55] Transgender people are regularly discriminated against regarding access to bathrooms, employment, health care, and housing.[56] The Trump administration has sought to reverse the US military's June 2016 decision for transgender people to serve openly. Implementation of the Presidential Memorandum of August 2017 was blocked by two lower courts, but in January 2019, the Supreme Court ruled that the ban on trans members of the military must go through the appeals process. In the meantime, the status of trans members in the military is uncertain.[57] What for transgender people is a natural identity, a correction of what was an inaccurate gender assignment for them at birth, is considered by many to be against nature. And when one is considered to be against "nature," which is often against a socially defined convention, one easily becomes "those people." Transgender identity remains a major source of Othering.

Despite the recent legal advances to recognize the rights of LGBTQ+ persons, there is a strong movement to reverse those gains. The Alliance Defending Freedom, with three thousand lawyers and huge financial support, is systematically working to deny those rights based on the First Amendment principle of the separation of church and state. They have been working at both state and federal levels to challenge laws that require persons or organizations to honor the various protections provided by existing laws if their religious beliefs conflict with those laws. An especially notable case is that of Jack Phillips, a Colorado baker, who refused to bake a wedding cake for a gay couple based on his religious objections. In 2018, the Supreme Court, by a 7-2 decision, ruled in his favor, but without deciding on the larger First Amendment issue.[58] Once again, religion is being used as a basis for Othering.

The Disabled

People with disabilities, whether mental or physical, are regularly treated as Other. A friend, who was a seminary president, was confined to a wheelchair with a severe genetic malformation. He was a brilliant, articulate leader. At a restaurant, the server turned to his wife and asked what the gentleman wanted for lunch. The assumption was obvious—he was discounted because of his disability. When my friend recounted the event to me, he said with sadness and anger, "Because I am confined to a wheelchair, some people think my brains are in my ass."

My awareness of the tendency to treat those with disabilities dismissively was raised when another friend, whose son was born with a crippling disease, challenged me for referring to his son as a cripple. He asked me to refer to his son as a boy with a crippling disease rather than as a cripple, and taught me to put the person first and the disability second. In defining his son by his disability, I had relegated him to the status of Other.

We have all seen people without a home sleeping on benches and in doorways, trying to find warmth and comfort. While some suffer solely from extreme poverty, many homeless persons are disabled. They are the mentally ill, returned veterans with PTSD, or those addicted to drugs or alcohol. During the day, they may stand at traffic lights with signs describing their plight or sit on sidewalks holding out a cup in the hope of a pittance. But at night, they return to a homeless shelter, if they are fortunate, or to a doorway, if they are not. Since our nation has deinstitutionalized their care, which is a structural form of Othering, they are forced to fend for themselves, depend upon the kindness of individuals or nonprofits, or end up in prison. There are so many, and their needs are so great, that it is easy to become overwhelmed, avert our gaze, and walk on by the Other.

The Elderly

Many elderly people suffer the ignominy of being treated as Other. While some voluntarily gravitate to their own cohort, many feel they have been marginalized through no choice of their own. Othering of the elderly is often reinforced in ways similar to prisoners. Facilities are built to separate them from the larger society; and while the accommodations and ambiance cannot be compared to a prison, their isolation is similar. As with many prisoners, out of sight is out of mind.

Older people today are particularly vulnerable to the accelerated change in information and technology, which often renders their knowledge outdated and frequently makes them seem "old-fashioned" or even "useless" in the eyes of younger generations. The traditional value of wisdom has been supplanted by information, so they are considered superfluous.

In addition, some younger persons resent "carrying" the elderly through their Social Security taxes; since there is an increasing number of elderly and fewer young people in the workforce, the expanding costs must be borne by the young. The supposed unfairness of this burden has been used by some politicians to further drive a wedge between the young and the old.

My wife, who has a master's degree in gerontology, frequently recounts the story of Pat Moore, a twenty-six-year-old graduate student at Columbia University who visited the cities of the United States and Canada disguised as an eighty-year-old woman. She encountered routine rudeness and disrespect; people deliberately shortchanged her and cut ahead of her in line. When she removed her disguise and returned to the same stores and same salespeople, she was treated courteously.[59] She was no longer considered Other.

Prisoners

Our prisons are the human garbage heaps of the nation, filled with persons society has branded "trash" and "scum." The mantra to "lock them up and throw away the key" is applied to those considered too evil to be allowed to walk our streets. In a previous book, I spoke of the "spirit of punishment" that is alive in our society and epitomized in the treatment of prisoners.[60] Those deemed most dangerous (the maximum-security prisoners) are herded like cattle, confined to small cells with no amenities, and sometimes placed in solitary confinement with no human contact. We have built a "correctional" system that discards millions of people from society. Because we fear or hate them, they are viewed as Other, fundamentally different from those on the outside.

A terminally ill prisoner at Sing Sing Correctional Facility who had been a student in my ethics class was transferred to a separately maintained corrections unit in a nearby hospital to undergo surgery. When I arrived at the hospital with flowers, an officer on guard stopped me and warned I could not take the flowers into the room. Realizing he might be concerned something was hidden in the flowers, I suggested putting them in a clear vase. He remained adamant and replied the prisoner didn't need flowers. When I responded "every person likes flowers," the officer retorted, "He's not a person; he's a prisoner," capturing our society's view of prisoners as Other.

Othering often involves making people invisible. Many new prisons are in rural areas, effectively separating prisoners from the broader society. For many years, the Maine State Prison was located on the main street in downtown Thomaston where it constantly reminded people driving on Route One that incarcerated people were housed in the town. Several years ago, that facility was demolished and a new prison was built on a remote country road in a rural area. While it is a far superior facility, it is hidden from sight. Assigning prisons to private, for-profit contractors is a disturbing trend that further removes them from public oversight.

Many states have built prisons in rural areas to promote sorely needed economic development. While there are many employment opportunities during a prison's construction, employment is limited to positions for corrections officers and support services once this construction ends.

Building prisons in rural areas frequently forces relatives to travel five or six hours round trip for a brief visit. In contrast, one of the appeals of Sing Sing prison, despite its aging structure, is its proximity to New York City where a majority of convicts resided, making travel for families easier. When prisoners are housed in rural facilities far removed from their neighborhoods, they are out of sight and out of mind, which contributes to their being viewed as Other.

Another consequence of building prisons in rural areas is that a majority of the corrections officers are white, while at least half of the prisoners are black. The *New York Times* has documented the extreme racial imbalance between officers and prisoners. For example, in the Clinton Correctional Facility in upstate New York, 997 of 998 corrections officers were white. Previously mentioned research by Eddie Ellis revealed 75 percent of all the black prisoners were from New York City. If one counts the metropolitan New York City area, the percentage of incarcerated black people is even higher. Given this grave imbalance, it is not surprising racism in the prisons is rampant. The article relates numerous stories of black prisoners and their treatment at the hands of white officers. David G. Larimer, a federal judge, concluded black inmates at Elmyra prison "were assigned the worst prison jobs, housed on the most decrepit cellblocks, and disciplined out of proportion to their numbers."[61] They were Othered within the Other.

One of the questions posed by the disabled, elderly, and prisoners is whether they continue to serve any purpose for those in power. They do, in providing labor to attend them, such as home care workers and corrections officers. But it is clear those who are cared for as part of the economy are largely considered Other.

Roma [pejoratively 'gypsies']

On trips to various European cities, I often have been warned to beware of pickpockets and swindlers, especially outside churches and tourist attractions. When I saw the people about whom I was warned, I assumed they were simply homeless or poor. However, I learned that many of them were Roma, one of the most maligned groups in modern history and pejoratively called "Gypsies." Their distinctive dress, nonconformity to the dominant culture, constant mobility, and designation as thieves has led to their ostracization by the dominant community.

In her deeply moving study, *Bury Me Standing*, Isabel Fonseca documents a pattern of mistrust, dismissal, prejudice, and violence toward them. Roma were among those targeted by Hitler in his attempt to purify Europe and, according to some studies, they were the second-largest group sent to concentration camps or killed on the spot; as many as 500,000 Roma or Sinti (who lived like them) were murdered during the reign of Nazi terror.[62]

The mistreatment of the Roma was not limited to the Nazis. Seeking to create a homogeneous nation, the postwar socialist government of Poland spoke of "the Gypsy problem" and an Office for Gypsy Affairs was established and operated until 1989. The Roma were considered outside the norm of what it meant to be an ethnic and nationalistic Pole. They didn't fit. The use of the phrase "the Gypsy problem" is eerily similar to "the Jewish question" that resulted in the Final Solution of the Holocaust.

Many Romanians were worried others in Europe might confuse them with the people they denigrated because of the similarity in the names *Roma* and *Romanian*. (Roma are a nomadic people living without national boundaries while Romanians are citizens of a nation.) Following World War II, Romania was an impoverished country and, in the minds of many, was second class; hence, they wished to create a distance between themselves and those they considered inferior. In her book, Fonseca reports one interviewee "considered it a horrifying notion that to the outside world Romanians were no better than a bunch of Gypsy panhandlers—or indeed than Gypsies of any description: no better, no different."[63] This attitude was underscored by the xenophobia of an elderly woman she interviewed who, while feeding her pigs, referred to the Roma as not human.[64] Her description echoes the Nazi reduction of the Roma and Jews to the status of nonpersons. They are Other.

The Roma are not just a European "problem." There are over a million Roma living in the United States, and their plight is severe.

Forty ethnic Roma were resettled by Immigration and Customs Enforcement in a town of 6000 in Pennsylvania. "We left our country not because we are poor; we left because of racism and we're seeking political asylum."[65] Unfortunately, they faced some of the same derision and rejection they had experienced in Europe. Some media called them "gypsies," a name they reject because of its pejorative connotation. They were misunderstood and judged unfairly. When people are new to a culture, it is to be expected that there will be some misunderstanding and friction. But the Roma have been systematically subjected to racist slurs, vitriol, and suspicion. Fox News spoke of the new arrivals in Pennsylvania in disparaging terms, maligning them with distorted allegations of defecating in the streets and beheading chickens.[66] Such a response is not an isolated incident. Roma in the United States have historically been viewed as thieves and beggars, bearing the burden of their European history. Until 1998, New Jersey had a law that allowed "local governments to craft laws and ordinances that specified where Gypsies could rent property, where they could entertain, and what goods they could sell. Facing such discrimination, the Roma learned to hide and blend in."[67] As a result, they remain mostly silent Others.

Shifting the Othering

One of the greatest ironies and tragedies is that people who have been treated as Other sometimes resort to Othering themselves. The early Irish immigrants, for example, were among the poor, struggling to survive. They were demeaned, treated as second-class citizens, and relegated to inferior housing—all experiences shared by enslaved black people and many free black people in the north. The Irish were sometimes referred to as "negroes turned inside out."[68] Despite suffering the same humiliation, many opposed the abolition of slavery, and some openly joined the ranks of the oppressors. According to one historian, when the Irish arrived in the 1800s, they turned their backs on their own history and identity as an oppressed people who had fought for their freedom. In the 1844 riots in Philadelphia, a conflict between Roman Catholics, a majority of whom were Irish immigrants, and Protestant nativists resulted in violence and destruction of buildings, with casualties also inflicted by the law enforcement and soldiers trying to quell the riots. Ironically, some of the Irish under attack then turned and attacked black homes, stores, and churches.[69]

Sadly, I have observed the same dynamic among some black pastors who, despite having experienced the rejection, humiliation, and perils of racism, nonetheless condemned LGBTQ+[70] or maintained the second-class status of women by denying their ordination and insisting on their subservience. My father's blindness to his own roots led him to take out his rage on those he considered inferior rather than understanding how class and family dynamics had shaped his life. Without self-awareness, it is frightening how common and even easy it is to shift the Othering to someone else.

The Complexity of Othering

In the preface to *Nobody*, an extraordinary exposé of the "War on the Vulnerable," Marc Lamont Hill describes how the state has systemically created the conditions that result in black people being treated as "nobody." He points to the discriminatory use of the law, the creation of disadvantaged neighborhoods, and the abandonment of the disenfranchised in its march to "promote private interests over the public good." The "nobodies" are disposable.[71]

While his book focuses on black people and ways in which the black community has suffered, he concludes the preface by underscoring how Othering is frequently multilayered. He draws upon two incidents. The first was the killing of Mya Hall, a black transgender person who took a wrong exit off the Baltimore-Washington Parkway in Baltimore, Maryland, on March 30, 2015. Since that exit led to the Baltimore headquarters of the National Security Agency, and Hall appeared to accelerate the stolen vehicle at the checkpoint, the NSA police assumed she was attempting to trespass and opened fire. The second was the case of Sandra Bland, who was jailed in Texas because she could not raise the $500 bail. She allegedly committed suicide; however, the jail staff was found guilty of negligence, the arresting officer was terminated, and the Bland family settled a wrongful death lawsuit for $1.9 million. In both those incidents, gender, race, and poverty were at play. These incidents underscore the complexity of treating people as Other. Hill says, "While Nobodyness is strongly tethered to race, it cannot be divorced from other forms of social injustice. . . . It would be impossible to examine the 2015 killing of Mya Hall by National Security Agency police without understanding how sexism and transphobia conspire with structural racism. We cannot make sense of Sandra Bland's tragic death without recognizing the impact of gender and poverty in shaping the current carceral state. To understand the complexity of oppression, we must avoid simple solutions and singular answers."[72]

The complexity of Othering is found not only in the structures of domination but also in our attitudes, beliefs, and values. The divisions in our world have multiple roots: both personal and systemic. I now turn my attention to understanding the complexity of our divisions.

2

The Roots of Othering

During my lifetime, I realized that discrimination was not accidental, that there were structural roots and causes to it.[1]

—Michelle Bachelet, former President of Chile

What leads us to think of others as "those people"? Most people are kindhearted, generous to others, and content to live and let live. Yet, as we saw in chapter 1, we invariably find ourselves viewing and treating some people as if they were not one of us.

Just as Othering is complex and can take various forms, its roots are also many and varied. My father's dismissal and demeaning of people were at least partly because of his attempt to overcome a sense of inferiority. My own racist and homophobic feelings and behaviors had their origins in my family, culture, and religion. But the Othering that characterized our lives was also rooted in extensive systems of domination. To understand Othering, it is important to get to the roots of this complex disease, which are both personal and structural.

How we talk about Othering matters. Michael Schwalbe traces the root of Othering to the basic dynamic of exploitation: the use or misuse of a person or group by one who claims superiority.[2] While I concur that the drive to exploit is a fundamental root of Othering, it seems helpful to acknowledge how other dynamics, both structural and personal, function to create and maintain our divisions. Like many other problems or issues, reducing something to a single cause may miss other important sources.

Throughout this book, I draw a distinction between nature and nurture, between our natural tendencies and the learned behaviors we adopt per our social circumstances. From our earliest age, we each define ourselves as beings distinct from others who are different from us, whether those differences are racial, gender, size, age, linguistic, and so on. These differences do not constitute Othering. Only as we attribute such things as inferiority, evil, or dehumanization to those who are different does it become Othering. The same pertains to group identities. It is natural to identify ourselves as "us" and others as "not us." We are United States citizens; they are Iranian citizens. We are different. But when our group differentiates itself at the expense of or with the denial of the full humanity for people who are different, we are engaging in Othering.

Fear

One of the most basic roots of Othering is fear: fear of the unfamiliar, fear of perceived threat, fear of insecurity, and fear of death. To be human is to experience fear. While fear is an innate human characteristic, its expression is socially constructed and can be exacerbated, overcome, or minimized. Fear, when shaped by forces around us, can lead to Othering.

When we are fearful, we readily turn to someone or something that can relieve our anxiety. For many, the escape of choice is drugs or alcohol, choices that may become addictive. But for the majority, it involves Othering. If we can reduce someone or some group to the category of animal, or if we can marginalize them so they no longer appear on our radar, or if we can exploit them for our purposes, we can limit their threatening influence.

The history of slavery is one of white fear, generated to maintain the system of slavery. White people were regularly subjected to images and narratives of black people as a threat to the peace-loving white nation. A distinction was made between good and bad slaves. "Good slaves" were portrayed as those who served their masters, worked hard, and didn't cause trouble. "Bad slaves" were portrayed as thieves, duplicitous, uppity, runaways, or, most terrifyingly, rapists of white women. The "bad" slaves were often described as fearsome animals. The fear was so deeply engrained that simply accusing a black man of raping a white woman was often sufficient cause for a lynching. In some cases, if a black man looked at a white woman, he was subject to beating or even death. On the other hand, it was permissible for white men to rape black women. "During America's chattel slavery system, white slave owners freely and legally raped the women whom they enslaved. They used rape to assert their power and authority over their property without accountability."[3]

Today, it is not uncommon for white people to fear black people not only for their personal safety, but also for their economic security. The rumor of a black family moving into the neighborhood often gives rise to the saying, "there goes the neighborhood," implying property values will decrease. The fear of economic loss due to the presence of black people in a neighborhood has emboldened some real estate agents to play upon those fears by creating "white flight" and profiting from the properties' turnover. Another damaging practice has been "redlining" in which banks, insurance companies, and mortgage lenders target certain areas for favorable loans to white people while refusing loans to black people, maintaining the division between black and white. And a similarly destructive consequence has been achieved through gentrification. Gentrification involves the buying of properties in depressed areas (inhabited primarily by people of color) by more affluent people (read white), thereby inexorably raising both property values and taxes and forcing poorer people to move out, exacerbating existing racial and class divisions.

It is remarkable how often those in power instill fear in people to control them. As mentioned in chapter 1, R. I. Moore's study revealed case after case of medieval rulers using the threat of heresy, leprosy, homosexuality, or Jewish avarice to create an enemy around which all would rally.[4] In part, this may be status anxiety, a fear about the loss of one's place in the world. But it goes even deeper to fearing not only what others think of us but fearing what "they" can do to "us." It is no different today, except some of the targets are different. Donald Trump's 2016 presidential candidacy was based on two principal appeals. The first was to promise the return of greatness: jobs, national prestige, and military might. This is an appeal to the lost status that many who have been left behind experience, and it can serve as a means of control by those in power. But the second strategy was to raise the specter of fear of what others might do to us: Mexican immigrants as rapists and murderers, and Muslims as terrorists. Fear continues to hold sway among his supporters, driving the wedge between them and those who are categorized as a threat.

Our foreign policy increasingly relies upon fear as a means of control, and the results are divisive. The threat of reprisal has sought to strike fear into the hearts of the Trump administration's enemies, such as North Korea or Iran. Trying to instill fear, however, is often counterproductive. The US threat to withhold funds from the United Nations for opposing our decision to move the US embassy in Israel to Jerusalem nevertheless resulted in a 128 to 9 vote against our action. A foreign policy that seeks to instill fear in other nations makes the divisions in our world more pronounced.

The forced removal of Civil War monuments and the Confederate flag has struck fear in the hearts of many Southerners and even some Northerners who perceive the removal of these symbols of the South's history as a threat to their culture and values. This fear is based on an idealized narrative, an ideology of a lost cause that camouflages racism under the guise of states' rights. In their minds, the federal government is acting as Big Brother and pursuing a course of persecution. Among the most dangerous responses have been the rebirth of the Ku Klux Klan, the rise of other nationalist movements, and the horrors of the deadly rally of 2017 in Charlottesville.

The consequence is a widening division and deepening fear in our nation.

The current War on Terror is another contemporary source of fear leading to division and mistrust. Ever since 9/11, many US politicians have promoted fear to get reelected. They often do so in the name of patriotism. The Middle East is portrayed as a cauldron of Muslim fundamentalists who hate the United States and everything for which it stands. Stereotyping an entire region and religion has generated an irrational fear of all Muslims. President George W. Bush's characterization of his War on Terror as a "clash of civilizations" was a revival of "Orientalism," a general denigration of Middle Eastern and North African cultures that should be subject to superior Western domination.

This dynamic is enveloping Western Europe and the United States. The presence of migrants is presumed to threaten jobs, the culture, and safety. The challenge to people's economic security raises enormous fear, especially at a time when the expectation that each generation will be better off than the former is fast disappearing. The presence of people with different languages, mores, dress, and values raises fear that our way of life is under siege. Because it is assumed that our customs and values are the norm, we are suspicious of anything that differs.

Linking immigrants with violence (rapists, murderers, and terrorists) strikes fear in the hearts of people in a world that seems overrun with violence. A friend of mine shared the fear she felt while traveling by train in Scandinavia when a young man she assumed was from the Middle East boarded the car and sat across the aisle from her. When he pulled the hoodie over his head and talked on his cell phone in a hushed voice for almost an hour, she became increasingly fearful he might be a terrorist. The story ended happily as he left the train and was greeted warmly by his family. Unfortunately, her response was not unusual. Much of the rising nationalism in Europe and the United States is built upon the fear of immigrants.

This is also fueled by a daily avalanche of possible threats to our lives from the movies, print media, and TV, where "if it bleeds, it leads." The top stories of the day consistently tell of violence, often identifying the violator by race. We are fed a diet of stories and fables that feed our tendency to create barriers between those who commit crimes and ourselves as potential victims. The closer the crime, the more fear it engenders. While news of a terrorist attack in another city or country will undoubtedly generate a sense of unease when we think of traveling there, the report of an armed robbery at a local store touches us even more deeply. It could literally have been us. We were there just yesterday. And with that possibility, our fear increases.

Fear is also one of the roots of ageism, which institutionalizes perceptions people have about the elderly, thus leading to Othering. As people grow older and leave the workforce, they relinquish a valued source of identity. Several years after I retired, I met a former student who asked, "Didn't you used to be Dick Snyder?" His question underscored the common tendency to assign primary value to the preretirement period and a concomitant sense of lost importance in retirement. Many elderly people experience the status anxiety that comes from the loss of role recognition with retirement. If I am no longer recognized as this or that, who am I? The problem is exacerbated when those viewing retirees assign them little or no value. If a person is of no value, then why acknowledge them, associate with them? And so, the elderly can be Othered, often walled off in separate communities.

Adding to the status anxiety that can lead to Othering is a fear of losing independence—a value highly prized in our society. Many years ago, I spent a week at Esalen, a center for Gestalt and other alternative therapies nestled high above the Pacific in Big Sur, California. While I was not elderly at the time, participating in a "blind walk" made me realize our deep fear of losing independence. I was blindfolded and took the arm of my guide. After a short time, I decided to walk on my own. The crashing surf below the cliffs was a reminder of how close danger lay. After realizing the peril of stumbling over some rocks, I asked her to give me her arm again. When she did, I began to cry. I had lost vision in one eye from an accident when I was twelve years old and always feared losing sight in the other eye. In that moment, however, I realized my real fear was not blindness but being dependent.

Many older people live with the fear of not being able to drive, manage their finances, or maintain their home. Becoming dependent can not only cause the older person to feel they are somehow "less," it can also cause others to reduce them to Other. And because each of us fears that happening to us, we tend to avoid those who remind us of that possibility by creating emotional and physical walls of separation.

It is interesting to note that loss of productivity, infirmity, and dependence are associated with the end of life. The gerontologist Erdman Palmore suggests an aversion to older people may be rooted in anxiety about death. Since death is greatly feared, so are elders because growing old is associated with death.[5] Perhaps it is the fear of death that leads many younger persons to refer to the elderly with negative stereotypes and to avoid them whenever possible. By treating the elderly as Other, they unconsciously hope to avoid being reminded of their own mortality.

Because fear is perhaps the greatest internal cause of Othering, many people are afraid of being treated or perceived as Other, and they go to great lengths to avoid all appearance of similarity to or contact with those who are different.

Ignorance

Sometimes Othering is caused by sheer ignorance. When I was young, I did not know the history of black people in the United States. I had no substantive contact with black people. There were no books about black history in my home, nor do I recall any discussions around our dining table about black lives, history, or culture. The absence of contact and reliable information, coupled with the overt racist views to which I was exposed and the dominant culture that portrayed white people as superior, allowed me to perceive black people as fundamentally different and inferior. As I grew older, information about black history was available, but I didn't pay attention; there were too many other things occupying my mind, such as sports, girls, grades, and automobiles. That ignorance allowed my distorted perception of black people to continue, albeit without malevolent intention.

With the emergence of the civil rights struggle, I had a choice to ignore what was increasingly evident or to take it seriously. Some of my friends chose to ignore it—a conscious refusal to know—and to label the civil rights struggle as propaganda, media hype, a Communist plot, or what today some would call "fake news." Absence of information, lack of contact through segregated neighborhoods and schools, failure to pay attention, intentional refusal to acknowledge the truth, or unwillingness even to consider the possibility of a different narrative all lead to ignorance that can contribute to Othering. And, it makes one vulnerable to propaganda by those who find it in their interest to exploit that ignorance.

When AIDS first came to the general public's attention, it was viewed as solely a "gay man's disease." Because of the stigma attached to homosexuality, it was assumed to be a befitting penalty for their behavior. Since gay people "deserved" the consequences of their lifestyle, there was limited attention to its cure. And because it was associated only with male homosexual behavior, most people failed to recognize that women, babies of mothers with HIV, and heterosexual people could also become infected.

As AIDS became more prevalent, the stigma increased, and the ignorance grew. Many people were fearful of even kissing a gay man on the cheek or of eating in a restaurant where a person with AIDS worked in the kitchen. Drinking from the common cup at communion became a serious concern in many churches, and some ceased the practice altogether.

People who had considered homosexuality unnatural or an abomination were now fearful of being contaminated by AIDS. Gay people were not just to be ignored or castigated, they were to be avoided. The marginalization of gay people intensified. There was a direct correlation between ignorance and Othering.

The narrative about Africa prevalent in Europe and the United States is another example of how ignorance leads to Othering. For years, Africa has been referred to as the Dark Continent, which is a metaphor for invisibility, vagueness, and ignorance. Since little or nothing was known of its inhabitants, they were assumed to be uncivilized savages as popularized in Joseph Conrad's *The Heart of Darkness*. Craig Murphy, a political scientist at Wellesley College, describes how European cartographers ignored the maps of earlier traders and provided detailed features only for the coasts, leaving the center blank, which gave rise to the notion of the Dark Continent.[6] Viewing the vast center of the continent as uncivilized and obscure led many to think of Africans as ignorant, primitive, cannibalistic, and violent, which helped them justify the slave trade.

While current maps of Africa no longer obliterate the center of the continent, it is interesting how many people today refer to Africa as a country or a nation rather than a continent composed of fifty-four nations. According to *The Economist*, it is larger than the United States, China, India, and Eastern Europe combined.[7] The continent of Africa remains largely unknown to most Westerners except as a locus of tribal conflicts, political corruption, and starving children. Its beauty, cultural richness, history, economic development, and friendly people remain unknown. One of the consequences is that its inhabitants are often considered Other.

The same is true with respect to Islam. Muslims are frequently looked upon with suspicion, and the West lives in fear of radical jihadists who believe the survival of Islam is dependent upon killing infidels. The 9/11 attacks and the rise of al-Qaeda, Islamic State of Iraq and the Levant (ISIL/ISIS), Boko Haram, and independent terrorist activities around the world feed the fear that all Muslims are our enemies, the evil Other. But we dare not permit ignorance to fan the flames of hatred and division. The label "jihadists" has been used to signify terrorists who seek to violently overthrow our way of life—hence Bush's "clash of civilizations." But the Arabic word *jihad* means struggle, and there are three kinds of struggle—only one is a holy war against infidels. First, Muslims are called to struggle against their tendency to fall short of the calling to be pure and do justice. This is an internal struggle many consider the most important form of jihad. The second struggle is to create a faithful Muslim society. The third struggle is to defeat those who seek to destroy Islam. While some Muslims have opted for armed response, the majority of Muslims throughout the world seek to live in peace. We must not allow the literal interpretation of portions of the Qur'an by fundamentalist Muslims to shape our understanding of Islam any more than we should allow literal interpretations of certain biblical texts by Christian fundamentalists to shape our understanding of Christianity.

It is also important to know many Muslims fear their religion and way of life are in danger of being eliminated. They know the wars waged and financed by the West have resulted in the death of Muslims throughout the world. Our drone strikes, bombs, and military presence cause them to see us as the evil Other. Despite this, the majority of Muslim leaders do not support a military jihad. While it is undeniable there have been egregious actions by some Muslims, our ignorance of their legitimate fears has led us to the verge of catastrophe. It is easier to view people as Other than to painstakingly pursue the truth.

In addition to personal characteristics of fear and ignorance that are fostered by social structures, there are social arrangements themselves that shape Othering.

Class

Discussions about class in our nation are often viewed as a throwback to a time when Communism appeared viable to many and Karl Marx was its champion. With the New Deal, World War II, the rising tide of wealth during the 1950s and 1960s, the collapse of the Berlin Wall, and the demise of the Soviet Union, one may conclude that class is passé. But class differences today are greater than at many previous junctures in history. Both Bernie Sanders and Donald Trump played to this fact in the 2016 presidential primaries and their campaigns for nomination/reelection in 2020. Trump focused on the difference between the common citizen and the elite Washington/New York insiders. Sanders also emphasized the division between common citizens and the elites. He went a step further by speaking about the enormous wealth gap between the one-tenth of one percent and the rest, and the ways in which the uber-elites exploit others for their benefit. Without using the term *class warfare*, both drew attention to the harsh class divide within our country.

The debate about class once again raises the question whether Othering is an essential element of our biological makeup or attributable to social factors. This is the classic "nature or nurture" debate. Marx claimed alienation (from ourselves, each other, our work, and nature) is rooted in the means of production and if we change our political economy, we can eliminate the basic experience of alienation. Others such as Hegel understood alienation to be an essential condition of humanity, a universally inherent idealistic human phenomenon that persists in all forms of societal structuring.[8]

The same debate occurs within Christianity among those who understand the human condition to be essentially one of innate depravity (human nature is fallen) versus those who believe in the essential dignity and worth of all persons and their freedom to choose good or evil. Like the latter, I don't believe human nature is inherently determined to create Others, incapable of choosing good because of an essentially evil nature, or destined for class conflict. So much depends upon the social context. Some German Protestants who had cordial and even friendly relations with Jews were gradually transformed into angry, hate-filled mobs as the culture changed under Nazi power. People are capable of both resisting and capitulating, and much is dependent upon the dominant culture.

It is critical to acknowledge the deleterious effects of class divisions that result in Othering. A study conducted in England about people who use food banks found that there was a consistent pattern of stigmatizing by those who were not in need of the safety net. In a number of cases, the stigma was so severe that some individuals actually starved themselves or rummaged in the garbage rather than risk being considered parasites. As the numbers of those needing assistance increased, so too did the general public's negative attitude toward the poor.[9]

The notion of "white trash" thrives today, and the link between poverty and laziness continues in the minds of many privileged white people, as well as in the minds of many poor white people themselves. Lisa Pruitt, a professor at the University of California–Davis, has studied the lives of poor white people and says that among them, work is associated with worth and only "white trash" take handouts.[10] Many others, like myself when my cousin came north from the hills of Kentucky, failed to understand those whom we labeled "white trash" had been marginalized and discarded. They were no longer needed as employees, and our contemptuous epithets only served to deepen their humiliation.

The debasing of impoverished Latin American migrants was similar. On Sundays when I was young, our family would often drive to visit my uncle who owned a cranberry farm in southern New Jersey where he employed migrant workers. He was a lay leader in his church, a respected member of the community who lived in a large, nicely appointed Victorian home. By contrast, the workers were housed in a basement with a damp dirt floor, and they worked long hours under difficult conditions. Yet, despite their hard work and hard life, he spoke disparagingly of migrant workers. He considered their poverty to be their own doing, discounting the substandard pay and working conditions the migrant workers experienced, including his own employees. He did not consider them worthy of a human relationship. They were just part of the machinery to harvest the cranberries. They were Other.

How often the poor are blamed for their circumstances is confounding. Laziness is thought to be inherent in their nature, even though, for example, some of the women serving as domestics in suburban homes arise before 5:00 a.m. to prepare their children's lunches and get them ready for school, then commute at least an hour to affluent neighborhoods, work a full day, commute home, prepare dinner, wash the dishes, and put the children to bed. These women are not poor because they are lazy. They are poor because they are not paid a living wage and have no health care or other benefits.

Many migrant workers are castigated for being poor, which is usually translated as "lazy" or "ignorant." They are portrayed as men lolling in the sun with sombreros over their eyes, waiting for mañana. For years, I served on the board of Rural and Migrant Ministry in New York State where I met a number of migrant workers, many of whom worked ten-hour days, six days a week, but still struggled to make ends meet because they owed their souls to the company store. The image of migrants as lazy and ignorant served the farm owners who hire them, the shopkeepers who sell them products, and the owners and shareholders of the companies that control the food systems. At no point along the food chain were they considered one of us. They were Other.

We live in a society in which upward mobility is both assumed and prized. The assumption is anyone who works hard can achieve their dream. Granted some have a greater head start: fine schools, well-connected families, adequate incomes. But according to the narrative, everyone, even those who must "pull themselves up by their bootstraps," has a chance. The myth of Horatio Alger is alive. In some instances, it is true, but even then, those who make it rarely rise above middle class.

There are several negative consequences in assuming ours is a nation in which anyone can become anything they dream. The first is those who don't make it up the ladder are deemed unworthy. They must not dream enough or work hard enough. They deserve to be poor because they are essentially inferior. This is "blaming the victim," a phrase popularized by William Ryan in the early 1970s in his book of the same name.[11] Blaming the victim allows us to view them as Other rather than blaming the system that has victimized them.

It is then easy to assume it is their nature, not the way things are organized, that accounts for their circumstance.

In addition to the assumption of deserved poverty, there is an expectation of upward mobility limited only by one's dreams and efforts. However, even if one advances a rung or two up the economic ladder, the most we achieve is the ability to consume a little more. But we have not gained more ability to decide or shape our world. Who among us would not eliminate poverty or end war if we were in charge? But we are not. Power remains in the hands of an elite few. The 2010 Supreme Court decision in *Citizens United v. Federal Election Commission* makes clear that those with unlimited funds have the legal right to exercise unlimited political power. The rest live as if this were the natural order of things. But it is not. Poverty and class divisions are the result of unjust power relations that benefit a few at the expense of the many.

Class differences often lead to stark divisions. Resentments run deep; blame is affixed on elites who control, the poor who seek handouts, or the government that fosters dependency or privilege at the expense of others. Othering runs in all directions.

Religion

As the Lebanese-born French journalist Amin Maalouf contends, there were times when toleration and coexistence held sway and other times when intolerance and totalitarianism were the norm within both Christianity and Islam. He documents how Christianity was intolerant of other faiths for many years, even totalitarian at times, but gradually became a religion of greater openness and tolerance. Islam on the other hand, took the opposite path, beginning rather open to other faith traditions, but becoming increasingly intolerant and totalitarian.[12] The contrast within Islam can be seen clearly in the experience of Al Andalus. Moors (Muslims) ruled much of Spain and Portugal for almost eight centuries (from early 700s to 1500), and during that time Jews and Christians enjoyed relative freedom. While they were taxed slightly more than Muslims, they were free to practice their faith, and some served in the government. That accommodation ended when Jews and Muslims were finally expelled by Christian monarchs Ferdinand and Isabella in 1492.

Tragically, there are roots of intolerance in the major Abrahamic religions that result in Othering. Earlier, I described the dividing line that biblical texts assert between the early Israelites and the Canaanites, a division that justified other conflicts for centuries. Of course, it is not just biblical stories that provided grounds for Othering. We have observed some ways Christian orthodoxy has created categories of heretics and infidels that have had dreadful consequences. Unfortunately, these divisions are not limited to the past. There are Christians today who draw upon their faith as a basis for Othering.

In a previous book, I claimed that popular Christian theology, especially in its Protestant form, contributes to the spirit of punishment similar to Max Weber's claim that the development of capitalism was deeply influenced by the theological ideas of Calvinism.[13] According to Weber, Calvinism provided a foundation for the idea that all work, including making money, was a legitimate calling and, hence, one should do one's very best. This notion of fulfilling one's calling by hard work was coupled with a strong asceticism that honored frugality and eschewed the ostentatious display of wealth. The result usually was the accumulation of wealth as savings or capital that, in turn, made investment possible.

Just as Weber understood Calvin's theology contributed to a developing capitalism, I explained how certain current theological teachings support a culture of punishment. In this book, I argue some interpretations and practices of Christianity provide roots for Othering. Obviously, there are Christians who seek to embrace rather than to exclude, but they often do so in spite of a commonly accepted theology that creates barriers between people.

This has occurred in a number of ways. Some branches of Christianity espouse a theological hierarchy of value: God, angels, humans, and animals, in descending order. Roman Catholicism has historically taught there is also a hierarchy among humans: clergy, monastics (such as nuns and friars), and laity in descending order. When we accept a hierarchy of value and worth, including proximity or access to God, it becomes easy to treat certain people as ontologically or essentially superior to others—men over women, white people over black people, straight over queer, the law abiding over the law breaking. It becomes us versus them.

Another significant way in which Othering is rooted in Christianity relates to the doctrine of sin. The most extreme notion of sin states we are born in original sin, are totally depraved and, therefore, eternally damned.[14] However, those who are saved have been born again, made new. And therein lies another potential for classification: some are lost, and some are saved. This is understood to be an ontological difference based on their condition: some will enjoy eternal bliss in heaven and others will suffer eternal punishment in hell.

Once we have accepted the idea people can be classified religiously, it is easy to embrace other classifications that are viewed as ontological differences. A contemporary division within our culture is the way we view those who commit a crime. "Murderer," "thief," or "felon" become a person's essence rather than aspects of a human being who has committed a terrible crime. The label becomes their identity, allowing us to see them as essentially evil, and thus less than human. We can then treat them as criminals and not as persons.

One important influence of Christianity on our culture is the notion of individualized salvation. Unlike the Jewish and even early Christian understanding that redemption involves the collective people—the nation or the community—much of contemporary Christianity views redemption or salvation solely in terms of the individual. When that is the case, it is a small step to viewing the wrongdoer as the sole source of the problem, ignoring how the decisions and structures of society contribute to crime and wrongdoing. When we treat individuals as solely responsible and ignore society's complicity, we are free to place the blame on the individual and label them Other.

Some radical jihadists similarly divide the world into a contest between them and us. Because they view Western civilization, including Christianity and Judaism, as diabolical, bereft of any redeeming values, and a threat to Muslim and Arab civilization, they believe it must be defeated at all cost. Why this apparently sudden rise of radical fanaticism?

According to Maalouf, Middle Eastern Arabs and Muslims have found their identity in a variety of social arrangements over the centuries: tribe, sultanate, religion, and nation.[15] Radical extremism was not the norm. While there have always been right-wing radicals within Islam who cite texts from the Qur'an that justify war on infidels, they were a small minority. Even today, the majority of imams and Islamic theologians affirm Islam is a religion of peace, and they reject the literalistic interpretation of passages from the Qur'an that call for or support religious war and killing. As Elise Boulding underscores in her study *Cultures of Peace*, there is a strong strain within Islam, including Sufism, and Baha'i for an emphasis upon the inner jihad.[16] Peace is the orientation of most of the approximately 1.5 billion Muslims, many of whom reside outside the Middle East in Africa, Asia, and elsewhere, including Indonesia, which has the largest Muslim population in the world. What we are experiencing in Islam now is the rise of a fundamentalist approach to religion. It is a tragedy that millions of peace-loving Muslims who have had to flee their country of origin to avoid being terrorized, or even killed by fundamentalist jihadists, are themselves considered terrorists by some citizens in the countries where they have sought asylum.

Maalouf, whose focus is on the Middle East, points out that prior to the rise of the extreme right in Islam, many Muslim and non-Muslim Arabs found their identity in Arab nationalism under the inspiring leadership of President Gamal Abdel Nasser, who led a military overthrow of Egypt's constitutional monarchy to end British occupation in 1952 and gave birth to a new nationalist pride.

They were nationalists, but not religious fundamentalists. But the potential of Arab nationalism came to an abrupt end with the decline and fall of Nasser and other Arab leaders. The undoing of nationalism was also accompanied by disillusionment with the atheism of Russian socialism and the failure of the West's liberal democracies—most especially the United States—to solve the problems of poverty, racism, and drugs. No longer able to find their identity in Arab nationalism, a deteriorating Communism, or a failing Western liberal order, many (especially the young) turned to religious radicalism for their source of identity, and beards and veils became prominent symbols of this new identity. Maalouf concludes their conversion to religious fundamentalism was a last resort.[17]

Lamentably, it is clear for many, categorizing and treating persons and governments as Other are inherent in a fundamentalist brand of religion.

While many Islamic clergy, theologians, and devout Muslims affirm their faith as a religion of peace, some texts in the Qur'an plainly label certain people as infidels who are to be killed. The terrorists who attacked the World Trade Center and the Pentagon, and who caused a plane to crash in Stonycreek Township, Pennsylvania, on 9/11 were significantly motivated by their faith and found justification for their violence in their understanding of early Islamic history when Muhammad called for raids against the Meccans. Comparative religions professor Hans G. Kippenberg analyzed the Spiritual Manual the 9/11 attackers relied upon as they prepared and carried out their assault on the United States. They referred to Q Tawbah 9:5, the so-called Sword Verse, in which faithful followers are commanded to slay the idolaters. As many interpreters have pointed out, this verse is not a carte blanche command for all times and places but was specific to the situation. However, fundamentalist followers have used this verse to justify killing all "infidels." That was the case with 9/11. In a summary of the theological understanding of the attackers, Kippenberg says the Spiritual Manual contains a ritual that removes the warrior "from everyday legal norms and turns him into a warrior-hero beyond the law. The people in the plane and the buildings are transformed into infidels deserving God's punishment."[18] For them, the infidels were Other.

One of the primary characteristics of fundamentalism is the literalistic interpretation of historic texts as holy and unchanging. In Christianity, biblical texts are deemed infallible or inerrant, not to be questioned, challenged, or reinterpreted. Islamic fundamentalists treat the Qur'an in the same way. This has led to many egregious acts, including suicide bombings, stoning homosexuals, and the suppression of women.

While, at times, religion has played a central role in fostering love, forgiveness, understanding, and community, it has unfortunately also provided the foundation for exclusion, rejection, and hatred that has created and perpetuated Othering.

Race

In chapter 1, I cite instances in which racism has been operative. The question is, how did race become a source of Othering?

One of the roots is a fundamental misconception about human nature. Although we are 99.9 percent genetically the same as all other people,[19] differences in skin color have been construed as evidence of an essential difference and have served as justification for racism. In 1972, Richard Lewontin concluded there are greater genetic differences within races than between races.[20] In 1994, the Human Genome Project similarly concluded there are more differences among individuals of the same race than between races.[21] Genetic scientists see race as one way of sorting or classifying persons, but it is not more essential than blood type, the shape of teeth, predisposition to certain diseases, or lactose intolerance.[22] But despite our genetic correspondence, pigmentation remains a major source of prejudice and has led to the perception of black people (and other people of color) as Other in the West. To understand how this has happened, it is necessary to understand the nature of racism.

In the West, racism is rooted in cultural perceptions that value white people more than people of color and that consider them superior. As Cornel West explains in his genealogy of racism, it is a combination of noneconomic and nonpolitical factors that provide the foundation for the culture of racism or what he calls "the structure of modern discourse."[23] He isolates three major historical developments in the rise of this culture: the scientific revolution that granted authority to observation and evidence; Descartes's philosophy that reinforced the critical function of observation; and the Classical Revival with its understanding of beauty as articulated by the Greeks. The emphasis upon observation, coupled with the Greek notion of beauty, eventually provided the foundation for delineation based on phrenology—lip size, forehead shape, eyelids, and so forth—with the conclusion of the observers (mostly white scientists and anthropologists) that white people constitute the natural form of humans and, hence, are superior to all others.[24]

Racism, however, involves more than prejudice or discourse. It is also an exercise of power: the power to create and enforce policies, to construct narratives, and to structure social arrangements. It is a system of power arrangements that oppresses black people and other people of color. Jim Crow laws were a legal form of power that maintained black people in their second-class status. As Michelle Alexander has documented, mass incarceration has become the new Jim Crow through its criminalization of black people.[25] This criminalization involves laws and policies that disproportionally arrest, convict, and sentence black people—a narrative that presents black people as a threat to safety and community—and social arrangements that systematically disadvantage incarcerated black people upon release.[26]

Class also plays a significant role in black people being viewed as Other. In 2015, the Federal Reserve Bank of Boston, Duke University, and the New School reported the median net worth of black households in Boston was $8 compared to $247,500 for white households.[27] Evidence of this enormous economic discrepancy contributes to the existing perception that black people and other people of color are inferior and that difference is attributable to the character of the races. But the real explanation for this lower-class status of black people is rooted in the historical use of power to discriminate and oppress.

During slavery, black people did not own land, houses, or even themselves. Laws were passed, such as Oregon's exclusionary laws, prohibiting black people from even entering the territory, and the Federal Donation of Land Act of 1859 that excluded black people from land grants, thereby ensuring white domination. Following the Civil War, an increasing number of states imposed a poll tax, effectively marginalizing black voters who initially thought the Union's Civil War victory had granted them full freedom. They were quickly disabused of this notion. During Reconstruction, there was a systematic pattern of taking land from black people. The promise of agrarian reform to allocate former plantation lands to black people, known as "forty acres and a mule,"[28] was an empty one for most, and many of those who did receive land were later evicted. This deprivation continued with racial covenants and real estate "redlining" that excluded black people from buying in certain neighborhoods, forcing them into ghettos. And it was exacerbated with the development of public housing that created inferior-quality, dangerous, and overcrowded dwellings into which many of the poor, especially black and Latinx people, were forced to live by default.

The result of the historic and systematic exclusion of black people from ownership has guaranteed the lack of assets to be passed down to future generations, which is a major source of wealth for white people. The Boston report indicates the racial gap in assets is primarily due to the lack of "inheritances, bequests, and intrafamily transfers" rather than to education, income level, or family life.[29] The myth that black people do not have money because of their lack of effort or frugality is inaccurate yet still active in supporting Othering.

While it is important to recognize the power dynamics of racism may exist without conscious prejudice, they are, nonetheless, damaging to persons of color. Racism can function without people intentionally wanting to harm anyone. My own ignorance of the injustices that gave rise to most black people living in separate, inferior housing in our suburb did not alter the facts. I did not see power dynamics, only skin color, making it easy for me to assume this was the "natural" order. I would venture most people I knew were unaware of the legacy, policies, economics, and culture that led to black people being treated as Other. One did not have to be consciously racist to assume that our housing pattern was simply the way things were. But that lack of awareness did not diminish the injustice of systemic racism and its deleterious impact.

There are, of course, many instances when racism is a conscious act—the result of a practice or a policy actively supporting injustice based on race. Many of the recent cases of police brutality toward black people have revealed prejudicial treatment, including the use of epithets and derogatory language. Even more damaging than personal invectives are the sustained practices built into current systems. An investigation by the US Department of Justice following the 2014 fatal shooting of Michael Brown in Ferguson, Missouri, found a "pattern and practice" of discrimination against black people. Attorney General Eric Holder accused the Ferguson police of routinely violating the Fourth Amendment. He pointed to a pattern of stopping drivers "without reasonable suspicion, arresting them without probable cause, and using unreasonable force against them."[30]

My socialized views and attitudes toward black people as a young person did not directly affect black people, as I had infrequent contact with them. More importantly, I was not in a position to exercise any power that might shape the relations between us. I did not control or influence policies regarding housing or employment, nor the practices of law enforcement and the justice system. I was too young to vote and did not have a voice in those decisions. At that early stage in life, I was merely prejudiced. But that prejudice served to support the racism of the status quo. Every joke, disparaging comment, or claim of superiority I made or let pass allowed things to go unchallenged and unchanged. My attitudes conformed to the racist culture that was telling me I was superior to people of color.

Are we born with an innate sense of racial superiority or inferiority? Is there something in human nature, in our biology or genes or psychological makeup that leads us to construct these evils, or does something else influence us to think and act in this way? Are we hardwired to be racists? Eric Knowles, a psychology professor at New York University who studies prejudice and politics, acknowledges while we are biologically disposed to dividing the world into "us and them," there is no evidence that racial divisions are endemic to our biological makeup. Rather, he concludes the drawing of racial lines is social, not biological.[31] Racism is a social construct that arises from our tendency to include some and exclude others. But there is no natural or inborn proclivity to draw lines based upon skin color. Those distinctions are ones we create.

Some would claim white people are born with prejudices that lead to both attitudes toward and treatment of persons of color as Other. But when we observe very young children in the play yard, we don't see them excluding or erecting walls. They play with whoever is present. Whatever racial differences exist among them are not a cause for treating some as inferior. They are all playmates. However, if a person they trust tells them not to play with someone who is "different" because of their race and suggests they are mean, dangerous, might carry a disease, or don't know how to play nicely (i.e., in a "civilized" manner), then the beginnings of racial prejudice occur. The social structure was there before the white child developed a sense that differences in skin color were a cause for distancing and feeling superior, for treating children of color as Other. Differentiating between those in the in-group and those who are not does not necessarily evolve from an innate racist sense. Who is in and who is out is socially constructed; it is part of the culture by which the child is being shaped. When the culture is racist, then the individual child's experience of difference, combined with a proclivity to draw lines, can easily become part of that racist culture.

Claiming racism is not innate is similar to the theological claim not totally depraved because of the fall of Adam and Eve. rth, we have the potential of doing good or bad. That is the h with which we enter the world. To the extent that the world t, it is exceedingly difficult to avoid committing unjust acts. In the same manner, to the extent that the world into which we step is racist, it is difficult not to succumb to racism. But such thoughts and actions are not innately predetermined.

Today, we live in a world that is shaped by systemic racism. Despite some changes and gains for black people and other people of color, many white people enjoy privileges that result from our racist structures. The ability of most white people to find employment, purchase a home, obtain an education, secure a loan, or enjoy retirement are privileges that are made significantly more difficult and are sometimes systematically denied to people of color. Unfortunately, this has led many white people to conclude that black people don't deserve these things because they are inferior. The irony is as more and more white people find themselves locked out of jobs, their mortgages foreclosed, and a comfortable retirement out of reach, they attribute their static or downward mobility to big government doling handouts to black people and other people of color. They now see the poor, and especially the government, as the reason for their own declining fortunes.

This dynamic is made clear in Arlie Russell Hochschild's study of Tea Party members in southern Louisiana.[32] She wondered why they vote against their own self-interests and why they blame government for their plight. They support legislators who want to roll back or eliminate the Environmental Protection Agency even though their lands have been desecrated by oil spills, their houses have fallen into sinkholes, and their rivers and lakes are so polluted they can no longer fish. They are against the federal government, although Louisiana receives 44 percent of its income from the federal government—one of the highest in the nation. The key to their vote is they believe the federal government's welfare handouts and affirmative action laws are allowing black people, women, refugees, and undeserving poor to cut in front of them in the line that leads to upward mobility. For them, the future is bleak and it's not fair. What Hochschild discovered was "[t]he shifting moral qualifications for the American Dream had turned them into strangers in their own land, afraid, resentful, displaced and dismissed by the very people who were, they felt, cutting in line." And the blame lay with the "supplier of the imposters—the federal government."[33] She goes on to say: "They'd begun to feel like a besieged minority. And to those feelings they added the cultural tendency to identify 'up' the social ladder . . . and to feel detached from those further down the ladder."[34]

Gender

Just as with skin color, there are clearly observable differences between men and women in body size, shape, composition, and strength. In this case, the biological differences are marked. According to Carothers and Reis, "we are more likely to categorize people based on gender than race. People use gender to sort individuals into categorical 'natural kinds' more than they use twenty other kinds of social categories."[35] These differences have led to many misunderstandings that resulted in the Othering of women. Women have experienced second-class treatment for centuries in the United States. Why has gender been a source of Othering?

There have been advocates of the inferiority of women for millennia. Classics scholar Mary Beard recounts how Homer's *Odyssey*, written approximately three thousand years ago, describes an interchange between Penelope and her son Telemachus. In response to her admonishing a musician for playing melancholic music, he silences her and orders her to return to her room, telling her, "Speech will be the business of men, all men, and of me most of all; for mine is the power in this household."[36] Aristotle viewed the natural order of things as a hierarchy in which children, slaves, and women were viewed as dependent upon men who were deemed to be more rational and better suited to lead. In the 1800s, Charles Darwin wrote *The Descent of Man*, positing the innate intellectual inferiority of the female based on his theory that men represent the apex of evolutionary development,[37] an argument that provided justification for the treatment of women as second class in Victorian England.

Even today, some suggest there are essential differences in temperament between men and women. Women are seen as nurturers, emotional, internally focused, and relational while men are considered aggressive, rational, problem solvers, and leaders. John Gray's extremely popular self-help book (fifty million copies sold), *Men Are from Mars, Women Are from Venus*, asserts men and women are essentially different psychologically and offers guidelines for negotiating the terrain between them.[38] This pop psychology, with its portrayal of the differences between the genders as essential, has many followers among the general public and some religious leaders. However, the preponderance of critics, including psychologists, psychiatrists, and scientists, make a distinction between differences that are essential—such as strength and anthropometric measurements—and those that are a matter of degree—such as empathy, caring, social relationships, mathematical versus linguistic orientation, and intimacy. These differences are substantially shaped by cultural norms, historic expectations, and systemic factors. There is extensive research corroborating the psychological differences pointed out by John Gray are not fundamental but are simply a matter of degree. The Myers-Briggs psychological test registers a mix of features: introversion and extroversion, thinking and feeling, intuition and sensing, judgment and perception. There is no "pure" type, and the types are not fixed by gender. Nonetheless, representing women as essentially or ontologically different from men continues to provide a rationale for Othering.

Religion has also been a major source of Othering of women. Judaism, Christianity, and Islam have texts that, when interpreted literally, treat women as Other. Both Jewish and Christian literalists believe the Genesis account of the fall places the blame upon Eve for the entrance of sin into the world. Because she listened to the serpent and then convinced Adam to eat the fruit of the tree bearing the knowledge of good and evil, the consequence of her action is "in pain you shall bring forth children, yet your desire shall be for your husband, and he shall rule over you."[39] St. Paul continued to uphold the subordinate role of women when he compared the subjection of women to men with the subjection of the church to Christ. "Just as the church is subject to Christ, so also wives ought to be, in everything, to their husbands."[40] Sharia Law in Islam also upholds the second-class status of women. "Men are the managers of the affairs of women for that God has preferred in bounty one of them over the other. . . . Righteous women are therefore obedient."[41]

These texts, and many others, have served as the basis for the contemporary treatment of women as Other by religious leaders and communities. Orthodox Jewish men are required to offer three prayers daily, the second of which is, "Thank G-d who has not made me a woman." In Orthodox Judaism, women are not permitted to become rabbis or to read the Torah in public services. Some Christian traditions refuse to ordain women. Roman Catholicism insists on a male priesthood since priests are in Christ's stead, and Jesus was a man. Under Islamic Sharia law, a woman must be fully covered, except for the eyes, when in public. One of the most horrific instances of strict Islamic law being used to treat women as Other occurred in 2002 when fifteen young Saudi girls died in a fire. They were not permitted to leave the burning school, nor were men allowed to try to save them, because they were not wearing the required headscarves and black robes.[42] They were not male, so they were allowed to die.

In my early socialization toward girls and women, I did not have the power to shape policies that affected women in relation to employment, compensation, or health care, for example. Nor did my attitudes and values constitute a developed ideology that explicitly aided and abetted sexist structures. But in uncritically accepting the world in which I was living, I was an unwitting supporter of the sexism of our culture.

Like racism, sexism involves not just prejudice based on assumptions of essential difference, it also involves power. Sexism is rooted in a hierarchical power dynamic that places fundamental control in the hands of men. This does not mean women have no power, but rather social, cultural, economic, and political control is largely dominated by men and operates for their benefit. White men, in particular, enjoy privileges our sexist structures make possible: the assumption of authority, greater mobility, higher pay, and the right to silence women. On Wednesday, February 7, 2017, Senator Elizabeth Warren was told to "sit down and shut up" by a male-dominated Senate when she dared to read a letter critical of Jeff Sessions who was being considered for appointment as attorney general. When Bernie Sanders later read the same letter, he was not silenced.[43] The contrast couldn't be clearer. When power resides largely in the hands of men and is coupled with the assumption of essential difference that is rationalized by pop psychology and religion, gender becomes a source of Othering.

Anti-Semitism

Anti-Semitism was not limited to Europe. Much of the United States' history is rife with persons, policies, and structures that have portrayed and treated Jews as second class and, in some cases, disposable.

One of the leading anti-Semitic voices in the early twentieth century was the industrialist Henry Ford. He epitomized the American dream for many; hence, his views carried a great deal of weight. His widely read four-volume publication of the 1920s, *The International Jew*, alleged a subversive conspiracy of Jewish imperialism that threatened to control business, media, the arts, and finance. The book became influential in the United States and also had a substantial impact on the rise of anti-Semitism among the Nazis. To propagate his views more broadly in the United States, he bought the *Dearborn Independent* newspaper that carried the same message.

When Kristallnacht signaled the full-blown onset of the Holocaust in Germany in late 1938, Jewish lives were at stake, prompting efforts to obtain US visas for them. For approximately the next six years, our government largely refused to provide refugee status for Jews fleeing Nazi threats. Though reports of the eviction of Jews from their homes and businesses, ghettoization, mass deportations, and, eventually, news of the death camps reached the United States, our government's focus was on winning the war, not rescuing the Jews. In the meantime, Jews were being slaughtered.

While not overtly stated, it became clear the rationale for ignoring the plight of the Jews was to avoid their migration to the United States. One of the reasons for this resistance was the Communist leanings of some of the Jewish intellectuals and leaders. Another possible reason was our government and businesses were run principally by white Christian men who may have wished to maintain power.

Evidence of the latter can be seen in our State Department's response to the plea for visas from its office in Switzerland. In reply, the State Department sent a cable instructing the office to suppress information about the extermination of Jews. They had received many reports from various private sources about the mass killings but were told not to release the reports. When the Treasury Department, under Henry Morgenthau Jr., discovered this, Morgenthau presented the evidence to President Franklin D. Roosevelt.[44] There was a clear, intentional plan to refuse both aid and admission to Jewish refugees. This refusal included forbidding a ship carrying Jewish refugees from Germany in 1939, the MS *St. Louis*, to unload its passengers in the United States or Canada.[45]

After years of pleading by the American Jewish community, Morgenthau, and others, President Roosevelt finally signed the War Refugee Board Act in January 1944. Despite this act, US response to the plight of Jews seeking escape from the Nazis was minimal. Funding was insufficient, and the State Department continued to drag its heels. In 1944, fifty-five thousand quota places were not used.

When the War Refugee Board asked the War Department to bomb the crematorium at Auschwitz, they were told the flight distance from England made it impossible. However, the bombers and their fighter escorts were regularly flying a greater distance from Italy and bombing the area around Auschwitz. Tens of thousands of lives could have been saved by destroying the crematorium. The US never did.[46]

The Jews were perceived as undesirable, a threat to our way of life, and ultimately, disposable. They were Other.

Colonialism

Another devastating root of Othering has been colonization. Major critics of colonialism such as Frantz Fanon[47] and Albert Memmi[48] make clear that colonialism is Manichean, i.e., a dualistic dynamic: colonizer and colonized, subjugator and subjugated, settler and native. These binary categories involve essential forms of Othering.

Colonization involves economic control and exploitation of resources by the colonizer. The economics of colonial control have, in most cases, resulted in the impoverishment of the native population. Land has been confiscated; local, sustainable, multi-crop agriculture has been replaced by single-crop economies controlled by foreign corporations; and natural resources, including food products, have been exported and then imported in boxes and tins at substantially higher prices. A few lines from Pablo Neruda's classic poem, "The United Fruit Company," convey the power and consequences of colonialism in Latin America.

The most succulent item of all,
The United Fruit Company Incorporated
reserved for itself: the heartland
and coasts of my country,
the delectable waist of America.
They rechristened their properties:
the "Banana Republics"—
And over the languishing dead . . .
they ravished all enterprise.[49]

The exercise of political control has been a critical element of colonization. In some cases, such as Britain's rule over India, the foreign power settled in the country and exercised direct control. In other cases, such as Iran during the time of the Shah, an internal oligarchy ran the country at the behest of the colonizing powers. Whether by means of foreign administration, the use of an internal ruling elite, or some combination thereof, political control has always been in the hands of the colonizing nation.

Colonization also often involves military violence to maintain control. Sometimes that control has been direct, leading to military intervention by the colonizing troops, as in India. At other times it was indirect, utilizing internal military as in the 1954 violent overthrow of Guatemala's Jacobo Arbenz. The democratically elected president was removed from power by a Guatemalan military coup demanded by external corporate interests and supported directly by the US State Department and the Central Intelligence Agency. Arbenz had been instrumental in giving back land to peasant farmers whose land had been confiscated by large corporations such as the United Fruit Company. His agrarian reform program challenged and threatened the colonial economic structure, thus resulting in the military coup.[50]

In cases of economic, political, and military control by a foreign power, the dualistic category of colonizer and colonized applied. Those categories were expanded to include exploiter and exploited, rich and poor, dominator and dominated. As we have seen, once people are consigned to categories, it is an easy step to Othering.

While economic, political, and military domination have been critical aspects of colonization, perhaps the worst consequence has been the diminishment and, in some cases, the destruction of the indigenous culture. As Federico Ferro Gay alleges:

> There is another bondage, which is much more profound in its roots, more general and mischievous in its effects, more difficult to eradicate, and more shameful for the countries subject to it, which can be identified with cultural colonialism. . . . This bondage consists in the imitation

of foreign languages, customs, and feelings, that is, in the absolute loss of the national idiosyncrasy.[51]

He also mentions a Mexican female entrepreneur who chose to give her newly created face cream an English name, fearing a Spanish name would not sell.

This cultural shaping has been accomplished through the substitution of narratives, heroes, images, religions, literature, media, cinema, and even language by the colonizing power. When central elements of a people's identity have been removed, erased, or debased and replaced by the colonizing power, the consequence is Othering.

Exceptionalism

Since its beginning, our nation has had a sense that it is exceptional. Uri Friedman has examined the ongoing reality of American exceptionalism, beginning with the Puritans' belief that New England was called by God to be a city set on a hill, a beacon of liberty for all to see. Their belief flowed from the biblical metaphor that a city set on a hill cannot be hidden. As we became a nation, that motif continued. And a 2010 Gallup poll found 80 percent of Americans "believe the United States has a unique character that makes it the greatest country in the world."[52]

The United States is not the only nation that has considered itself exceptional. When Barack Obama said he believed in American exceptionalism, he added other countries, including Britain and Greece, each believe in their own exceptionalism. Louisiana governor Bobby Jindal criticized him for failing to see US exceptionalism as truly exceptional; nevertheless, Obama was correct.[53]

Many nations and empires have considered themselves to be exceptional. For religious Jews, for example, Israel has a sense of its exceptionalism based on the biblical view that the Jews are God's chosen people and have been granted the land of Palestine by divine mandate. While there are also secular interpretations of their exceptionalism that grow out of the Jewish people's survival of the horrors of the Holocaust and other historic persecutions, the religious foundations have significantly shaped Israel's self-perception.

Britain understood itself to be exceptional in its economic development and international reach that created colonies throughout the world. Nazi Germany considered itself exceptional based on the ideology of the Aryan race's superiority and Germany's responsibility to restore the purity of the race.

In these cases and others, the notion of exceptionalism entailed both the idea of superiority and a sense of responsibility. If the nation is a beacon of liberty, chosen by God, racially pure, or advanced beyond all others, then, other than for isolationists, it has a responsibility to bring its purportedly civilized way to the rest of the world. Claiming it had a God-given responsibility, the United States applied the doctrine of Manifest Destiny to justify its expansion, first across the continent, and then in the late 1800s across the Caribbean and Pacific islands.

Belief in American exceptionalism continues in the contemporary calls for the United States to spread democracy and the American way of life to other nations. The belief our form of democracy and culture is superior to others is based on the notion of our exceptionalism. Even if we grant other nations also think of themselves as exceptional, we believe we are more exceptional than others.

In a dire warning against our nation's assumption, former ambassador Charles Freeman said:

> For more than two centuries, American exceptionalism has appealed to the angels of humanity's better nature. But, as the twenty-first century advanced, foreigners began to see American claims to political privilege and demands for legal immunity as instances of assertive irresponsibility. The result is steadily reduced foreign support for the hegemonic privileges and double standards to which America had come to feel entitled.[54]

Unfortunately, our nation's sense of being exceptional, along with the concomitant responsibility to show others the way, has often come with a feeling that other nations and people are benighted, bound, impure, lost, uncivilized, or underdeveloped. As Edward W. Said exhaustively documented in his account of Orientalism, one of the results of our exceptionalism is Othering.[55]

This certainly does not exhaust the roots of Othering, but it addresses some of the more fundamental elements. These roots are both personal and systemic. Each of us is capable of exclusion or embrace. In a culture shaped by dominant powers seeking their own benefit, the potential for Othering is exponentially expanded. In the next chapter, I will examine some of the forms Othering takes.

3

The Forms of Othering

Ideas, cultures, and histories cannot seriously be understood or studied without their force, or more precisely their configurations of power, also being studied.

—Edward W. Said, *Orientalism*

To understand how people are Othered, it is critical to pay attention to the various forms in which this happens. Some of those forms are quite obvious, such as demonization. Calling someone evil or demonic relegates them to a status qualitatively different from the denouncer—as inhuman or unredeemable. Other forms are much more subtle and can even appear to be innocent, such as the medical profiling to predict potential disorders. But the consequences for the person or the group being profiled can result in Othering. For example, women's medical problems were diagnosed as hysteria for many years, eventuating in the dismissal of their illnesses and personhood. It is important to understand the multiple forms Othering takes so we are not limited to noting its more obvious occurrences.

Another reason to be alert to the ways in which Othering occurs is the malleability of its forms. Just when one form of Othering has been denounced as unethical or socially unacceptable, it can reappear in a different form.

For example, when slavery was abolished, racism was reformulated through the institution of Jim Crow laws that treated black people as inferior, to be feared, and relegated to second-class status. When the civil rights movement of the 1950s and 1960s eliminated Jim Crow laws, they were replaced by the mass incarceration of black people, resulting in the criminalization of black people with consequences similar to those suffered under Jim Crow laws. In other words, while the forms of racism have differed over time, the effects are the same.

Without attempting to prioritize or chronologically order its various configurations, the following examples are some of the more important and often insidious forms Othering has taken and continue to occur.

Demonization

Historical enemies are commonly demonized, labeled as evil or agents of the devil. Generally speaking, the notion of the demonic has been a religious concept or at least one with religious implications. Those labeled demonic may be considered to be doing the devil's work or, in some cases, such as the Salem "witches," thought to be possessed by a supernatural demon. To demonize a person or a group is to allege they are fundamentally evil and must be exorcised or destroyed.

The biblical injunction for the Israelites to reject false gods is closely tied to instructions to annihilate the people who serve those gods after the God of Israel defeats them and settles the Israelites in their place.[1] Accounts of such total destruction are familiar in the description of Joshua at Canaanite Jericho, among others, lest the continuing presence of alternatives to the God of Israel lead them astray. These stories, although not supported by archaeological evidence, did and do have a significant impact on future audiences.

One of the tragic misconceptions resulting in the Christian demonization of Muslims, and to some extent Jews, is the belief they worship other, false gods. As historians of religion recognize, however, Allah in Arabic means simply "God," and Muslims believe they are following a more recent revelation to the Prophet Muhammad by the same God worshipped by Jews and Christians. They enacted this belief in areas governed by Muslims by granting special, more favorable status to the other "people of the book." Their common heritage was difficult to maintain in practice, however, when European Christians took military action against Muslims in the Crusades and later made territorial claims after World War I. Not until the late nineteenth and twentieth centuries did many Middle Eastern Jews leave their long-established residences in Muslim cities and resettle in what became modern Israel.

The history of Christianity is replete with demonization. Elaine Pagels points out that as Christianity matured, the notion of satanic enemies included many opponents: the Romans, who were persecuting the Christians; Jews, who were considered the killers of Jesus; and eventually, those Christians who were deemed heretical. Heretics were those who, claiming to be Christian, did not accept the doctrinal formulations of orthodoxy. The demonization of Jews and heretics did not end with the early church. "In the sixteenth century, Martin Luther . . . denounced as 'agents of Satan' all Christians who remained loyal to the Roman Catholic Church, all Jews who refused to acknowledge Jesus as Messiah, all who challenged the power of the landowning aristocrats by participating in the Peasants' War, and all 'protestant' Christians who were not Lutheran."[2] These agents of Satan were considered Other.

In the late 1600s in Salem, Massachusetts, a number of women, men, and girls (as young as four years old) were accused of being possessed by the devil and causing harm to other people. For a few months, pandemonium ran rampant as the Salem witch trials were held. Accusations were made, trials were hastily held by a specially appointed court, and fourteen women and five men were convicted and hanged by the time the panic ended. Others died in prison.

The Nazis often associated Jews with the devil, using the language of the demonic to depict the Jews as evil. One of their posters portrayed the devil removing a mask that covered the face of a

Jewish person. Another referred to a Jewish person as an evil spirit or even Satan himself. The November 1937 issue of the Nazi propaganda paper, *Der Stürmer*, published "Demon Money," a cartoon of a Jewish person as a monster greedily encircling the world. One of the Nazis' most demonizing claims was that Jews ritually murdered Christians to use their blood in their religious rites.[3]

A more recent example of demonization was the 2002 accusation by President George W. Bush that North Korea, Iran, and Iraq constituted an Axis of Evil. Although there were clearly other nations with whom we had severe grievances at the time, these three were considered to be in a different category for sponsoring terrorism and developing weapons of mass destruction, leading up to the 2003 invasion of Iraq.

Demonizing people has been a frequent form of Othering.

Animalization

Often persons considered Other have been portrayed as animals. World War II was a time of rampant animalization. Early Nazi propaganda posters portrayed Jews as avaricious rats seeking to devour good Germans, as worms creeping to get what they want, and as serpents threatening to attack Germans. During World War II, the Japanese were routinely depicted in US propaganda posters, cartoons, and comics as monkeys or as rats with huge teeth. These conscious attempts to portray the enemy as nonhuman took hold throughout our nation.[4]

There have been more subtle instances of animalization as well, particularly in children's literature and film. At a very early age, children learn to erect walls as they receive lessons from the culture around them. Parental prejudices are quickly absorbed, as well as the alienating messages in the media. One of the dominant influences on very young children is the cartoon portrayal of certain people as Other. Maggie Griffith Williams and Jenny Korn show how the popular 2009 British children's film, *Hero of the Rails*, embodies a latent communication of Othering, masked by the message of the benefits of friendship.[5]

With the exception of the dominant railway manager, each character is portrayed as a railroad engine. The voices and color of Thomas, the protagonist, and the other engines are clearly Anglo and in good running order. But Hiro is different: he is broken and in need of help. That is not all that differentiates him from the others. Williams and Korn identify at least four ways Hiro is Othered in the film: "(1) his glamorized description as 'strange,' (2) his heavily accented voice, (3) his Japanese origin story, and (4) his pigmentation and powerlessness."[6] Denigration of Hiro and his symbolism as Asian, which is conflated with Japanese in this movie, are promoted. While not animals, the engines do serve to express inhuman stereotypes.

It is easy to dismiss such stories as merely innocent; indeed, it is conceivable the writer was oblivious to the message it latently conveyed. But the absence of intention does not absolve the story of its negative influence.

Animalization has been notoriously used as a depiction of black people, particularly during the days of slavery and Jim Crow when they were commonly portrayed as monkeys or apes in cartoons and literature. "Biological determinism" differentiated the origins of the various races. Each was viewed as being biologically distinct from the other, and black people were said to have developed from apes and monkeys. This approach was popularized by Josiah C. Nott and George R. Gliddon in their publication, *Types of Mankind*, in 1854.[7] Interestingly, this was just a few years before Darwin's *On the Origin of Species* in which he made the opposing claim, that all people were of the same origin and differences were determined by evolution. Despite Darwin's thesis, the identification of black people with apes and monkeys was indelibly fixed for many, providing the rationalization for psychological and physical violence toward them. If they are not really human, then they can be treated inhumanely.

For most people today, such an overt identification would be considered racist. Nonetheless, according to research published in

2008, many white participants associated black people with apes, even though few knew the history of that association.[8] This association has had an impact on some juries that, in identifying black people as apelike, have handed down verdicts leading to their execution.[9]

Another form of animalization occurred during the Vietnam War—a time of incredible tensions as police and protestors faced off against one another. TV and magazines showed images and reported stories of police brutality, including the killing of four and wounding of nine college students at Kent State in 1970. Their killing intensified the characterization of the police as pigs. Protestors carried signs with pictures of a police officer with the face of a pig while others made pig-like oinks to convey the message. Categorizing police in this way allowed the protestors to avoid dealing with them as fellow human beings. Many of the protestors had little or no familiarity with the police outside the antagonistic dynamics of the protests or what they saw on TV or read in the papers. Like most forms of Othering, the great distance between the two groups facilitated categorization. To the protestors, the police were "pigs." The fact some knew an officer personally and thought of them as a good neighbor or friend was considered the exception. In general, they were lumped together and categorized as animals.

Numbering

I first became aware of numbering as undermining people's identity during the years I taught in New York Theological Seminary's master's degree program at Sing Sing Prison. The men's names were important to them. One man proudly used his surname that denoted his family's status and wealth. Others changed their names when they converted to Islam, signaling an affirmation of their new identity. However, for the prison system, the prisoners' names were irrelevant. Each class session was interrupted by a corrections officer conducting a roll call: "Prisoner Number 596, answer if present." No names, just numbers.

Similarly, Nazi captors knew millions of Jews only by the numbers tattooed on their arms. The faceless prisoners were divided into groups: those who were temporarily useful and those who were to be exterminated immediately. The concentration camps needed physical laborers to do the work the Nazi themselves would not do. Those who could provide physical labor were serviceable and given a number. Those who were judged unnecessary were executed. To this day, Jews with a tattooed number on their arm remind us of the horrors of a system that designated those deemed "not pure," but temporarily exploitable, as Other. The purity rationale may have disguised another number, the belief Jews controlled disproportionate wealth that could be confiscated.

Our culture lives and dies by the numbers. Some numbering is simply for convenience, such as waiting in line at the motor vehicle office. Although it may make a person feel somewhat less significant, we are prepared to accept our number and subsequent wait as a necessary annoyance. Some numbering has a more deleterious effect on people, though not designed to Other. In a few cases, it serves as a marker of unworthiness, of not meeting the expectation of others. The Scholastic Aptitude Test (the SAT) for college admission can function that way. One of the most frequently heard questions on high school campuses is, "How did you score on the SATs?" Anxieties run high and there are stories of students committing suicide due to their sense of failure.

The SATs do not test equitably or effectively, advantaging some and disadvantaging others. Many students from lower socioeconomic backgrounds are significantly disadvantaged since they often cannot afford special tutoring, preparatory books, or repeat tests many of the economically privileged students use. The publishers also have acknowledged a male-oriented bias in the math section of the test, which they have subsequently sought to mitigate.[10] While the consequences are not systematically intended to negatively impact disadvantaged students, they nevertheless unintentionally harm millions of students who are left behind in the competitive marketplace of college education and subsequent employment opportunities. This may not rise to the level of Othering, but it fits comfortably with our Othering culture and systematically sorting people as worthy and unworthy, based on numbers.

Women are often reduced to numbers. Beauty pageants judge women on numeric scales. While no one who scores low on the scale is invited to enter the pageants, the winner is the one with the highest cumulative number. Unfortunately, this numbering scale has become an accepted part of the broader culture and is not relegated to only pageants.

The 1979 movie 10, starring Bo Derek and Dudley Moore, portrayed a man suffering from midlife crisis who fixated on a beautiful young woman. The movie plods along with scene after scene focusing on the woman's physical beauty, accompanied by Ravel's "Bolero" on the soundtrack. While it received only a 53 percent rating from Rotten Tomatoes, the message was a hit—namely, the numbering of a woman on the beauty scale.

A woman who rates a ten is considered beautiful, desirable, and a winner. A woman who ranks low on the scale is considered (even sometimes called) ugly, disgusting, and a loser. When debate moderator Megyn Kelly confronted presidential candidate Donald Trump with his having called women fat pigs, dogs, slobs, and disgusting animals, he facetiously said, "Only Rosie O'Donnell."[11] He was greeted with uproarious laughter. But it is not a laughing matter. His demeaning words fit well with the inclination to rate women by numbers.

In a study of the beauty ideal in children's fairy tales, the authors conclude the emphasis on the beauty ideal may "operate as a normative social control for girls and women."[12] While they reject the idea of a conspiracy among publishers to promote sexist values, they find the impact upon girls and women often does just that. When authors or publishers gauge girls or women on physical beauty, they reinforce a sense of who is valuable and who isn't.[13]

Profiling

One of the most common forms of Othering is profiling. According to the Oxford Dictionary, profiling is a process that involves "the recording and analysis of a person's psychological and behavioral characteristics, so as to assess or predict their capabilities in a certain sphere to assist in identifying a particular subgroup of people."[14] While this definition involves recording and analysis, ordinary people often engage in profiling when they assign characteristics or predict behaviors based on limited knowledge or biases. Profiling without careful recording and analysis can be detrimental.

Many years ago, while walking in Harlem, I encountered a black man whose appearance struck fear within me, a feeling I acknowledge with remorse. I had no basis for my response other than profiling. But I decided to say "Hi" and when I did, he broke into a huge smile and said, "Hey bro, how are you?" I realized in that moment how easy and destructive it can be to profile.

Technical profiling, done by professionals, can sometimes be useful. The medical profession often engages in profiling, alerting them to patients who may be prone to specific illnesses. Psychiatrist Sally Satel defended patient profiling in a *New York Times Magazine* article in 2002, citing cases in which physicians indicated how racial profiling can offer important clues for medication and treatment. She quotes a professor emeritus from Morehouse School of Medicine, a school that primarily matriculates people of color: "Drugs can stay in the body longer when their metabolism in the liver is slower. We know this can vary by race, and doctors should keep it in mind."[15] Despite the Human Genome Project discovery that everyone is 99.9 percent genetically identical,[16] providing foundation for the claim racial differences are a social construct, she affirms the importance of controlled racial profiling for clinical purposes: "As rough a biological classification as race may be, doctors must not be blind to its clinical implications. So much of medicine is a guessing game—and race sometimes provides an invaluable clue. As citizens, we can celebrate our genetic similarity as evidence of our spiritual kinship. As doctors and patients, though, we must realize that it is not in patients' best interests to deny the reality of differences."[17]

On the other hand, sometimes medical profiling can lead to serious mistakes. Dr. Renate G. Justin pointed out that some physical problems suffered by women have been attributed to hysteria, leading to treatment for psychosis rather than physical causes. Imagine if the same symptoms were suffered by a man? Would he have received the same diagnosis or prognosis? The elderly similarly complain that medical caregivers often attribute physical problems to their advanced ages, without further diagnosis. The same results occur when unexamined assumptions based on a person's race lead to an erroneous diagnosis or dismissal. In cases of profiling, Dr. Justin cautions such bias can significantly affect not only the diagnosis but also the communication between patient and doctor.[18]

While there are some circumstances in which profiling is beneficial, most profiling does not involve careful recording and analysis. Rather, it is rooted in prejudice, unwarranted assumptions, and power relations that privilege the profiler. This can be true of both professionals and ordinary citizens.

There have been numerous documented instances of police profiling black and Latinx people. Being stopped for DWB ("driving while black") is a common occurrence. Michael Eric Dyson recounts when his son, Matwa, a medical doctor, was pulled over by a police officer, without explanation. The officer's threatening behavior frightened Matwa's son who was in the back seat. After excessive verbal abuse, Matwa was given a ticket and told to park the car and not drive it that night. Within seconds, the cop stopped another black driver. That night, the little boy in the back of the car learned the meaning of profiling. "To this day," Dyson confides, "my grandson is worried every time he sees a cop. He fears the cop will arrest him and his father. He can't understand why the color of his skin is a reason to be targeted by the police. Mosi is only seven years old."[19]

Black people have also been stopped for walking, standing, sitting, or sleeping—in other words, just for being black. New York City's notorious "stop and frisk laws" allowed the police to stop and search anyone they considered potentially dangerous. Originally instituted to ferret out gun possession to prevent violent crimes, Matt Taibbi reported in 2011 "New York City police stopped and searched a record 684,724 people. Out of those, 88 percent were black or Hispanic . . . they found guns in less than .002 percent of stops."[20]

When I was in high school in the 1950s, we were offered the choice of two tracks: college preparatory or vocational. In many cases, that choice was significantly influenced by race, gender, class, and earlier educational experiences. What I didn't realize was tracking had been going on from my earliest days in school. Children who received preschool or kindergarten preparation were more likely to perform well and be recognized by their teachers as promising students. Those who did well in their classes were generally paired with other students who performed well and, conversely, those who did not fare well were paired with students with lower grades. Eventually this became a self-reinforcing dynamic; and by the time most students reached high school, the die had been cast.

In its most basic form, educational tracking involves sorting children according to their expected success in school and separating the high achievers from the lower ones. Often the school curriculum reflects this kind of presorting or profiling. Educational tracking often steered poor white people, people of color, and women into manual work and the service sector through courses such as auto repair, carpentry, and home economics, leading to jobs that are often less valued and less remunerated. Privileged white males, on the other hand, were groomed for the professions by college preparatory courses such as languages, history, mathematics, and science. Obviously, there were many exceptions, but profiling frequently fostered predictable futures.

Educational tracking has been highly criticized, and since the 1980s and 1990s has been eliminated or greatly curtailed. Many educators now recognize the importance of providing preschool and early school children with opportunities to overcome a disadvantaged background. However, the current well-intentioned advanced placement courses, magnet schools, and charter schools often constitute new and modified forms of tracking that provide additional advantages to those already privileged, exacerbating the existing divisions within our society. There is a role for constructive profiling in education, but it is critical that such profiling be carefully analyzed for its impact on those who have been disadvantaged. Our history reminds us that profiling too often has been a source of Othering.

Instrumentalization

When persons are reduced to their instrumental function, they are viewed primarily, or exclusively, in terms of their service to the user. One of the most egregious forms of instrumentalization in US history was chattel slavery. Chattel, from the French "property," refers to any portable property such as a horse or a plow, but not to real estate that is fixed. Chattel slavery in the United States gave the right of ownership and transfer of the enslaved to the slaveholder. Because they were treated as property rather than as persons, the enslaved could be bought and sold for their value as workers or procreators. It did not matter that the sale or purchase of an enslaved person might separate a parent from a child or a spouse from a partner. They were exploited for their economic value without regard to their family ties, background, or dignity. An enslaved person was just another instrument.

The infamous *Dred Scott v. Sanford* decision by the US Supreme Court in 1857 put the imprimatur on the concept of an enslaved person as property. After an eleven-year battle to be freed because the family had moved into free states, the court decided an enslaved person of African descent was not a citizen, that they should be defined as "an ordinary article of traffic and merchandise," and, consequently, had no rights to sue. He was an instrument of his owner. When that owner sold him to the son of a former owner, that man freed him.

Women have often been treated as instruments. Patriarchy (from the Latin word *pater*, meaning father) is an enduring social system that privileges male control over women. Essentially, it is about power; the power of men over women, both individually and socially structured. Women were systematically excluded from voting or owning property. Although the term is based on ancient family structure, it also applies to denying women's broader political and economic rights. Viewing women as instruments has been reinforced in the Christian tradition by selectively highlighting biblical passages that women are to be subservient to their husbands. Given this patriarchal legacy, it is not surprising some men view women principally as their servants, the bearers of their children, and instruments of their pleasure.

One of the most sordid modern cases of women's instrumentalization is their use as drug mules—carriers of drugs. The news media are filled with stories of women from Central and South America being arrested in US airports as carriers. While some women have become drug traffickers by choice or are persuaded by their "lovers" to do this for them, many have been coerced or threatened lest they or their children be killed. Sometimes, drug mules carry the drugs in suitcases; but often, they are forced to conceal the drugs in their body cavities or by swallowing plastic bags that are expelled when they defecate. If the bags break, the women die of overdoses. They are treated as human suitcases.

The development of the sex slave trade is another way in which women are being used and treated as Other. Sex trafficking is big business. In 2017, it is reported that 99 billion dollars in profit was made from the sexual exploitation of women (and children) who were bought and sold for the purpose of men's sexual pleasure.[21] While it differs in some ways from the enslavement of black people, it constitutes a modern-day version of slavery, another form of Othering.

Workers, too, can be reduced to their instrumental function through the development of the assembly line and mass production that mechanizes people. As a teenager one summer, I was employed by a machine shop that manufactured screw products. Although almost everything was mechanized, the studs had little burrs that the machines didn't remove. My job was to hold the stud to the grinder and "de-burr" it. Needless to say, standing in front of a grinder all day reduced me to an extension of the machine. The monotony of the work soon led to boredom and eventually to sleep, causing me to run my finger into the grinder, necessitating several trips to the emergency room. After the second mishap, I was transferred to the shipping department. Most people don't get transferred. They just fulfill their role as an instrument.

Ostracism

Shunning is a form of ostracism that occurs among a number of religious groups, including the Amish, Jehovah's Witnesses, and some Orthodox Jews. When a member of the group marries outside their religion or renounces their faith, they may be shunned by their family, the religious community, businesses, and friends. They are ignored, not spoken to, and excluded from all family or community activities. The phrase, "you are dead to me," epitomizes shunning. Shunning is not only religiously motivated, it can also occur when communication is cut off with a family member because of a fight or misunderstanding, casting the cut-out person as Other.

People who are convicted of a crime are shunned and banished to prisons where they are cut off from the outside world, surrounded by walls, watched over by guards, and frequently incarcerated at great distances from family, making visitation extremely difficult and sometimes impossible. Except for an occasional riot or hunger strike that creates headlines, prisoners are out of sight and out of mind.

Inside the prisons, many inmates experience the additional banishment of solitary confinement. Those placed in these extreme "cages" are denied all human contact and let out to exercise alone for only an hour a day. At mealtime, their plates are shoved through slots so that the one giving and the one receiving never connect. Their ostracization is total. Fear of being sent to "the hole" is used as a deterrent, and the reasons for being sent can be as seemingly inconsequential as an off-color remark heard by a guard. Many experts consider lengthy time in solitary to be a form of torture.

We also ostracize those who remind us of our own potential frailty and mortality. The mentally ill are banished to asylums, the frail elderly are placed in nursing homes, and many of the dying are isolated in hospital rooms where they die alone. The elderly are often treated as Other. Older people were once honored and respected, but now a number of negative stereotypes captured in phrases such as "over the hill," indicating cognitive and physical decline, and "you can't teach an old dog new tricks," suggesting that the elderly are useless in a technological world.[22]

My wife told me about a woman she observed who was regularly wheeled into the common area in a nursing home with her head down, her eyes closed, and her hearing aid turned off. When the therapist asked why she had turned off her hearing aid, her response was revealing: "I didn't think anyone cared." Many of the elderly feel like Other.

For years, gay, lesbian, bisexual, and transgender people lived in "closets" created by our society and often maintained by themselves. People of my generation pretended they were invisible, knowing all the while we ignored them because they were "different." Closeting people allows us to pretend there is no connection between us.

I live in Midcoast Maine where, because of its scenic beauty and proximity to the water, many people live in a bubble, ignoring the rampant poverty in the rest of the state. Just a few miles from our town, families live in dilapidated houses or ramshackle trailers without adequate food or health care, as well as few prospects to escape their condition. I spent time with a family who lived in a rented two-bedroom trailer. Their four children slept on mattresses side by side on the floor in the same bedroom. The living room furnishings included a broken-down couch, a rickety table, and four mismatched chairs for dining or homework. The kids' toys, books, and school backpacks were stashed on the floor in a corner. There was a hole in the outside wall covered in a makeshift manner to keep out the cold. It was home for them, and those who drove by probably never noticed it. Nor did anyone, other than a social worker, go out of their way to discover what life was like for that family. They were out of sight and out of mind.

Keeping all those who are Other out of sight and out of mind allows the rest of us to live in our bubbles.

Winners and Losers

The emphasis placed upon winning and losing in contemporary sports in Western society is one of the most seemingly innocent yet insidious ways in which Othering can function. I say this as one who has participated in competitive sports all my life. In each sport, I tried to win and, even when losing, I found enjoyment in playing the game. While winning wasn't everything, it was always something.

There is nothing wrong with wanting a team to win or doing one's best in a game that is designed to create a winner. But the desire to win at all costs has sometimes morphed into cheating, aggression toward those we wish to best, and treating opponents as enemies to be conquered—even hated.

Some fans get caught up in the brutality and vitriol, describing the opposition and its supporters as the enemy. While sports have many positive effects, sometimes they perpetuate a binary approach to life that can influence young children. Taking their cues from adults who divide sports into winners and losers can engender hatred of teams and players. In his extensively researched analysis of "fandom," George Dohrmann tells of a five-year-old boy obsessively crying and screaming when the Patriots beat his favored Eagles. When asked by his father why he was so angry at Tom Brady, the boy screamed, "Because I hate him."[23]

Winning and losing in sports has become a metaphor for life and especially for politics, which has always involved winners and losers. We are now in a time of extreme division between the political parties and between liberals and conservatives. In the United

States, the route to winning in politics has increasingly been marked with portraying the opposition as corrupt, evil, or the enemy.

Differences of policy are no longer debated in a bipartisan way but presented as a zero-sum game. For one side to win, the other must lose. Regardless of the attempt to portray the 2017 federal tax cuts as a win-win policy, there are clear winners and losers. The pittances doled out to the lower and middle classes in the short run are far outweighed by the enormous long-term gains for the very wealthy. President Trump told those gathered at Mar-a-Lago, "You all just got a lot richer."[24] The ultra-rich are the winners and the poor are the losers.

Ostensibly, winning has been equated with receiving the most votes. That is no longer the case. In the 2016 election, although Hillary Clinton won almost three million more votes than Donald Trump, the electoral college system led to a decisive win for Trump. And to obtain the most electoral college votes, many districts had been gerrymandered. In these cases, winning isn't something; it's everything.

In sports, you win or you lose. Even in the sports where ties can occur, one team is crowned the victor at the end of the season. However, in a democratic society, politics often involves compromise, which is how most legislation is achieved. The problem is the political divisions today are more than just traditional party politics or arguments over policies, both of which require compromise. They are about basic identities: good versus evil, just versus unjust, and caring versus uncaring. Under such circumstances, compromise is perceived as losing, giving rise to identity politics in which winning at all costs becomes the goal. The money and benefits involved in politics today also make winning a matter of personal gain, thus impeding compromise for a larger good.

Many rural white people feel left behind, forgotten, and without a future. As Arlie Russell Hochschild documented, government, in their minds, has allowed immigrants to take their jobs, supported immoral policies such as abortion and gay marriage, and given their tax money to the unfit. They see the cities and urban poor (which the media has primarily defined as people of color) as the undeserving recipients of government handouts and feel they are losing and "those people" are winning.[25] They believe President Trump represents a new kind of leader whose business experience will turn things around. They identify with him because they believe he identifies with them. He is their identity politics president, deserving of their loyalty, regardless of how distasteful some of his language and personal actions might be.[26]

On the other side of the divide are those who have experienced centuries of suffering and second-class citizenship, immigrants who have fled persecution and economic disaster, and progressive supporters. They identify white Trump supporters as racist, homophobic, and xenophobic.

And therein lies one of the most dangerous and contrived binary divisions: lazy people of color who only want a handout and white racists who would banish people of color if they could. Increasingly, politicians and parties are defending one side or the other of this divide—each an identity that excludes the other. Having created and benefited from the false binary, those in power continue to be the real winners, while both people of color and poor white people end up the losers.

Maybe these divisions are easier to notice in countries with autocratic dictators. There, the winners remain in power through the overt use of police and military power, intimidation, imprisonment of dissenters and opposition leaders, economic benefits offered to their supporters, control of the media, and even murder. But it is not just occurring in dictatorships. We are witnessing the perilous rise of identity politics in our own nation where winning at all costs has become the paradigm. Our polarization is not limited to one party. We are increasingly living with the intentional ostracism of the opposition political party by both sides. E pluribus unum has given way to exclusionary politics.

In a society that perpetuates the notion we live in a dog-eat-dog world, it is not surprising that winning at all costs can involve treating even those with whom we disagree as Other. Judging our worth by our victories can prove to be short-lived, while creating enemies can have long-term consequences.

Bullying

"No bullying will be tolerated in this school" is a familiar sign one sees in public schools today. Some may consider bullying rather innocent and wonder why so much is made of it. After all, "kids will be kids." When I was in school, students commonly referred to one another in terms that would be considered bullying today. Even when the language got a little rough, it was accepted as the permissible norm. So, it may seem to some that this is a case of political correctness run wild. But reducing the concern about bullying to political correctness misses a critical point.

"Sticks and stones can break my bones, but words will never hurt me." When I was in seventh grade, a fellow student whom I admired commented on my flannel shirt that my parents bought from the local army-navy store. I was proud to be wearing it. When he said, "Hey, I'd like to have two of those shirts," I was really pleased. When he continued, "One of them to shit on and the other to cover it up," I was devastated. I didn't consider it bullying at the time, but the memory still remains with me after all these years. Words can have power.

C. J. Bott defines bullying as "any repeated behavior that is intended to harm a targeted individual who has less power."[27] From this perspective, bullying always involves creating a dividing wall of superiority and inferiority and exercising power over another—both of which are central components of Othering. However, the behavior need not necessarily be repeated, as Bott asserts, since the threat of repetition may be sufficient to intimidate the victim.

Members of the LGBTQ+ community are among those often targeted for bullying, especially in schools. One young male student in a local high school told me he had been constantly harassed for his sexual orientation, was called a faggot, pushed around, mocked, and placed upside down in a trash can where he was told he belonged. He changed schools in the hope of finding a safer space, but, even there, he could not fully escape the bullying.

People of color have routinely been the objects of bullying. Michael Eric Dyson tells of his experience as a seven-year-old: "I remember the first time I heard the white world call me 'nigger.' I say white world because it was not an individual saying that to me, mind you, even though the words came from his mouth. This man was simply repeating what he had been told about me. I was every black person he'd ever met. We were all the same. That's what nigger meant. That's what it still means."[28]

In Maine, one of the whitest states in the Union, Somalian immigrants are increasingly the objects of bullying. A high school student told me on her first day at the new school, a group of white boys accosted her at the bus stop. The boys mistook her for a Mexican and told her to go back to Mexico where she belonged. When she replied she was from Somalia, a country in Africa, they called her a nigger. Since that day, she has been wearing the hijab as a symbol of her identity, but she is afraid to eat in the lunch room, and her mother is fearful of attending any events at the school.

While bullying is especially a concern in schools today, it can also occur in offices, on dates, in sports, in fraternities and sororities, in marriages, and on playgrounds. Recent reports of men harassing and sexually abusing female coworkers and interns have resulted in the expulsion of prominent men from the entertainment industry, the news media, corporations, and politics. Acquiescence to the men's advances often resulted from fear of losing a job or career. A *Guardian* survey found 81 percent of the fifteen hundred respondents who work in the UK National Health Services had experienced bullying at work. The harms experienced included silent suffering, the need for mental health treatment or counseling, and job loss.[29]

The 2016 presidential campaign was characterized by excessive bullying. While ad hominem attacks are not unknown in politics, the prevalence and ferocity of the attacks were extreme. Donald Trump attacked opponents with demeaning labels: "Lyin' Ted," "Crooked Hillary," "Lil' Marco," and "Low-Energy Jeb." He assigned the label of rapists and murderers to Mexican immigrants, cast Muslims as terrorists, and insinuated that debate moderator Megyn Kelly was an "out-of-control, menstruating female."[30] David Von Drehle underscored the divisiveness of such bullying when he said, "Trump serves as a magic decoder ring for our seemingly incomprehensible twenty-first-century politics. With reptilian clarity—hopeless on strategy, but instinctively keen—he seizes on the binary basics of our endless combat: To survive, one must have a foe."[31]

Bullying can also be done verbally and through cyberattacks. When we were kids, bullying was primarily confined to school. But today, there is no escape with the constant bombardment in cyberspace. Twitter, Facebook, Snapchat, Instagram, and other internet sources are a staple of young people and provide 24–7 opportunities for bullying. The use of cyberspace to bully is not limited to youth, and it is not unusual for persons who did not originate the bullying, sometimes referred to as bystanders, to share the negative messages with others.

It may be difficult for those of us who have never experienced cyberbullying to realize the devastating impact of name-calling, innuendo, stalking, or direct threats. The negative portrayal of the victim on websites exposes them to potentially greater abuse than face-to-face bullying. The victim is hung out to dry for the larger public to see and sneer. Cyberbullying is a modern-day version of the coliseum in which victims are made public spectacles.

And bullying is not always confined to one-on-one attacks. When a number of people are involved in bullying, it is called "mobbing." The gay high school boy I mentioned was consistently bullied by a group of boys. In some cases, the mob includes the state. Black people have experienced state-sanctioned bullying—slavery, Jim Crow, and mass incarceration. And because of the legal and moral permission by government, white racism has been expressed by groups of individuals such as the Ku Klux Klan, skinheads, and other white supremacist groups. As Michael Eric Dyson indicated, the individual who demeaned him was speaking for a mob.

Comedy

Comedy can cut both ways. Some humor is truly funny and not made at the expense of others. Some comedy creates or increases Othering.

Humor has the ability to hang out the dirty laundry for all to see, undercutting people in power, and targeting existing norms, policies, and practices. Political satire, in particular, has this effect. The nightly talk shows have become the source of many people's news, exposing the clay feet of those in power through the use of satire. But satire also can reinforce our divisions and fail to construct a new reality. As Stephen Marche quoted in an opinion piece, "Jonathan Swift said that satire was a mirror in which viewers discovered everybody's face but their own; its pleasure is the pleasure of othering. The act is inherently tribal, as well as political, and social media exacerbates the tribalism."[32]

Comedy also has the ability to present viewpoints and facts commonly buried. The documentary *In Stiches*, produced by Hannah Raskin and Meg Robbins, features black South African comedians performing in their tribal language, offering a historical and contemporary critique of the treatment of people of color by white people. It was both an act of resistance and an affirmation of their tribe's identity and worth.[33]

Much comedy, however, reinforces existing stereotypes, denigrating and humiliating persons who are different from the comedian or those in the audience. One of the earliest and most destructive forms of comedy in the United States was the minstrel show. Developed in the 1800s and continuing into the early 1900s, minstrels depicted black people according to racial stereotypes. White comedians blackened their faces, dressed in tattered clothes, and affected the dialect and vocabulary of black people, routinely portrayed them as buffoons, illiterate, and docile. They "shucked and jived," messed up their words, and offered simple-minded responses—all to make white audiences laugh. It is important to understand the historic denigration of black people that blackface represented. Behind the laughter was the sense black people were inferior.

One of the most influential comedic portrayals of black people—first on radio (1928–1960) and later on television (1951–1953 plus reruns)—was *Amos 'n' Andy*. The show was written by two white men who were the voices of Amos and Andy on the radio. Kingfish was portrayed as conniving, money-grubbing, and manipulative; Andy was lazy, stupid, and gullible. And Lightnin' was bumbling, confused, and often messed up. This drew uproarious laughter from white people, and even from some black people, but for different reasons. For some black people, these characters provided momentary relief from the horrors of Jim Crow. For most white people, the show confirmed the worst stereotypes. With comedy, the question is always whether we are laughing *with* or *at* the object of humor.

Blackface was used by young men in college or medical school in the 1980s, as has been revealed in the case of the governor of Virginia.[34] A decade later, Roger Ebert reported on Ted Danson's use of blackface at the 1993 Friars Club roast of Whoopi Goldberg, a traditionally anything-goes comedy roast of celebrities. A significant number of people, black and white, cringed at his put-downs of black people and constant use of the N word. According to Ebert, the audience groaned, and some walked out.[35]

For a short time when I was in college, I did stand-up comedy. Remarks or heckling from the audience became fodder for my routine. Realizing much of the comedy involved put-downs and stereotyping, I soon gave it up. Since then, I have become increasingly sensitive to using comedy to Other.

Even some comedy writers understand how divisive comedy can be. Eric Pfeffinger's comedic play, *Human Error*, critiques the use of comedy. The play begins with a fertility doctor's error in transplanting the embryo of a liberal couple into the womb of a woman who shares her husband's right-wing perspective. The ensuing nine months depict the struggle of the two families to form a friendship for the sake of the child. While side-splittingly hilarious, it also reveals both couples' deep-seated prejudices and judgments. During the play, the liberal husband offers some conclusions about his research into comedy, to which the right-wing husband responds with incredulity:

KEENAN: Comedy is primarily a divisive force. It splits people into factions. It's Balkanizing.

JIM: But—People get together, it's fun, they laugh together.

KEENAN: Ah! Laughing, yes. At what? A caricatured representation of someone who isn't them.

JIM: Naw, 'cause, getting together in one place, havin' fun, laughing—y'know, at foibles. All our foibles. Bunch of people laughing at a sitcom—

KEENAN: And that experience reinforces their tribal affiliation. Think about it: a comedy protects the family by transforming outsiders into laughable caricatures.[36]

Much of the humor that makes us laugh reinforces Othering. Sexual jokes frequently speak of women either as servants and vessels for men's pleasure or as "bitches," often confirming the traditional notion of women as virgins or whores. Gay men are routinely depicted as having feminine mannerisms and speech. In the comedic movie, *The Birdcage*, Robin Williams's character is loving and caring, but also "swishy." When he shows his partner how to act "straight," the stereotype of gayness becomes pronounced.

In many comedy films and television sitcoms, Latinx people are replacing black people as menial laborers. Jennifer Lopez's portrayal of a hotel maid in *Maid in Manhattan* symbolizes such stereotyping. The contrast between the opulence of the hotel and its socialite patrons, and her own humble life and menial work sets the stage for much misunderstanding, humor, and romance. The plot ends with the maid and the powerful politician living happily ever after. Once again, the damsel is saved by the powerful white man—a Cinderella story updated. In this case, the damsel is a Latina woman. Granted, the movie also shows her gumption, solid values, and her ability to rise above her station. And there are some hilarious scenes. But despite its predictable romantic comedic outcome, it is fraught with stereotypes. The fact she is an exception only reinforces the stereotypes portrayed by the drudgery of her own work and the condition of her colleagues in the basement who have no shining knight to save them.

It is possible, of course, to focus on the negative aspects of comedy and miss some of its beneficial contributions. *I Love Lucy* provided a positive view of a woman who could stand up to her man. But despite her constant ability to outsmart her husband, Ricky, she is also portrayed as a ditsy redhead, conforming to the patriarchal idea that women are emotionally unbalanced (i.e., hysterical) and naïve. And despite the fact Ricky is portrayed as a successful Latino man, his broken English, frustrated attempts at control, and frequent ineptness or stupidity reinforce the dominant culture's notion that Latinx people are second class in most things, except music and sports.

The use of stereotypes and prejudice in a society structured to treat those who are different as Other can have drastic consequences. While not necessarily intending to contribute to Othering, demeaning people and reinforcing existing divisions through comedy can significantly buttress the walls. There is much to laugh about in life. A good joke is one thing, but Othering someone is significantly different.

Militarization

War has been one of the principal tools of foreign policy throughout history. Tribes, rulers, and nations have relied upon the military for the conquest and occupation of territories and people. War has also been a principal means to foster patriotism and nationalism. To win the hearts and minds of its citizens, a government can character-ize the enemy as Other. We have already noted the way in which enemies have been demonized—characterized as satanic or evil. But there are other ways that have been used to create a boundary between us and "those people" to justify war.

The military has historically called the enemy by derogatory names that help mask their humanity. In World War I German troops were called "Huns," referring to Attila the Hun and his atroc-ities. In World War II, our troops routinely referred to Germans as "krauts," reducing them to what they ate, or "ratzy," as a com-bination of rat and Nazi. During the Korean War, North Koreans were derisively called "gooks." In the Vietnam War, the enemy was given the name Cong, or Charlie, or "slopes." Enemy soldiers are called "targets," and the number of enemy killed is antiseptically called "body count" to avoid speaking of them as persons. Use of a derogatory nickname or euphemism makes it easier for soldiers to kill another human being, who is made faceless by being reduced to Other.

Sometimes governments use euphemisms as a substitute for what they wish to cover up.

Euphemisms have been used extensively to assuage civilian anx-iety or resistance to military action. The word *torture* has been replaced with "enhanced interrogation methods." Surgical strikes have been portrayed as offering laser-like precision that eliminates or at least minimizes civilian deaths. Perhaps the most egregious euphemism is the term *collateral damage*, referring to the number of civilians erroneously killed in a military action. According to a comprehensive 2018 study by the Watson Institute at Brown Uni-versity, "All told, between 480,000 and 507,000 people have been killed in the United States' post-9/11 wars in Iraq, Afghanistan, and Pakistan." Of these, about 250,000 are civilians. Almost 7,000 US military personnel have died. "Most direct war deaths of civilians in Afghanistan, Pakistan, Iraq, and Syria have been caused by mil-itants." This is considered an "undercount" and does not include indirect casualties and refugee displacements and hardships.[37] But somehow, the enormity of this tragedy is swept under the carpet. If those who are killed are deemed collateral rather than seen as mothers and fathers, children, or brothers and sisters, it becomes easier to accept. Collateral is Other.

Nationalism and Xenophobia

Nationalism is on the rise. Nationalist parties have gained significant electoral power in recent years in many countries, including France, Britain, Germany, the Netherlands, Hungary, Poland, Turkey, and the United States. Vladimir Putin's ethnic nationalism has led to Russian annexation of Crimea, the overt support of separatists in the Ukraine, and the rise of anti-Muslim feelings and actions. China's sense of nationalism is behind its staking claims in Thailand, its refusal to recognize Taiwan's independence, its increasing clampdown on Hong Kong, its territorial claims in the South China Sea, and the domination of ethnic groups by the Han Chinese.

In each of these cases, much of the fervor of nationalism has been linked with xenophobia. There are almost daily reports of people and parties lashing out at refugees or even immigrants who may have lived and worked in their country for years. The campaign slogan "Make America Great Again" played on the sense of loss experienced by many in the American middle class who perceived the flight of jobs abroad and competition from immigrants to be the cause of their diminishing financial security and future hopes.

The Trump administration's executive order to exclude immigrants from six primarily Muslim nations in 2017, augmented by six more nations in 2020, played on the fears of "Islamic terrorism" and encouraged anti-Muslim attitudes of many white Christians in the United States. Similar anti-Muslim fervor has been growing in Western Europe, Russia, and China.

We should not confuse patriotism with nationalism. Patriotism is a love of one's country and a willingness to defend it. It involves a sense of pride in a nation's history and place in the world, but it does not seek to cut itself off from the world either literally or in terms of identity. True patriotism includes a concern for the common good and recognition we are part of the global community.

Nationalism is totally self-absorbed. It emphasizes protecting ethnic identity and fearing those who are different. As David Brooks points out, this is the stance of the Trump administration. He refers to two of Donald Trump's early advisers, H. R. McMaster and Gary Cohn, who said, "The president embarked on his first foreign trip with a clear-eyed outlook that the world is not a 'global community' but an arena where nations, nongovernmental actors, and businesses engage and compete for advantage." Brooks continues, "That sentence is the epitome of the Trump project. It asserts that selfishness is the sole driver of human affairs. It grows out of a worldview that life is a competitive struggle for gain. It implies that cooperative communities are hypocritical covers for the selfish jockeying underneath."[38]

In the United States, concern for the global community and the planet has given way to a xenophobic nationalistic chauvinism that threatens to undo longstanding treaties, alliances, and cooperation. To date, we have witnessed our withdrawal from the 2016 Paris Agreement on climate change, the 2015 Joint Comprehensive Plan of Action (Iran Nuclear Agreement), and from much of our military presence in Syria. Protectionist trade wars are increasing. We are witnessing the rise of a negative nationalism that is neither civic-minded nor willing to recognize the larger world community. Our nationalism is rooted in and exacerbating our antipathy toward those who are ethnically, religiously, and racially different. The walls are growing higher.

Tribalism

According to Edward O. Wilson, we are instinctively predisposed to form groups and then to favor our in-group over other groups. But this natural tendency is also culturally shaped. The example of very young children at play presents us with the dynamic between natural and learned behavior. For Wilson, tribalism is both genetically and culturally formed. He calls it the "gene-culture co-evolution"[39] and offers two genetically based instincts that have been variously shaped by culture—lactose tolerance and the prohibition against incest—as proof of his argument that human nature includes some elements that are instinctual but also malleable.

As I have argued elsewhere, we may be born with natural tendencies, but they play out in different ways, given the circumstances and influences. Tribalism is a case in point. Tribalism is the gathering of people into groups on the basis of such things as shared experiences, religion, race, ethnicity, language, gender identification, cultural affinities, or class. In addition to offering its adherents a strong sense of identity and belonging, it also can attract uncritical followers and foster resentment and hostility toward those outside the group.

Tribes as a form of organizing human society are described by Jared Diamond as a kinship-based association on a scale ranging through bands, tribes, chiefdoms, and states, the last having developed as early as 5,700 years ago in Mesopotamia.[40] But there is a difference between tribes and tribalism. It has been erroneously assumed by many that with the rise of the nation state, tribes have become a thing of the past. That is not the case. There are currently an estimated three thousand tribes in Africa, most of which existed before colonialism; and while there were occasional wars between them, they were far fewer before the advent of colonialism. The artificial national boundaries created by the colonial powers for the purpose of maintaining control over the people, land, and resources forced disparate tribes to coexist under the rule of the colonial power and to assume a new and artificial identity; at the same time, escalating tensions among tribes often led to tribal wars. Many of the wars, including those in Rwanda and Sudan, were genocidal.[41]

Tribalism is increasingly evident in the United States. Most of us don't think of ourselves as tribal. We view ourselves as rational, balanced, and commonsensical, but we may actually view those with whom we disagree as deluded, emotional, and blinded by loyalty.

This tribalistic attitude is a significant component of everyday life for many people in our nation.

As mentioned, sports illustrate one way in which we have become tribal. Sports fans form tribes based on their allegiance to a particular team, in some cases even bearing American Indian tribal names such as Chiefs, Redskins, Braves, or Indians (the use of these tribal names has proven offensive to many American Indians and in some cases their protests have resulted in the elimination of those names). Fans share the experience of watching their team live or die on the big screen, wear clothing and logos that identify them as fans, communicate with shorthand phrases, refer to players by their first names, and quote statistics unfamiliar to those outside the tribe. Loyalty runs deep and fans commonly find their identity in the team, which can sometimes devolve into viewing opponents as enemies.

Our politics are increasingly tribal. In a discussion between Mark Shields and David Brooks on the PBS *NewsHour*, Brooks lamented the rise of tribalism in our political system, pointing to the change in attitudes toward marriage with someone from the opposite political party: In 1960, approximately 95 percent said they wouldn't mind interparty marriage compared to approximately 60 percent now. He went on to state both Democrats' and Republicans' descriptions of opposing party members are identical: they speak of each other as "immoral . . . lazy . . . stupid . . . closed minded . . . people [who are] moving to people like themselves, part of the same political tribe. . . . It's now tribal. And tribal is basically political."[42]

Our population is deeply divided into political tribes: Democrats versus Republicans, liberals versus conservatives, progressives versus the Tea Party. Each holds firmly to its values and denounces the other. The Left cares about health care for all, taxing the wealthy, and caring for the environment. The Right cares about less government intervention, lower taxes, preventing abortions, and the right to own guns. It can be described as a divide between individualism and the common good. Increasingly, this is translating into a political tribalism that cares primarily about defeating the other party at whatever cost. President Trump's support for Roy Moore, the 2017 Alabama Republican candidate for the US Senate, is an example of this. Trump, along with others, was willing to support a man accused of having sex with multiple underage minors rather than accept a Democrat winning that seat.

"It's both parties," said Republican strategist Jon Seaton. "You can't get one Democratic vote in either house on the tax bill, so it's not just our side. The country is really hunkered down, everyone's gone to their respective corners. And so, while maybe there's some hope [now] that Roy Moore didn't win, I still think tribalism is something we're definitely going to be dealing with in the short term."[43]

Amy Chua, who has conducted extensive research into the development of political tribes in the United States, contends tribalism develops when democracy is overshadowed by a "market-dominant minority—a minority group, perceived by the rest of the population as outsiders, who control vastly disproportionate amounts of a nation's wealth."[44] She likens our nation's recent rise of a market-dominant minority to the ethnic control of Indonesia's economy by a tiny percentage of Chinese and the former Sunni control of the vast oil wealth of Iraq under Saddam Hussein. This, she says, has led to resentment of elites by many "real Americans" who have turned to what they see as a populist movement that is essentially tribalistic: the tribe of those wanting to take back our country versus the tribe of the elites. That perception remains despite evidence the 2017 tax cuts by the Republican administration overwhelmingly benefited the wealthy elite at the expense of wage earners and the national debt.[45] Each of these tribes views themselves in a battle for the future. Each categorizes its adversaries as Other.

Religiously based tribalism also exists. Freemasonry has been viewed by the Roman Catholic Church as a satanic tribe intent on overthrowing the church. In 1958, Pope Pius XII said the "roots of modern apostasy lay in scientific atheism, dialectical materialism, rationalism, illuminism, laicism, and Freemasonry—which is the mother of them all."[46] As recently as 1983, Cardinal Ratzinger (later to become Pope Benedict XVI) called membership in a Masonic order a mortal sin.

While the natural tendency to identify with one's group or tribe can be benign, in its negative manifestations, it reduces those who are not part of the tribe as Other.

Ethnic Cleansing

Ethnic cleansing is the elimination of the presence or existence of a group deemed Other. The preamble to the Stockholm Accords on Ethnic Cleansing offers this definition: "Ethnic cleansing is the systematic annihilation or forced removal of the members of an ethnic, racial, or religious group from a community or communities to change the ethnic, racial or religious composition of a given region."[47] Ethnic cleansing can occur for various reasons, including economic, religious, political, and ideological, and can be accomplished by driving people out of a region or by extermination.

In 1994, extremist Hutu ethnic cleansing of the powerful minority Tutsi and Hutu moderates in Rwanda was the result of longstanding political rivalries. The Nazi ethnic cleansing of Jews, Roma, the physically or mentally disabled, and homosexuals was purportedly to guarantee Aryan purity, but it also had economic incentives. The United States removed American Indians from entire areas of the country or killed them to provide land for the economic development of white settlers. The list is endless.

According to Gregory Stanton, the president of Genocide Watch, there are ten stages of ethnic cleansing. Among them are: classifying people as fundamentally different from us; exclusion from civil rights; what I call animalization, polarization, persecution, extermination; and, finally, denial. He describes how such ethnic cleansing is organized, legally defended, and covered up.[48]

The forms of Othering vary from time to time and place to place, ranging from the obvious to the subtle, deliberate to unwitting. Demonizing a person or group is an obvious and deliberate attack, while participating in the numbering of people can range from intentional to unwitting. In a society structured to build walls that divide us, even such "normal" behaviors as prejudice and profiling can become ways in which people are categorized as not merely different but as another order of being that can result in their treatment as Other. What each form of Othering has in common is the treatment of those who are different as inferior and even disposable, whether figuratively or literally.

And, as we shall see, the consequence of this is inevitably violent.

4

The Violent Consequences
of Othering

Visiting the iniquity of the fathers upon the children to the third and
fourth generation.

—Numbers 14:18

The consequence of Othering is always violent—whether intentional or unintentional, subtle or overt, physical or psychological,
individual or institutional, the result of a policy or practice. Since
violence is ubiquitous, it is easy to become inured, blinded to its
presence, and anesthetized to its impact.

The 2002 *World Report on Violence and Health* defines violence as
"the intentional use of physical force or power, threatened or actual,
against oneself, another person, or against a group or community,
that either results in or has a high likelihood of resulting in injury,
death, psychological harm, maldevelopment or deprivation."[1] In the
minds of many, violence implies only physical harm. The addition
of psychological harm, maldevelopment, and deprivation helps us
understand the complexity and extent of the harm certain actions
can cause. While violence is often thought of as only physical, it
is important to recognize the variety of ways that people can be

treated cruelly, brutalized, and even destroyed in both body and spirit.

Many definitions, including the one above, state violence must be intentional. But even if intention is not present, the result may be violent. Within our legal system, intention is an important consideration. There is a dramatic difference between intentional murder and unintentional manslaughter caused by negligence or accident. Unless it can be proven that the automobile driver intended to run over the victim, or that the doctor knowingly prescribed a medication whose interaction had fatal consequences, the driver or doctor will be charged with manslaughter rather than first-degree murder, and the consequences will be less severe. However, the consequences for the person killed are the same, whether intentional or not. When Othering occurs, whether intentional or not, harm is done, which I classify as violence.

Intentional violence is easiest to spot. When someone abuses another person—whether verbally or physically—when a bomb is dropped on an enemy, or when someone is executed on death row, the intent to harm is clear. However, people are often violated by unintended actions or attitudes. When an idea offered by a woman, person of color, or young person is ignored, but is later recognized when presented by an older white man, it violates the worth of the individual, even if unintentionally. Similarly, to be ignored in a gathering or to be in a conversation with someone who is scanning the room for someone else can feel like an affront to one's self-worth. Being silenced, ignored, or treated as invisible can create a feeling of being violated, which often precipitates internal rage.

Overt violence is obvious. As Mark Taylor points out, our contemporary death sentence executions are public spectacles designed to show justice is being carried out.[2] These spectacles are similar to lynchings and witch-burnings that allowed violators to feel vindicated. We are inundated with images of physical violence every day, from video reports of war-torn Syria to action movies and TV shows that spill blood and guts across the screen. It is also evident in the bruised face of a battered woman or the lash marks on a slave's back.

Subtle violence is less obvious and often hidden from the public. The massive use of plea bargaining in our criminal justice system often results in people confessing to a crime they did not commit to avoid more serious charges of which they may also be innocent. For those who are innocent, the punishment either of jail, prison, or probation is violence. Unfortunately, plea bargaining disproportionately affects people of color. Jenn R. Borchetta and Alice Fontier draw upon a study by Carlos Berdejo of Loyola Law School who discovered that not only are white people more likely to have charges dropped, but white people with no criminal history were also 24 percent more likely to have charges reduced than black people who also had no criminal record. This suggests, as Berdejo concludes in his report, prosecutors use race to judge whether a person is likely to recidivate.[3] Plea bargaining can be a form of racial Othering, since it usually results in incarceration or, at least, in a criminal record.

Another form of violence is psychological. This harm is far more difficult to detect, but the cumulative and long-lasting effects of being demeaned, disparaged, and dissed run deep and impact how people see themselves and respond to others. Living in the closet for fear of discovery has cast an indelible shadow over the lives of many LGBTQ+ people. Similarly, many women have taken a back seat in life because of a deep-rooted sense of inferiority resulting from how they have been treated.

Both individuals and institutions carry out violence; however, violent behavior by individuals is more often noticed. Videos of black people killed by police officers flood the media, riveting our attention. But institutional violence is subtler and often rooted in policies. For years, the penalty for possessing a gram of crack cocaine was 100 times greater than for possessing a gram of powder cocaine. This disproportionate punishment put the offender, rather than the policy, on center stage, leading the general public to assume black people who smoked crack were more vile and dangerous than white people who snorted cocaine.

Dom Hélder Câmara, the former archbishop of Olinda and Recife, Brazil, identified three forms of violence he referred to as the spiral of violence.[4] The first, institutional or structural violence, is exemplified by war conducted by governments. Câmara also includes poverty and the withholding of funding for education as forms of institutional violence. This gives rise to the second violence he calls "counter-violence," represented by riots and revolutions, followed by the third form of violence—the repressive violence of the police or military to quell counter-violent actions. The repression often leads to more violent protests and, as Kurt Vonnegut often said, "so it goes."[5]

The 1984 Dr. Seuss book *The Butter Battle Book* related the story of the Yooks who buttered their bread on the top and the Zooks who buttered their bread on the bottom. Each considered the other wicked. The grandfather Zook spoke of the Yooks as having "kinks in their soul." The enmity between them leads to ever-escalating violence and ends with each possessing a weapon capable of utterly destroying the other.[6]

Both Câmara and Seuss characterize the unending spiral of violence; once it is unleashed, it inevitably escalates. The Bible recognizes the futility of violence, predicting the iniquity of the fathers will be visited upon the third and fourth generation. The future will be shaped by the violence of the present.

The consequences of a policy or action may be violent, even if unintended, and the violence can spiral out of control beyond the initial circumstance or purpose. While the intent of most sports fans, for example, is to support their team, enjoy camaraderie, and have a good time, the fervor sometimes breaks out into violence. In the same way, the intent of most who enslaved black people was not violence, but economic gain—regardless of the consequences to the enslaved. While some slaveowners resorted to physical violence as a means of control—and some even derived pleasure from such brutality—it was their understanding of the enslaved as property and as means to a financial end that induced violent consequences.

Sometimes, violence is viewed as a necessary means to a desirable end. Nations and religions have waged wars with the stated intent of securing peace; offenders are incarcerated to create safer neighborhoods; capital punishment is defended as a deterrent and to offer closure for the victims; and inquisitions are held to save the souls of the heretics and lost. But since these actions are founded on the assumption those being violated are inferior, evil, and in some cases, not even human, the intention is never achieved. There is no peace, no security, no repentance, and no closure. Violence begets violence. It is futile; it never ends.

Violence is the unavoidable consequence of Othering. It is important to reiterate Othering is not simply the recognition of difference, which can be enriching. Othering includes the full range of treating others as "those people," from denigration to extermination, from casting them as inferior to considering them inhuman. In every case, a division is created and harm is done—violence ensues. The following are some of the violent consequences of Othering.

The Violence of Bullying

Bullying among young people can sometimes result in suicide, or bullycide as it is termed. Jonathan Hewitt's HuffPost blog recounts the tragic story of Steven, a slight seventh-grader who was a little different. After years of relentless teasing, some bullies "set him on fire . . . recorded their attack on a cell phone, and posted it on the internet. Later that evening . . . Stephen took his own life."[7]

As Jenna Russell reported in the *Boston Globe*, there are many long-term, traumatic effects of bullying, including self-doubt, regret, fear, and withdrawal. A fifty-five-year-old man confided his experience of being bullied left him filled with rage. "Now, if I even suspect someone's disrespecting me," he related, "it's only with the greatest self-control that I don't assault them. It comes from being mad at myself for not standing up for myself as a kid."[8] There is evidence many harbor and later give vent to that built-up rage; the battered, whether physically or psychologically, often become the batterer. According to the Secret Service, about 71 percent of school shooters felt "persecuted, bullied, threatened, attacked or injured."[9]

While there are certainly other factors involved in school shootings, being bullied has played a major role.

Prior to a restorative justice circle for a middle school student who had been expelled for breaking a classmate's nose after being spit upon, the student's father agreed to meet and seek reconciliation between his son and the other boy. When we came together in the circle, the father ranted he taught his son to beat up anyone who treated him disrespectfully, and he claimed that the victim was a no-good punk who deserved to have his nose broken. When I inquired whether he thought violence could solve things, he came toward me, fist clenched. Several people in the circle rose to stop him, but he caught himself and returned to his seat, all the while defending his son's behavior. It was obvious the father's rage had been transferred to his son. A correctional officer who was present later remarked that people who abuse or bully frequently have been abused and bullied in their youth, lending credence to the maxim the iniquity of the fathers will be visited upon the third and fourth generation.

The spiral of bullying violence often continues unabated. Some victims internalize the violence, becoming inwardly enraged. That violence and its long-term results are described by Michael Eric Dyson. His experience, when he and his family were referred to as niggers and refused service, filled the then seven-year-old with a rage that can be detected today in the honest and deeply bitter sermons he offers to the white community.[10]

Bullying can have a corrosive effect on society. Donald Trump's repeated bullying of candidates, Mexicans, Muslims, and women released a cascade of hatred, intimidation, and violence that has spiraled throughout our nation. According to the Southern Poverty Law Center, there were 867 hate incidents within the first ten days after his election, many of them involving verbal, psychological, and physical abuse.[11] Their data did not include cyberbullying. Many of the incidents unleashed by his bullying were directed at black people and, increasingly, at Jews. The synagogue killings in Pittsburgh and Poway, California, were tragic cases of anti-Jewish violence fueled by bullying language. Bullying and violence go hand in hand.

There are additional costs to bullying. People who are bullied at school or in the workplace often feel trapped and fearful, spending much time planning how to defend themselves to prevent the bullying. This results in less attention to the task at hand, lower grades at school, or less productivity at work, often leading to absenteeism.

There also can be long-term effects for the one who bullies. Some studies report a strong correlation between childhood patterns of bullying and the use of aggression in adulthood.[12] For example, studies have also shown a correlation between adult criminality and psychiatric disorder, and childhood cruelty to animals.[13]

Given the research and analysis cited in the preceding chapters, it is clear issues of control and aggression are inextricably related to racial, gender, religious, class, and other divisions in our world. Children who learn to rely on bullying may become the adults who thrive on war, the officers or inmates in prison who brutalize others, the predators of children and abusers of women, the religious leaders who browbeat their followers with rigid orthodoxy, or the politicians whose goal is winning at any cost.

People who are different or considered to be different are vulnerable to being bullied. The harm done to them, whether psychological or physical, needs to be called what it is—violence.

The Violence of Enslavement

Slavery is violent. During eighteenth- and nineteenth-century America, black people were instruments or tools of the landowner, in many ways indistinguishable from a mule or a plow. The basic intent of the slaveholder was to keep his slaves docile and physically fit to complete the work for which they had been purchased. While some slaveholders were extremely cruel, especially when an enslaved person got "uppity" or out of line, it was in their self-interest not to harm them. However, the enslaved commonly experienced harsh working and living conditions, were separated from their families, had restricted social mobility, and were prohibited from reading (except certain sections of the Bible chosen by white people) and gathering in meetings (except church services that were controlled by white people). Even when physical violence was not intended, there was a constant and encompassing violation of black lives.

Being treated as a tool rather than as a human being, having one's family torn apart, being sold and bartered as livestock, standing naked before potential buyers while being visually and verbally dissected for one's usefulness, suffering the loss of one's birth name and cultural heritage, and constantly being reminded one was property, all constituted enormous and sustained violence, even for the enslaved who were "treated well."

One of the ongoing forms of slavery today is the sex trade of women and children. The commercialized enslavement of children (mostly girls, averaging twelve years of age) is an international tragedy. Estimates of child sex trafficking run as high as one million children per year.[14] While the motivation for those engaging in the enslavement of children is profit for the purveyor and pleasure for the procurer, the consequence is violence for the children. Their childhood and innocence are torn away; they are exposed to AIDS and other sexually transmitted diseases that often cause deformity or death. They are vulnerable to beatings, rape, and drug addiction to keep them enslaved. And should they survive, they will eventually be discarded when they are no longer useful and suffer depression, low self-esteem, or hopelessness.

Women who are forced into prostitution and become enslaved to their pimps are similarly exploited for economic reasons. They no longer control their own bodies: physical abuse by their pimps and customers is common, and they are often coerced into using drugs, becoming addicted and further dependent on the pimp. For them, as for child sex slaves, diseases are rampant; and when their serviceable life is over, they, too, are discarded on the trash heap of humanity.

Both psychic trauma and physical wounds can last a lifetime.

For example, even after many years, the few surviving World War II "comfort women" from several areas under Japanese occupation continued to live with the pain and humiliation of their enslavement.

Sexual Violence

It is critical to acknowledge that Othering often results in sexual violence. Viewing a person instrumentally as a means of pleasure or profit is one of the most common ways sexual violation occurs. Those who pay to use young children for their perverted sexual pleasure are guilty of viewing the child as simply a sexual tool who is reduced to Other, thought of only in terms of the buyer's pleasure. The trafficker views the child as an instrument for financial gain. In both cases, the child is considered an "it" rather than a human being with aspirations, dreams, and potential for a good life. One can only speculate about the motivations behind the sexual abuse scandals involving Roman Catholic priests. Whatever the reasons, there has been a flood of charges against priests for abusing young boys. In 2017, NBC News reported almost 1,700 priests and other Roman Catholic clergy are considered to be "credibly accused of child sexual abuse."[15] Many women, girls, and young boys have also come forward alleging sexual violence by Protestant pastors. Digging deep into the horror of sexual violence, *USA Today* reported "more than half of American Indian and Alaska Native women will experience sexual violence in their lifetimes, according to the Department of Justice."[16]

While sexual violence can take many forms, it often involves rape. Rape discounts the feelings, needs, and humanity of the victims for the sake of the rapist's own satisfaction. The victim is only a vessel for the perpetrator, an object who exists for the rapist's pleasure. The prevalence of rape under slavery makes twisted sense because the enslaved were considered chattel, property. Women were subjected to various forms of sexual violence, ranging from the seemingly more "humane" use of black women as mistresses to the more overt violence of rape. In all cases, however, the women were treated as objects, as Other, an instrument for one's satisfaction, without boundaries. The USA Today article cited above also reports one-third of Indian and Alaska Native women will likely be raped. Sarah Deer said, "Native women have told me that what you do when you raise a daughter in this environment is you prepare her for what to do when she's raped—not if, but when."[17] Even within the bounds of marriage, men sometimes demand certain acts by their spouses, something that can only occur in a relationship of domination rather than mutuality.

Sexual violence is really about power more than pleasure—the power of the violator over the victim. It can be as subtle as the power of a coach, trainer, or doctor over a young and vulnerable athlete, or the imbalance of power of teacher over student. It may be the elevated status of the priest or pastor above the laity. It can be the power of slaveholder over the enslaved. It can be the demands of an employer who controls the financial and professional future of an employee. The #MeToo movement has released hundreds of testimonies about prominent men and a few women who have used their power to coerce or seduce women into serving them out of fear of reprisal should they refuse.

The sexual violence of Othering is not limited to women and children. Men, too, are raped. There are reports about male prisoners who are humiliated and made sexually submissive by more powerful ones. They become the rapist's "bitch"—which denotes power over and also reinforces a common Othering of women. For some, the alternative to being raped has been to "choose" the protection of an individual and become their "wife," which means becoming totally subservient. Rape has also been used as a weapon of war. Terrorists use rape to intimidate civilian populations and to humiliate the men, and prisoners of war have been raped. The Guardian noted that "a study of 6,000 concentration camp inmates in Sarajevo found that 80% of men reported having been raped."[18]

In all these cases, and others like it, violence that is expressed sexually demands the victim be considered less than fully human: an object, an instrument, chattel, subservient, the enemy, lower in the hierarchy, not equal in position or knowledge. The victim is viewed as Other.

The Violence of Tribalism

In a previous chapter, I noted how our culture's emphasis on winning often leads to viewing the opponent as the enemy.

In some sports, the violence between teams is plain to see. Pro football has become increasingly violent, necessitating rules designed to protect players from serious injuries, sometimes to little or no avail. Tackling to injure the other is routine, and players may be out for entire seasons or permanently because of those injuries. Concussions resulting in long-term brain injury are legion. Dr. Ann McKee reported in the *Journal of the American Medical Association* that all but one of 111 donated brains of deceased NFL players showed signs of brain injury that resulted in cognitive and behavioral problems and, in many cases, dementia.[19] Many of the men died prematurely.

Ice hockey is, perhaps, the most blatantly violent team sport, routinely involving fistfights, high sticking, and punishing body slams. Even the supposedly limited contact sport, basketball, has become brutal, often causing serious injuries. Because intentional fouls are an ever-present danger, the league has had to institute the category of "flagrant fouls" to try to limit the risk many players face. Even in the "gentlemanly" game of baseball, pitchers often intentionally hit batters, bats are slung at opposing players, and base runners spike infielders. A recent baseball game between the New York Yankees and the Detroit Tigers involved fistfights and an all-out brawl, resulting in eight players and coaches being ejected from the game.[20] In these sports, and others, we are witnessing increasing deliberate violence as players are urged by their coaches, fans, and their own inner drive to win by any means necessary. And some fans are attracted by the violence.

Unfortunately, violence is not limited to the players. Fans scream vitriolic barbs at the opposition team. Black outfielders have been called horrible names and had trash and flashlight batteries thrown at them from the bleachers. Soccer matches have sometimes ended in full-blown riots and even deaths, and some stadiums now have moats and fences constructed to prevent fans from streaming onto the fields and creating mayhem. After the Philadelphia Eagles won the 2018 Super Bowl, the exultant fans rioted in the streets, smashing windows, tearing down streetlamps, and lighting fires. The *Washington Post* noted many possible factors leading to the riots, including elevated testosterone, strong identification with a winning team, alcohol, peer pressure, and, perhaps, most important, mob psychology.[21]

Political tribalism also can lead to violence. Electoral politics is inherently competitive, and, when conducted humanely, political contests have produced policies that hopefully benefit the people. However, when personal attacks are used to demean and denigrate one's opponents, as was the case in the 2017 Venezuelan presidential race or the 2016 Republican primary, the election often cascades into violence. In cases when a dictator has had control, the opposition is frequently forced into exile or killed. In our more "civilized" style of politics, the opponent's integrity and reputation are attacked; scapegoats, such as Muslims or immigrants, are created to generate voter support; and brawls are encouraged or treated lightly. Reporters have been increasingly maligned; in one case, a reporter was body-slammed by Greg Gianforte, a congressional candidate in a special election in Montana. He won despite having been arrested by the sheriff.

The rise of tribalism in politics has also been accompanied by increased economic violence. Silencing or marginalizing people who are poor is a form of violence. The vast financial resources poured into campaigns by wealthy donors frequently overwhelm small individual donations and the interests they represent. In defining money as speech, the Supreme Court decision in favor of Citizens United granted unlimited power to the rich, allowing huge amounts of money from billionaires such as the Koch brothers, George Soros, Sheldon Adelson, Tom Steyer, Peter Thiel, Donald Sussman, Michael Bloomberg, and Robert Mercer to be funneled into both Republican and Democratic presidential and local campaigns. The consequence is the marginalization of the majority, especially the poor—a form of violence.

There is also violation of the truth. In win-at-any-cost politics, we've become accustomed to a certain amount of "spin" by politicians and, perhaps, even somewhat tolerant of it. We take it as part of the game. But when totally false claims are offered as truth, the truth is ravaged beyond recognition. When politicians distort the facts to serve their interests, they violate not only their opponents, but also the truth. In his 1949 dystopian novel, *Nineteen Eighty-Four*, George Orwell captures the falsification of the truth by quoting the slogan on the facade of the Ministry of Truth: "War is Peace, Freedom is Slavery, Ignorance is Strength."[22] As history has shown, violation of the truth can lead to fascism, with its inevitable increase in violence.

When winning is reduced to a zero-sum game in which one tribe must lose for the other to win, violence is the result.

Inquisitions and Pious Violence

Claiming to be caring for the souls of Christian heretics and nonbelievers, Roman Catholic inquisitors who presided over hearings to examine and judge people's beliefs felt obliged to punish individuals who refused to renounce their heresies or who maintained non-Christian faiths. Such tribunals were held from the 1200s through the early 1800s in Europe and the New World. The Dominican Order, largely responsible for the Inquisitions of the Middle Ages, emphasized the connection between ecclesiastical and divine judgment in its enforcement of orthodoxy and believed the Inquisitions were a necessary discipline to care for people's souls.

While the authenticity of the heretic's confession and contrition was thought to be revealed only to God, the inquisitors believed the heretic's actions revealed the intention of the heart, thereby justifying their acceptance or rejection of the confession. Claiming to be God's delegates, the inquisitors used psychological manipulation and physical violence on heretics and infidels, including fasting, hair shirts, floggings, and imprisonment. The specter of death always hung over the heretics and nonbelievers should they fail to be genuinely contrite. Many thousands of people were examined. The number of executions cannot be verified above a few thousand from qualified church Inquisitions, but other tribunals may be responsible for a great many more.[23] Nonrepentant heretics were handed over to the secular authorities for punishment. While the friars were prohibited from killing, they frequently allowed and supported the actions of secular authorities, well aware death was probable.

Christine Caldwell Ames alleges the Inquisitions of the Middle Ages were not merely based on power dynamics, as R. I. Moore claimed, but also upon religious beliefs she characterized as "pious violence." "By the early fourteenth century, Dominicans had fashioned a seamless garment of earthly and divine justice and violence, in which execution, appearing to some as most 'unchristian,' putatively reinforced the Inquisitor's claim to holiness."[24] According to Ames, inquisitors viewed the heretics as either redeemable through discipline and punishment or destined to eternal hell because of their refusal to repent and recant. Since those who refused were considered destined for eternal punishment by God, death in this world was deemed a comparatively minor fate.

Some monastics inflicted self-punishment as a form of purification and, hence, considered it appropriate to inflict punishment upon those coming back into the fold. For those who refused to renounce their heresy, and for the nonbelievers, the violence sometimes involved death. To keep the church pure, impurities had to be rooted out, whether in the inquisitors themselves, or in others.

It is an unresolved question whether people's deeply held beliefs and traditions could be changed by the inquisitors' violence. Out of fear, some people capitulated to be restored to the church's good graces. Especially in Spain, some Jews and Muslims agreed to baptism to preserve their lives and circumstances, but they were always under suspicion. To the extent they had been genuinely committed to beliefs the church deemed heretical, in confessing and showing contrition they may have offered an outward renunciation while holding silently to their beliefs. Living with a sense of guilt for that renunciation could have engendered its own form of violence.

While doing some ancestral research, I discovered my lineal descent from Richard Stockton, a signer of the Declaration of Independence. Stockton, who was in Princeton University's first graduating class and became a lawyer with a promising future, was sent to Scotland at age twenty-seven to persuade John Witherspoon to become the university's next president. In 1777, he was captured by the British, tortured for months, and forced to renounce his loyalty to the Independence cause and to pledge allegiance to the British king. However, upon his release, he repudiated his enforced loyalty pledge and signed an oath of allegiance prescribed by the New Jersey legislature. His story obviously substantiates the futility of forced change.

Scholars who have studied the use of torture in modern times conjecture those who have been tortured (disciplined, in inquisitional language) may finally say what they think the torturer wants to hear, regardless of its truth. Brian Foley has evaluated the effectiveness of torture by the US military on prisoners at Guantanamo. "The upshot is that coercive interrogation techniques virtually guarantee a certain proportion of false confessions. . . . Most people who are 'water-boarded,' beaten, deprived of sleep, and attacked by guard dogs—or who are simply threatened with such treatment—will, at some point, decide that it is in their interest to acquiesce to their captors, telling them what they know, agreeing with the accusations interrogators make against them, or even concocting stories that they believe will please their interrogators."[25]

Regardless of how violent the Inquisitions became, not everyone relinquished their beliefs, even when threatened with death. The violence of the inquisitors sometimes led to counter-violence. While the inquisitors believed the church must be purified of heretics who were instruments of Satan, their antagonists portrayed the inquisitors as unjust (a behavior) and evil (a character description) to be resisted at all cost. At the end of the seventeenth century, the Waldensians, a Protestant sect on the French-Italian border, engaged in military resistance against the Duke of Savoy who required, as the church had pursued for many decades, that they renounce their erroneous beliefs. Although the conflict was complicated by religious and political interests from surrounding areas as Protestant and Catholic rulers competed for alliances, the Waldensians are often held up as an example of armed resistance to religious persecution. Caught in the dynamics among conflicting rulers, they lost many people and territory, yet survived. In 2015, Pope Francis asked for their forgiveness.

In the name of God, the Inquisitions led to violence.

The Violence of Mass Incarceration

Most people presume the purpose of incarceration is manifold: to punish, rehabilitate, and maintain society's safety. The reality is quite different. Tragically, punishment, with its inevitable violence, is the primary and, often, the only goal. The motivation to punish is to get even, to inflict on someone who has caused harm a similar or worse harm. A state system operates on behalf of the citizens, so they will not take private revenge into a vicious, unending cycle, but retribution is still active. While our justice system is ostensibly based on the notion of fairness, both in terms of proportionality and innocence until proven guilty, we are failing miserably.

As noted, our nation incarcerates more than two million people, the highest per capita rate in the world. If we add those who are on probation and parole or awaiting trial, the number at the end of 2016 increased to around seven million under some form of correctional control, or more than one out of every fifty persons.[26] Among them, a disproportionate number of blacks and Latinx are caught up in our criminal justice system.[27] No society can escape devastating consequences when such a huge proportion of its people is trapped in the criminal justice system. When the majority are people of color, the violence of Othering is clear to all but the willfully blind.

As Michelle Alexander points out, our "colorblind" justice system is a modern-day version of Jim Crow, having its greatest effect on black people and people of color. Even though justice is supposed to be blind and the scales of justice are to be balanced, black and Latinx people are disproportionately incarcerated. The War on Drugs, with its unequal punishment for possession of crack versus powdered cocaine, resulted in more arrests, convictions, and longer sentences for people of color than for white people. The 1973 Rockefeller Laws for selling and possessing illegal drugs mandated minimum prison sentences of fifteen years to life. Almost 90 percent of those incarcerated under these laws were black or Latinx. In a futile attempt to control the flow of drugs, we have responded with mass incarceration of persons of color. However, the war on drugs, like so many of our wars, has proven ineffective. Even though our prisons are overflowing disproportionally with persons of color, drugs remain rampant.

The violence of incarceration spreads like a cancer, impacting the incarcerated, their families, and the larger society. There are many ways in which the violence is experienced. The most obvious violence is that suffered by the person incarcerated. Despite the name "Correctional Facility" given to many prisons, correction is not what they do. Instead, they punish—even when not intending to do so. The violence prisoners experience is extensive, especially the violence of separation. When people are incarcerated, they are removed from their family, neighborhood, work, school, friends, and life as they knew it. In some cases, that may be for the better; but in most cases, separation is damaging.

There is also "contagious" violence—some persons who are incarcerated for minor convictions learn physically violent behavior inside the prison that they carry with them when released. Several prison wardens have remarked housing a person convicted of a minor offense with someone who has committed a more serious crime frequently has a negative influence on the lesser offender, prompting prisons to be called "training schools for crime."

As I mentioned in chapter 3, one of the most shocking developments in incarceration has been the extensive use of solitary confinement where prisoners are locked up in a tiny cell without human contact, other than an occasional encounter with a corrections officer. The isolation can last from days to years, depending upon the prison, the inmate, and the staff. There is no consistency in this treatment, and prisoners can be sent to solitary for a range of behaviors, from posing a serious threat to oneself or other prisoners, to breaking a minor prison rule or displeasing an officer. The suicide rate for those in solitary confinement is much higher than the general prison population, and severe mental illness and even insanity are common.[28] In some cases, the psychological and mental damage caused by solitary confinement is manifested upon their release. How can we expect people who have been so damaged to not act out when they are released?

Recognizing the violent consequences of solitary confinement, in September 2017, Rick Raemisch, the executive director of the Colorado Department of Corrections, instituted the Nelson Mandela Rules that set a maximum limit of fifteen days in solitary (any lengthier time is considered torture).[29] Since that time, the number of prisoners in solitary confinement in Colorado has dropped dramatically from 1,500 in 2011 to just 185 in 2016.[30]

Even if a former prisoner is able to find work, fulfill probation requirements, and rebuild their life, they endure constant stares, suspicion, and whispers; the stigma of conviction follows them everywhere. Some men have confessed to intentionally being rearrested and sent back to prison because they felt they could not make it on the outside. As strange as it may sound, they said they wanted to be back in prison where they knew where they stood. For them, the violence on the inside was less than on the outside. The violence continues after release because of the stigma of incarceration.

I have used the term *released* rather than *freed* because far too often they are never free from the violence brought about by incarceration. For many, there is an internal violence that results from incarceration. Despite having served their time, some are never able to erase the stigma. One man who had been released for a number of years recounted to me: "No matter what clothes I wore or where I lived, I had the letter 'C' for convict on the inside of my head and it would not go away." He did not need anyone to tell him he had failed.

The violence continues beyond prison. In some states, former prisoners are prohibited from voting, further accentuating their status as second-class citizens. The odds are against someone who is released back into the community with little or no education, no resources to help them deal with an addiction, and scant skills to help with activities of daily living. Whatever resources the released prisoner may possess are systematically thwarted, and the community is deprived of their potential contribution to the common good.

Even if there were no racist intent behind the mass incarceration of black people and other people of color, the violent consequences for the families of the incarcerated are enormous. The absence of a parent (usually the father, but increasingly, the mother) leaves any family without a major breadwinner and the children without one of their parents—a recipe for disaster. Today, more women are being incarcerated than in the past, many of them mothers of young children. The Sentencing Project reported the number of women incarcerated rose over 750 percent between 1980 and 2017 and 60 percent of those in state prisons had children younger than eighteen years of age.[31] The impact on the prisoners' families is seldom taken into consideration when looking at evidence-based results of imprisonment.

Just as there is intergenerational poverty in society, so too, there is intergenerational crime. A study conducted by Murray and Farrington concludes "parental imprisonment is a strong risk factor (and possible cause) for a range of adverse outcomes for children, including antisocial behavior, offending, mental health problems, drug abuse, school failure, and unemployment."[32] They also are more likely to end up in prison themselves. The Texas Department of Criminal Justice undertook a study and discovered "nationally, 7.3 million children have at least one parent in jail or prison. Sadly, 70 percent of these kids are doomed to follow in the same footsteps as their parents, becoming imprisoned at some point in their lives. The violence continues. In fact, children of incarcerated parents are five times more likely than their peers to commit crimes."[33]

So many of those imprisoned are poor, and the economic realities of poverty contribute substantially to their risk. One aspect of our criminal justice system that can result in serious harm is the public defender system, in which the court appoints a free public defender when a person cannot afford their own lawyer. While many public defenders are genuine advocates, they are working against tremendous odds and, in comparison to other lawyers, are grossly underpaid, often carry two to six times the recommended caseload, have no funds for private investigators, and frequently have limited time to prepare a defense. Regrettably, those negative odds, sometimes combined with negligence and failure to adequately represent the accused, have resulted in wrongful convictions and even death sentences.

Bryan Stevenson, the attorney whose book is now the powerful film *Just Mercy*, has defended people on death row and seen many die or waste away for years because of inadequate or no counsel. In a case of a juvenile convicted of rape, the prosecution illegally withheld and destroyed physical evidence, and the circumstantial evidence it presented included dubious eyewitness accounts. The youth might not have been convicted and sentenced to life in prison had his court-appointed lawyer done his job. Stevenson's assessment of the lawyer was blunt: "There was a great deal to say that was never said."[34] The State of Florida eventually suspended the lawyer, and he was not reinstated.

Often overlooked, another violence of our criminal justice system related to poverty is the cash bail system. Millions of persons are consigned to our jails each year because they are poor. According to *The Nation*, "Seventy percent of people in jail haven't been convicted of a crime. They just can't afford bail."[35] They remain confined until their hearing, which could be as long as four months. The report focuses on the Orleans Parish Criminal District Court and Judge Harry Cantrell's refusal to set bail lower than $2,500 regardless of the seriousness of the charge. That amount is well beyond the means of the majority of those arrested. A person who cannot afford bail may be charged with only a minor offense, such as running a stop light; but if they cannot pay the bail, they are placed in jail with, and treated the same as, others who may have committed serious crimes. In addition to the negative impact jail can have on the prisoner, some jurors may be influenced negatively if the accused has been incarcerated, possibly influencing them to view them as guilty when they are eventually tried.

The fact those who can afford bail are released while those who cannot must serve time in jail or prison is an indictment of our justice system. Many of the poor who cannot afford bail are black. It's little wonder the Vera Institute found black Americans are jailed at approximately four times the rate of white people,[36] and a great majority of those incarcerations are due to an inability to raise bail money. The cash bail system "Others" the poor and, disproportionately, people of color, leading them to suffer the violence of incarceration and the indelible stain on their records.

The impact of poverty of so many leading up to their incarceration is unabated following their release. One of the most egregious kinds of violence is the financial hardship that almost guarantees a downward free fall. It is extremely difficult to find work, especially if one must check the box indicating they have been convicted of a felony. While some employers do not let that affect their ultimate decision, far too many don't get past that question. The door is slammed shut and the obstacles continue. Often, work requiring certification or professional licensing is banned for felons. Depending upon the state, such jobs as school bus driver, physician's assistant, veterinarian, or real estate agent may be closed to them. Those who do find employment often earn less than persons with comparable skills. Since black people constitute the largest percentage of our incarcerated population proportionally, it is important to recognize the effect this has upon them. Bruce Western notes, "For those (less-skilled black people) with a prison record, hourly wages were reduced by around 15 percent and annual earnings fell by 30 to 40 percent."[37] They also are barred from public housing, making it difficult to find affordable shelter.

Many prisoners who are released are placed on probation, and while probation is intended to help them succeed—and many probation officers work hard to ensure success—it can hang over a prisoner's head like a sword of Damocles. They are required to report regularly to their probation officer and usually face certain restrictions. It is not uncommon for a person serving probation to commit a minor offense such as missing an appointment, drinking a beer, staying out past a curfew, or driving without a license (even though that may be the only way for them to get to work). The "three strikes and you're out" laws in several states mandate that a former felon guilty of two previous offenses be returned to prison, regardless of how minor the third offense, including violating probation requirements. So, even when released, many live in fear of "messing up."

But the violence does not end here. The harm to the larger society is another way in which the consequences of incarceration wreak harm. The enormous cost of maintaining our current carceral system is diverting money from critical arenas of the common good such as education, affordable housing, public transportation, infrastructure, and health care. A recent study has shown diminished access to health care for the general population because prisoners who are released are forced to draw upon more costly emergency room care, reducing the money available for health care for others.[38]

Black people have suffered a tragic history that has cumulatively resulted in extreme imbalances in income, educational opportunities and levels of achievement, housing, health care, and police protection, to name a few. By incarcerating so many black men, we have stigmatized them as both moral failures and criminals, reinforcing commonly held racist attitudes. When incarceration is piled upon people who are already at a distinct disadvantage, the result is further violence. The violence begun by incarceration radiates unendingly outward throughout our nation.

The Violence of Capital Punishment

From its beginning, our nation has supported capital punishment, a violence frequently justified as mandated by God or necessary for the common good. Daniel A. Cohen has documented the dominant role clergy played as cheerleaders for capital punishment in Puritan New England.[39] Their reasons were often supported with biblical quotations. For example, Numbers 35:16 says someone who murders another with an iron object "shall be put to death," and Leviticus 24:17 commands "he who kills a man shall be put to death." While the Numbers chapter also described "cities of refuge" to which perpetrators of unintended deaths may flee, the Leviticus verdict is unconditioned.

A more secular and moralistic rationale for capital punishment gradually developed among the clergy during the later Revolutionary-era years following law enforcement's concern with public safety, order, and the protection of property. As a result, deterrence came to play a more dominant rationale for them as the culture of criminal justice changed.

Cohen's conclusion is damning: "The clergymen, as a group, were less firmly committed to a particular line of defense, than to the effective vindication of penal severity through the most compelling arguments available at any given time. . . . Like the criminals whose cases they addressed, New England's orthodox ministers were, in the end, constrained only by a line firmly attached to the gallows."[40]

Their endorsement of capital punishment was based upon the belief those who committed murder (or increasingly, property crimes) were of a different moral order and standing before God. They were the lost, the unredeemed who were destined for eternal punishment and warranted violence in this life. While the argument for the common good eventually replaced the religious basis for capital punishment, differentiation between those who lived orderly lives and those who threatened public peace and safety was also based on an essential distinction between good and evil. Those who committed such acts were considered evil.

The correlation between racism and the violence of capital punishment is obvious. Capital punishment has perpetuated enormous violence on the black community. In the 1800s, enslaved black people could face the death penalty for a wide range of crimes, from simple theft to murder; today, black people constitute 41 percent of those on death row even though they are less than 13 percent of the population. To add to the disparity, it is killing white people that generates a disproportionate number of death sentences. "Over 75 percent of the murder victims in cases resulting in execution were white, even though nationally only 50 percent of murder victims generally are white."[41]

From this, one would have to conclude black lives don't matter as much as white lives, either as victim or accused. Given the historic Othering of black people, it is reasonable to conclude the racist perception of some juries also accounts for black people's disproportionate representation on death row. As Lynch and Haney report, "Although some of the racial disparity in how death sentences are meted out is the product of prosecutorial decision making in seeking the death penalty . . . studies continue to demonstrate that jurors' death sentencing behavior is significantly affected by the race of the defendant and the race of the victim in the case."[42]

Of course, many white people have been executed or currently await execution and, in their case, poverty, rather than race, is often a factor. Jeffrey L. Johnson and Colleen F. Johnson have documented the disproportionate number of poor individuals facing the death penalty, showing the link between class and capital punishment.[43] For those with money, the best lawyers and investigators are secured; for those without money, the court appoints attorneys to defend them, often providing substandard or overwhelmed representation as noted earlier. The consequence is the poor of every race are disproportionately sentenced to death.

One of the dubious arguments for capital punishment is it deters crime. In Elizabethan England, when pickpocketing larger amounts became a capital crime, thieves took advantage of crowds gathered to watch hangings as a perfect opportunity for plying their nefarious craft. They were undeterred by the possibility of execution. Even if capital punishment is a deterrent in some cases, what are the tradeoffs?

Evidence that many persons have been mistakenly sentenced to death made the risk of maintaining the death penalty too great for Illinois Governor George Ryan. After having already set a moratorium on executions in 1999, he made a momentous announcement at Northwestern University Pritzker School of Law just before leaving office in 2003. He acknowledged that following the reinstatement of the death penalty in Illinois, for ninety-three people the state had "rescinded the sentence or even released the prisoners from custody because they were innocent." He also said that, in the United States, the overwhelming majority of those sentenced to execution have been poor, abused, psychotic, alcoholic, addicted to drugs, or mentally unstable. He concluded, "Our capital system is haunted by the demon of error in determining guilt, and error in determining who among the guilty deserves to die."[44] With that, he commuted the sentences of all death row inmates in Illinois to life sentences.

In April 2014, a mathematical modeling study published in the *Proceedings of the National Academy of Sciences* (PNAS) estimated "if all death-sentenced defendants remained under sentence of death indefinitely at least 4.1 percent would be exonerated."[45] Given juries' reluctance to use the death sentence, the study concluded "the rate of innocence must be higher for convicted capital defendants who are not sentenced to death than for those who are. The net result is the great majority of innocent defendants who are convicted of capital murder in the United States are neither executed nor exonerated. They are sentenced, or resentenced to prison for life, and then forgotten."[46] A number of wrongfully convicted inmates have been waiting on death row for many years with the specter of execution hanging over them. The *PNAS* study found exonerations usually occur only under threat of execution. "Except for those who are exonerated—and a very small group who are resentenced to lesser penalties and eventually released—all prisoners who are sentenced to death do ultimately die in prison. They all start out on death row, some stay there until death by execution by other means, and the rest eventually are moved to the general prison population where they remain until they die."[47]

In 2017, 61 percent of those on death row were placed in solitary confinement for at least twenty hours a day.[48] They lacked almost any human contact, often inducing a mental disorder that has been described as "death row syndrome." Even those who were later released because they were found innocent often suffered from extreme psychosis. The violence of the death penalty, or years spent by innocent persons on death row, cannot be undone.

In their position paper against the death penalty, the American Civil Liberties Union (ACLU) recounted stories of innocent persons who were sentenced to die. They conclude these miscarriages of justice result from "overzealous prosecution, mistaken or perjured testimony, race, faulty police work, coerced confessions, the defendant's previous criminal record, inept and under-resourced defense counsel, seemingly conclusive circumstantial evidence, and community pressure for a conviction, among others."[49]

Someone who murders should not be excused without consequences, but I am opposed to capital punishment under any circumstance. No matter the many offered justifications, the wide margin of error should be sufficient to end it. Killing innocent persons who have been erroneously or maliciously convicted, no matter how few, is unjust. To do so sanctions violence begetting violence.

In warfare, which I discuss later, our nation subscribes to one of the central principles of just war theory: avoid taking the lives of noncombatants. In other words, innocent civilians should not be killed to win a battle. If the same principle is applied to the death penalty, we must conclude taking the lives of innocent persons to deter further murders—if in fact it is a deterrent—should not be permitted. But the study cited above exposes the likelihood that is precisely what our country is doing. Deterrence at the expense of innocent lives is a violence that should not be tolerated.

In addition to the moral argument against taking innocent lives, the financial cost must be considered.[50] If the intention is to deter murder and other crimes, then it is critical to assess where we get the most cost-effective benefit. Rather than spending enormous amounts of money on the death penalty, the nation should be addressing the causes of crime. As Governor Ryan concluded, poverty, substance abuse, physical abuse, and mental illness need to be addressed. The cost of each death row inmate (including trials, appeals, and death row incarceration) in some states is three times greater than for life without parole, which substantially reduces funds for rehabilitative programs.[51] Our money can be spent more effectively by investing in preventative measures that deal with the root causes of crime and funding rehabilitative programs that lower the possibility of further criminal behavior, rather than futilely spending taxpayer money on executing the few. The violence perpetrated by our financial priorities is futile.

While capital punishment has been historically considered either as state-sanctioned revenge or as a deterrent, increasingly it is proposed as a method to engender closure, especially for the victims. In her extensive research, Susan Bandes concludes pushing for closure in response to murder actually helps continue our retributive instinct: "The language of healing and closure has provided a way to soften the retribution rationale. If the death penalty can help survivors heal, then retribution can be viewed as therapy rather than bloodlust. Thus, the notion of closure provides a rationale for our continuing commitment to the capital system."[52]

Since it often takes ten or twenty years before a convicted person is executed, where is the closure when the victim's family lives in limbo for all those years? Does closure mean the victims will be able to live normally? How can one ever be the same when a loved one is killed? And what about families of victims who demanded the death penalty only to regret the decision when it is too late?[53] Is closure the final step in revenge?

The idea of closure allows us to ignore the most important questions facing capital punishment: racial disparity, poverty, mental illness, and mistaken convictions. This is particularly true with respect to race. According to the 2018 Death Penalty Information Center's compilation of the National Association for the Advancement of Colored People (NAACP) data, as of July 2017, more than 2,700 persons were awaiting death in the United States.[54] And black and brown persons account for a disproportionate number of those 2,700. When we consider just the percentage of black people in a few states and compare that with the percentage of black people incarcerated, the figures are striking. In Louisiana, black people are about 32 percent of the population but about 66 percent of those on death row. The disproportion is similar in South Carolina: 27 percent of the population are black, but they constitute 54 percent on death row. Pennsylvania is the most disproportionate: 11 percent of the population are black while 54 percent of those on death row are black. It is similar in other states with large numbers of inmates awaiting execution.[55] These statistics raise concerns about who is being executed to bring about "closure"; how many black or Latinx people are convicted by all-white juries; and where is "closure" for the families of black victims? In about half of all murders, the victims are black but the number of capital sentences when the victim is white is over four times greater than when the victim is black.[56] How can there be "closure" when there is such a disproportion of arrests, convictions, and death sentences for black people?

A subject that should be a national priority is often overlooked in discussions about the death penalty—gun control. Addressing underlying causes of capital crimes must also include confronting the weapons used, both in actual crimes and in the all-pervasive media displays and gaming platforms that promote desensitization to their effects. Gun-promoting lobbies and legislation must be subject to greater scrutiny for the common good if we are serious about reducing violence.

There are some hopeful signs. By the end of 2019, "half of U.S. states have now either abolished the death penalty or halted executions. Executions and new death sentences remained near historic lows for the fifth consecutive year. For the first time since Gallup began asking the question in 1985, a majority of respondents (60 percent) believe that life in prison without parole is a better approach for punishing murder than the death penalty."[57]

Terrorism and Violence

Since 9/11, the United States has declared a War on Terror and devoted enormous resources and military efforts to stamping it out. But despite our investment of money and blood, terrorism persists. It is one of the consequences of Othering.

Terrorism as a form of violence differs from war, often targeting noncombatants in the hope of spreading fear or engendering support. It is a political act meant to change the existing social or political arrangements rather than an effort to promote self-gain or exact revenge. The *New Fontana Dictionary of Modern Thought* defines terrorism as "the systematic use of coercive intimidation . . . to publicize a cause, as well as to coerce a target into acceding to the terrorist's aims."[58]

While the focus of US attention in the past twenty years has been largely on foreign terrorism, the truth is we have had internal terrorists throughout our history, most notoriously the Ku Klux Klan (KKK). The KKK was formed to strike terror into the hearts of black people and white people who supported the Reconstruction movement following the Civil War. They intimidated through lynchings and cross burnings as they sought to undo the legislative changes they believed would destroy their way of life, which was based on white supremacy. Their reign of terror initially focused on black people but expanded to include Jews, immigrants, Catholics, organized labor, and more recently LGBTQ+, each of which they deemed threatened white supremacy.

The terrorism born out of the fears of white people is resurgent in the United States today. In response to the warnings by Trump about the "invasion" of foreigners, tweets to "send them back" (congressional representatives of color), and constant references to immigrants as rapists and murderers, white nationalists, neo-Nazis, and other white supremacists have been emboldened, resulting in an exponential increase in white terrorism. The "manifesto" of the white terrorist who killed twenty-two people at a Walmart in El Paso, Texas, in 2019 revealed his hatred for and fear of the "invasion" of Latinx immigrants. It is essential we recognize the rise of terrorism within our own nation before we cast our sights outward to external enemies.

Terrorism, of course, is in the eye of the beholder. Attempts by colonized persons to resist their oppressors have been labeled terrorism by the colonizers. On the other hand, those seeking to break free of the colonizing fetters see themselves as liberators and the dominating power as terrorist. Some terrorism is overtly state sponsored, such as the Nazis' "Final Solution." Other terrorists have sought the mantle of state sponsorship as a means of legitimacy. While ISIS has referred to itself as a caliphate, asserting its legitimacy as a state actor, it has not been recognized as such by most of the world and is seen, instead, as a terrorist organization. US support of military operations that inflict large civilian casualties has also been labeled terrorism, whether siding with right-wing Contras against the Sandinistas in Nicaragua in the 1980s or supplying weapons and logistics for Saudi attacks against rebels in Yemen's civil war since 2015. Efforts in Congress to remove this support from the military budget have been unsuccessful. In light of US conflicts with Islamist terrorists, it is important to understand why we have come to this point.

As mentioned earlier, Edward W. Said's analysis of Orientalism[59] reveals the historic ways in which Westerners have viewed Muslims as different, categorized them as inferior, and even threatened them as a civilization. In the face of this Othering and domination, extremists have used terror as a means to assert their identity and cripple Western attempts to conquer through colonialism or neocolonialism. The Othering of Muslims has not been confined to those who live in the Middle East. In Europe, and increasingly in the United States, Muslims have endured mistreatment, including disproportionate arrest and incarceration, inferior housing, lower wages, hate crimes, demands to dress "Western," and to take pledges of nonviolence.

It was not always this way. Amin Maalouf claims when the adherents and leaders of Islam have felt safe, their religion has been open toward others, but not when it is endangered. During the Middle Ages, the Moors (Muslims) created a substantially inclusive society in Al Andalus (southern Spain and Portugal). For hundreds of years, the Islamic rulers offered freedom and protection for Christians and Jews that resulted in relative harmony. In contrast, Malouf points to the contemporary status of Muslims who feel under attack and endangered. They are "poor, downtrodden and derided . . . when I look at the militant Islamic movements of today I can easily detect . . . the Third World theories that became popular in the 1960s. . . . Such movements are not the product of Muslim history; they are a product of our time, with all its tensions, distortions, stratagems, and despairs."[60] This is the soil out of which terroristic violence often grows.

Lamentably, victims' responses to terrorism can sometimes be violent. Peter O'Brien identifies three basic approaches in European responses to terrorist attacks on their own soil.[61] Two use what he describes as "soft power." The first is the guarantee of equal rights, respecting and affirming the dignity of all Muslims, just as for non-Muslims. This assumes persons treated fairly will adopt European values and act in lawful ways. The second is to support Muslim organizations so they may, in turn, support the peaceful coexistence of Muslims in a non-Muslim country. The third is "hard power," namely the use of "surveillance, search and seizure, arrest, prosecution, conviction, and imprisonment or deportation."[62]

Even though there has been significant success with the soft approaches, there still have been a number of deadly terrorist attacks, including the London Tube bombing in 2005 in which fifty-six people died, the Russian plane crash in the Sinai that killed 224 people in 2015, and the November 2015 Paris attacks that killed 129 people. The notoriety of the attacks has generated enormous fear and hatred and given rise to governmental law-and-order responses that often violate legal rights: stop and search of Muslim-looking youth, temporary imprisonment without access to a lawyer, deportation, and, on occasion, shooting or even killing suspected terrorists. Terrorist attacks have also contributed to the rise of hate speech, mistrust of all Muslims, and even nativist attacks on Muslims, as was the case in the mass killing of fifty-one worshippers at two mosques in Christchurch, New Zealand, in 2019.

As ways of life are perceived to be threatened, fear and hatred of the Other too often give rise to terrorism.

The Violence of Trauma

One of the increasingly recognized violent consequences of war is the trauma suffered by combatants. Exposure to the violence of death and destruction has a deep and lasting impact on many veterans who live with flashbacks of the violence. According to the US Department of Veterans Affairs, the National Vietnam Veterans Readjustment Study estimates 30 percent of Vietnam War veterans suffered from post-traumatic stress disorder (PTSD).[63] The numbers for those fighting in Iraq and Afghanistan are lower, but still significant. If untreated, PTSD can cause recurring nightmares, paranoia, and murderous or suicidal thoughts. This trauma often leads to dependence on alcohol or drugs to mask the pain.

In the worst cases, trauma victims act out in ways that lead to incarceration. Drawing upon the experience of Dr. Judith Broder, director of the Soldiers Project that offers free psychological services to veterans, Matthew Wolfe concludes, "The combination of unemployment, substance abuse, mental-health issues, and a shortage of adequate counseling creates, Broder said, a 'perfect storm' for sending vets into the criminal-justice system."[64] If they abuse substances or commit criminal acts, they no longer fit into our notion of normality, of what it means to be a civilized member of society, and they become viewed as Other.

It is not just the violence of war, however, that causes trauma. Trauma can also result from being treated as Other.

Some women who have been raped report lifelong anxiety about men. People whose loved one was murdered report reoccurring visions of the tragedy. Some LGBTQ+ people who have been bullied and ostracized constantly feel they are being watched and judged. Many black people carry the disgrace born of racism deep within them. Some children who were laughed at and disparaged in school bear the stigma throughout their lives. Each of these traumas is related to being Othered.

The physical violence associated with bullying, lynching, terrorism, or war can visibly mar a person—limbs lost, vision damaged, or faces disfigured. But even if the physical scars disappear, violence experienced as trauma can mar a person's identity for life, even if it's carried in silence and hidden from others. One of the heartbreaks of trauma is that the experiences of Othering become buried deep within the psyche, often emerging unpredictably and sometimes with no precipitating event—what Freud referred to as "latency."

Toni Morrison's harrowing novel *Beloved* offers a graphic image of the internal devastation caused by trauma. Paul D, the protagonist, shares the pain he suffered as an enslaved person, but he suddenly stops:

> Just as well. Saying more might push them both to a place they couldn't get back from. He would keep the rest where it belonged: in that tobacco tin buried in his chest where a red heart used to be. Its lid rusted shut. He would not pry it loose now in front of this sweet sturdy woman, for if she got a whiff of the contents it would shame him.[65]

To live with trauma is to live with internal violence. While often maintaining outward normality, one's identity and the meaning of one's life is distorted. The violation of being treated as Other can last a lifetime.

The Violence of War

I am reminded of the 1960s British satirical revue, *Beyond the Fringe*, in which an officer tells a foot soldier the war is not going very well and a sacrifice is needed. "'Perkins,' he said, 'I want you to lay down your life. We need a futile gesture at this stage. It will raise the whole tone of the war.'"[66]

Despite its futility and destructiveness, war has been a principal form of domination by nations. Characterizing those against whom a nation goes to war as evil and using euphemisms such as collateral damage for civilian casualties reduces them to Other, making it easier to create support for its actions. The obverse is also true. Othering can give rise to war in the first place. Indeed, war is one of the most devastatingly violent consequences of Othering. The twentieth century was the most violent in modern history. The enemy is frequently portrayed as being of a different order, which inevitably leads to dismissing enemy combatants, and even noncombatants, as humans. Treating the enemy as human is considered either soft-headed or an impediment to victory.

The violence of war is all-encompassing. No one escapes the violence, whether it is the enemy, our own troops, or innocent victims. The soldiers largely come from the ranks of the poor. Families on both sides of the conflict are torn apart and shattered by the loss of loved ones. And the killing, however carefully controlled, cannot be limited to the combatants but always spills over to noncombatants.

Some suggest we are hard-wired to be aggressive, based on the evolutionary history we share with animals that attack one another to survive. But, at most, this means we have a propensity under certain circumstances to respond in a war-like manner. If we consider the spectrum of evolutionary development, however, we find animals also have the capacity to care for one another, even, in some cases, across species. *National Geographic* reported on a number of cross-species adoptions by both domestic and wild animals.[67] Suggesting we go to war because we are biologically predetermined to fight is to ignore the equally true reality that humans are also capable of embracing and cooperating with one another.

But is war always futile? The term and main principles of just war theory are credited to St. Augustine of Hippo in the early 400s. He acknowledged there are circumstances in which violence, although always a last resort, is necessary. While we understand the survival of human life and our planet dictates nonviolence should be our primary leaning, there may be instances in which self-defense or saving the life of an innocent victim may call for the use of force. Just war theory specifies, among other things, it be defensive; a last resort; proportional, that is, involve no more force than necessary; and avoid killing civilians.

While just war theory is concerned with the behavior of a legitimate authority, such as a nation, its principles may also guide individuals. If we can save an innocent child from molestation or murder, we may feel morally justified. But in doing so, we should be guided by the same constraints just war theory places on nations—namely, asking is there another way to stop the violence; how much force is necessary in this case; and will my action further endanger the victim?

The stated reasons for war have been numerous: defense against an aggressor (the US response to the Japanese attack on Pearl Harbor), revenge (Russian brutality toward German prisoners of war as payback for Germany's destruction of their homeland), competing ideologies (the Cold War), and "Lebensraum" (the Nazi claim for more living space). Each of these appears to be a defense against a threat.

But nations and people often go to war also for exploitative reasons: to dominate, expand territory, or secure resources. One has only to look at some of our nation's interventions in Central America that sought to obtain or maintain US corporations' exploitation of the natural resources of a country. A recent example is the clandestine Obama-supported military coup in Honduras that has weakened regulatory protections and has allowed the violation of minimum wages, both of which contribute to the profits of US corporations.[68]

Woodrow Wilson's intention that World War I would be "a war to end all wars" was a most admirable goal. If, in fact, a war could bring an end to all future wars, we might consider it worth the cost. But that goal has never been achieved. Tragically, World War I did not fulfill President Wilson's dream. It is estimated ten million soldiers lost their lives, twenty million were injured, and millions more civilians were killed. That enormous and futile sacrifice did not prevent World War II.

Even if one is inclined to acknowledge the value of just war theory and support the use of violence in certain extreme situations, there is a radical difference between the kind of violence engaged in under the terms of just war theory and the violence resulting from Othering. The violent outcome of Othering has no purpose other than to differentiate, demean, defeat, or destroy those whom we consider inferior or evil. It blinds us to the reality we are inextricably connected. It fails to acknowledge our complicity in the divisions that are generally the stated cause of war. And it allows us to assume our power to violate others is because of our assumed moral superiority.

A fundamental question that must be raised with respect to war is whether it is possible to avoid Othering. Can anyone or any nation engage in war, despite the best intentions and purest motivation, and still consider the enemy to have human worth? The use of the word *enemy* conveys an undifferentiated mass and allows them to be treated as Other.

It has been said our entrance into World War II was "just." Unfortunately, our entrance into the war was not primarily out of compassion for innocent human beings who were being persecuted, forced from their homes, and murdered. While the extermination of millions of innocent people by the Nazis needed to be halted, our reason for entering the war was not primarily to save the lives of those deemed expendable by the Nazis such as Jews, Roma, and homosexuals; it was primarily to respond to the Japanese attack and to stand with our allies. The atrocities of the Nazi "Final Solution" were initially ignored or even denied by many who supported our entrance in the war. As Ervin Staub points out, during the war the United States admitted only 10 percent of our legal allotment of refugees, and President Franklin D. Roosevelt did not establish the War Refugee Board until 1944, years after he'd learned of the horrors being suffered by Jews under Hitler.[69]

Further, we failed to acknowledge our own complicity in accelerating the rise of the Nazis, including terms of the post–World War I Treaty of Versailles that redrew German borders, imposed unrealistically heavy reparations on Germany, and contributed significantly to their severe economic hardship. Nor did President Roosevelt's call for unconditional surrender, which strengthened the Nazis' resolve to fight to the death, fit the goals of the just war theory.

Even if we were to grant our government's intentions for entering the war were compatible with the just war theory, as the war progressed our actions became increasingly at odds with its principles. Two major bombing campaigns near the end of the war, in Europe and the Pacific, seem contrary. Did the saturation bombing of Dresden that killed at least twenty-five thousand civilians (some estimates run as high as one hundred thousand) and destroyed much of the city's architecture strengthen the case for German surrender? Did the atomic bombs dropped on Hiroshima and Nagasaki, killing and maiming hundreds of thousands of civilians, persuade Japan to surrender rather than engage all its citizens in a fight to the death after an expected invasion? In these cases, the decision of the military and our politicians ignored the ethical guidelines of a just war, ostensibly for other goals. Once engaged in the violence of war, excessive violence inevitably occurs.

Too often wars have been initiated based on ideological rationales when other options were available. Our leaders subscribed to the Cold War domino theory that if Vietnam fell to the Communists, it would be the beginning of an exponential spread of Communist evils throughout Southeast Asia and beyond.

We entered that war based on lies about the cause of the fighting in Vietnam and the pretext of an attack in the Gulf of Tonkin. We prolonged the war based on persistent false information about the conduct of the war; the portrayal of the Viet Cong as degenerate, sadistic people; the political opportunism of some South Vietnamese leaders; and the unwillingness of those in our military and government to admit they had made a mistake. The result: at least three million Vietnamese and fifty-seven thousand US military lost their lives. Our use of Agent Orange contributed to the deaths of many Vietnamese civilians, as well as destroyed millions of acres of forest and arable land, significantly reduced wildlife, and created lifelong diseases for more than a million Vietnamese. The violent effects of our use of Agent Orange continue in Vietnam and within our own nation to this day, long after the war officially ended. Our government has recognized a number of fatal or debilitating diseases suffered by our troops who were exposed to the defoliant and is offering compensation as a result.

The Vietnam War also further divided our nation. While our government and many people supported the war, many others supported draft evaders, burned draft cards and the flag, and destroyed military property. Riots occurred, protestors were killed, and returning soldiers were harangued. The violence spread from Vietnam to our own towns and cities.

Thousands of our troops returned home with PTSD, a debilitating psychological disorder that caused psychosis, suicide, and even murder; disrupted families; and cost the country hundreds of millions of dollars in medical care.

More than $170 billion (over $1 trillion in today's terms) was spent on the Vietnam War—money that could have been invested in education, health care, housing, food security, infrastructure, and economic development. This misappropriation of money had violent consequences for the poor in our own country who, as a result, suffered from malnutrition, lack of access to health care and affordable housing, inferior education, and a crumbling infrastructure.[70]

We have not learned from the tragedy of the Vietnam War. Suspicious of Saddam Hussein after his aggression leading to the Gulf

War, and eager to believe he had weapons of mass destruction—perhaps even enlisting post-9/11 fervor against a leader who had not been involved—the United States' "Shock and Awe" campaign began in 2003. Saddam was killed in 2006, and people in the United States celebrated by destroying effigies with devilish masks. Meanwhile, ISIS has arrived, and our Kurdish allies have reason to doubt US commitments to them.[71] In 2011, we killed Osama bin Laden but remain engaged in regional efforts against the Taliban and al-Qaeda. Our wars have no exit strategy. Once again, the cost in military and civilian lives has been enormous. Once again, massive financial resources have been diverted from rebuilding our cities, infrastructure, public education, health care, and rural economies. Once again, many of our troops are returning with PTSD. Once again, our nation and world are dangerously divided.

Some have argued our failed wars in Iraq and Afghanistan have given rise to ISIS and other radical extremists by leaving a vacuum that they have filled.[72] Many conclude our wars have served as a recruiting stimulus for these groups, leading to and exacerbating dangerous divisions between Sunni and Shia Muslims, and between Christians and Muslims.

One of the violent consequences of Othering is the demand for unconditional surrender following the defeat of an enemy. Unconditional surrender involves removing all control from the defeated, leaving them at the total mercy of the victor. At his meeting with Winston Churchill in Casablanca in 1943, President Roosevelt insisted on unconditional surrender by the Germans. According to Brian Villa, his intention in doing so was to solidify our relations with our allies and to terrify our enemies.[73] He concluded Roosevelt was clear "he would accept no restrictions whatsoever on the victor, from Geneva or elsewhere. 'Please note,' he once angrily stated, 'that I am not willing at this time to say that we do not intend to destroy the German nation.'"[74] He would accept no limits on the potential maltreatment of the defeated enemy, even to the point of their total annihilation. The US military, on the other hand, was fearful that insisting on unconditional surrender would convince Germany to fight to the death since they did not know what their situation would be after the war. The military's assessment proved to be correct.

Unconditional surrender involves control over the defeated enemy in a manner that almost certainly will lead to humiliation and further alienation, often ensuring the defeated will rise again to fight another day. It is one of the consequences of viewing the adversary as Other who deserves whatever abuse the victor might heap upon them. And it is a guarantee the violence will continue.

War and Othering are umbilically connected.

Genocide

One of the most devastating forms of violence is genocide, the attempted destruction of a people based on their race, nationality, religion, or ethnicity. Genocide is the extreme result of Othering. While the term has been used to describe numerous situations in which people have been killed, Article II of the UN Genocide Convention designates two elements that must be present:

1. A *mental element*: The intent to destroy, in whole or in part, a national, ethnical, racial or religious group, as such.

2. A *physical element*, which includes the following five acts, enumerated exhaustively:

   ◦ Killing members of the group

   ◦ Causing serious bodily or mental harm to members of the group

   ◦ Deliberatively inflicting on the group conditions of life calculated to bring about its physical destruction in whole or in part

   ◦ Imposing measures intended to prevent births within the group

○ Forcibly transferring children of the group to another group[75]

The twentieth century was the most violent in history. According to the Stockholm Accords, "By some estimates as many as 170 million human beings died from ethnic cleansing, genocide and political mass murder in the twentieth century alone."[76]

The experiences of the twentieth century also contributed to understanding a progression of events leading to genocide, identifying stages that can be used as warning signs and opportunities for intervention. In 1996, Gregory Stanton, former professor at George Mason University and founder and president of Genocide Watch, proposed a list of eight stages, later expanded to ten, with the understanding they are not totally separate nor linear in development.[77] His work remains useful and has been applied to recent worrisome situations such as the persecution and expulsion of Muslim Rohingyas in Myanmar.

The warning signs now include the following characteristic behaviors, each of which is a process: classification, symbolization, discrimination, dehumanization, organization, polarization, preparation, persecution, extermination, and denial. All of them are recognizable as familiar traits of Othering.

The consequences of Othering recounted in this chapter make clear that Othering begets violence. This cannot be the last word. Is there another way?

5

Voices of the Moral Imperative

I call heaven and earth to witness against you today that I have set
before you life and death, blessings and curses. Choose life so that you
and your descendants may live.

—Deuteronomy 30:19

The horror of violence caused by Othering has led to a cacophony
of voices calling for a different way of being in the world. It is a call
to embrace rather than to exclude, to reach out rather than to shun,
to care rather than to dismiss, to resist rather than to capitulate, to
transform rather than to accept.

In this chapter, I offer voices that raise the moral imperative to
embrace for the sake of our souls, psyches, democracy, species, and
planet, as well as voices that call to resist divisive structures. Each
voice on its own is powerful; together, they form a choir. They range
from mystical to political, from aboriginal to philosophical, from
the marginalized to the privileged, and from religion to science.
These are not the only voices, but they are some of the ones I find
compelling.

These voices do not call for a simple recovery of an assumed lost
past. Our search will not be rewarded by reclaiming a discarded
past, a paradise lost, or a mythic time when all was in harmony with

others and with nature. While there is no historical record of such a time, the existence of such stories does reveal a universal longing deep in the human soul. But we must look cautiously at the notion of a virtuous golden age standing in stark contrast to the present. This is what the Tea Party wishes to do, what the fundamentalist religionists wish to do, what those who fear losing their privilege and power wish to do—namely, to go back to the way things were, or at least as they were imagined to be. "Make America Great Again" uncritically assumes a static past of unequal relations of race, justice, and power.

It is not an overstatement to say the way forward demands a radical transformation—transformation of our imagination, our consciousness, our reasoning, our behavior, and our social structures. Anything less will fall short. We may be tempted to fix or modify the violent consequences of Othering by returning to the old days, but doing so will not address the heart of our problem.

So, where do we turn? We need a new imagination, a total reorientation. The idea of "again" is a chimera. Thomas Wolfe claimed, "You can't go home again."[1] Many of my born-again friends refer to Jesus's admonition to Nicodemus that he must be born "again." But there are several problems with thinking in terms of "again." It assumes there was a time when things were the way they are supposed to be—in the garden before the fall of Adam and Eve, in Camelot, in Milton's *Paradise Lost*, in Shangri-La. "Again" too often substitutes nostalgia for historical accuracy.

We can't go home again because home never had the complexity, the racial/ethnic mix, or the reality of a global world we now have. As Langston Hughes poetically penned, "O let America be America again—the land that never has been yet—and yet must be—the land where every man is free."[2] We need to distinguish between nostalgia for an illusory past and hope for a new world.

Many Christians interpret the words of Jesus to Nicodemus about being born again as essential for salvation.[3] A closer look at that challenge reveals a better translation and an even deeper requirement. One must be born from above; that is, to be captured by a transcendence that goes far beyond mere longing for a lost morality and culture. Nicodemus's response was limited to a return to the past—to ask how he could enter a second time into the womb. But to be born from above is the promise of something totally new, a transcendence of the past rather than simply a recovery and repetition of what was. What many of the born-again preachers are calling for is a return to a time when marriage was only between one man and one woman, abortion was illegal, the Bible was read in the schools, and the church was the center of life.

As Andrew Murray points out, two giants of our nation's attempted rebirth, Frederick Douglass and Abraham Lincoln, lamented the racial divisions born of slavery and looked to a new day rather than a return to the past. They understood to make America great, there must be a transformation to something genuinely new:

> The pillars must be replaced, certainly, in order to buttress the nation's founding principles, but they will be hewn from different materials than those supplied by the founders. In such a way, the task of the founders will be advanced in a new setting. For Lincoln and Douglass, the nation's promise lay in its ability to grow out of its earlier shortcomings.[4]

Murray concludes:

> So long as what is essentially American is located in a Christian consensus among northern European white Protestants, pluralism in the American religious and political landscape can only appear as a falling-off from those standards of purity, and never as a new and vibrant cultural production in its own right.[5]

And while legislative changes sometimes achieve desirable results, often those changes merely mask an underlying reality that does not change. The ending of slavery, for example, did not eliminate racist treatment of people of color. There have been legislative changes along the road, as slavery was replaced by Jim Crow, and Jim Crow by the War on Drugs and the resultant mass incarceration. But racism continues. While the Civil Rights Acts led to some improvement for black people, they didn't fundamentally change the beliefs, attitudes, and values of many white people. At the structural level, the guarantee of the right to vote has been circumvented by gerrymandering, identification requirements, reducing the number of convenient precincts, and shortening registration and voting periods. Despite legislation, racism remains.

And the Equal Rights Amendment, ratified by enough states but not yet certified to make it part of the Constitution, has not ended the mistreatment of women. Allowing a few women to rise to the top of the corporate ladder does not change the underlying sexism of a male-dominated culture, as we have witnessed with the steadily increasing accounts of sexual abuse by men against women, and lower pay for women for comparable work. The suit being brought against the US Soccer Federation by the world champion US women's soccer team alleges institutionalized gender discrimination, including significantly lower pay than for the men's team.[6]

American Indians have witnessed scores of legislative actions to correct their mistreatment, but they remain marginalized and largely impoverished. And while legislation has created more educational programs for prisoners and has reduced recidivism, it does little to change our society's perception of prisoners as undesirable people who must be kept away from us "good" people.

New technologies are often praised as the way to a genuinely new future, but, too often, they fall short of the promise. This is especially evident in the development of military technology. Drones have been developed with the promise of surgical strike capacity, thereby minimizing or even eliminating civilian deaths. But the "collateral damage" of civilians continues and the advent of drones does not change our view of the enemy as evil and deserving of death. What we have created is a technologically advanced form of warfare. The technology may have changed, but wars and a war mentality continue.

The dynamics of social change inevitably involve both personal morality and social structures. Martin Luther King Jr. claimed that those who insist we cannot legislate morality are speaking a half-truth. The whole truth is more complex, as he recognized when he said:

> Morality cannot be legislated, but behavior can be regulated. Judicial decrees may not change the heart, but they can restrain the heartless. . . . Those dark and demonic responses will be removed only as men are possessed by the invisible, inner law . . . that all men are brothers and that love is mankind's most potent weapon for personal and social transformation. True integration will be achieved by true neighbors who are willingly obedient to unenforceable obligations.[7]

Nor is it my intention to ignore the role transgressive memory can serve, highlighting actors and movements that resisted divisions and their underlying systems. Their voices and sacrifices offer us a different understanding of the past and what is needed to transcend our divisions. The moral imperative must involve both embrace and resistance, two sides of the same coin.

This chapter focuses on the importance of our moral imagination. For real and lasting transformation to occur, we must address the foundations of our morality—our way of understanding the world, and the processes that shape our understanding. The fundamental roots of the disease we face are our readiness to treat people as Other and the systems that create and use Othering. The path forward must address this moral failure.

Black and Maori Voices

While some enraged voices have called for revenge and even violence, others have sought to embrace their oppressors. Their strength to claim hope in the face of both historical and current racism has been astounding. Two people who have most deeply affected many of us are Martin Luther King Jr., who was attacked, jailed, and eventually murdered, and Nelson Mandela, who spent twenty-seven years in prison. Despite the racist brutality they endured, each called for the embrace of those who had benefited from the unjust arrangements and of those who had been its witting or unwitting supporters. But, the call to embrace came after significant acts of resistance by both King and Mandela. King insisted on a nonviolent resistance to the evils of segregation, and it was only after his call to resist that he called for love of the perpetrators. Further, it is doubtful whether King's consistent call for nonviolence and embrace of oppressors would have been as powerful if they had not been rejected by Malcolm X's calls for resistance by any means necessary.[8]

Mandela's power to negotiate the end of official apartheid and the embrace of all South Africans as one nation came undoubtedly from the years he had been a radical resistor, calling for the violent overthrow of the white regime. He had come to understand the embrace of the Afrikaners was strategically necessary if his nation was to avoid a bloodbath.

A Single Garment of Destiny, Martin Luther King Jr.

Born in Atlanta and a graduate of Morehouse College, Martin Luther King Jr. earned a divinity degree at Crozer Seminary in Chester, Pennsylvania, and a PhD at Boston University. He could have remained in the north, but even before his degree was finished, he accepted the call to be pastor of the Dexter Avenue Memorial Baptist Church in Montgomery, Alabama. And so began his baptism by fire.

His years of leadership were characterized by three primary commitments: freedom for the black community from the injustices suffered, resistance through nonviolent civil disobedience in the face of unjust laws, and the embrace of all people—black or white, friend or enemy.

King, himself, often experienced treatment as a second-class person—in housing, public transportation, and public accommodations. He was frequently enraged as he witnessed the ways in which black people were demeaned and discriminated against. He was sickened by the brutality of the police and "the abyss of injustice" black people had long suffered. Yet despite his anger, he did not think evil was inevitable. He rejected both the liberal notion that humans are inherently good and the neo-orthodox notion that humans are inevitably evil. He believed firmly in the possibility the vilest persons could be transformed because "every man is an heir to a legacy of dignity and worth."[9] He constantly reminded people the Declaration of Independence states "all men are created equal." For him, "all" meant *all*.

Nor would he allow his critics to dismiss him as one who was not included in "all men." Despite having been accused and jailed for being an outside agitator, his letter from the Birmingham jail declared, "We are caught in an inescapable network of mutuality, tied in a single garment of destiny. Whatever affects one directly affects all indirectly. Never again can we afford to live with the narrow, provincial 'outside agitator' idea. Anyone who lives in the United States can never be considered an outsider anywhere in this country."[10]

How could King speak of love for those who had so severely injured him and other black people? Yet his challenge to embrace our enemies with love is at the heart of his vision for a just world. He said in a sermon we should love our enemies because "love is the only force capable of transforming an enemy into a friend."[11]

In one of his most memorable speeches, he spoke of his dream for a nation in which all would be embraced. His dream envisioned the formerly enslaved and slaveholders sitting down together in brotherhood, and his children being judged by the content of their character and not by the color of their skin. But he did not stop there. His dream extended beyond the American South and even the United States, "The American dream will not become a reality devoid of the larger dream of a world of brotherhood and peace and good will. The world in which we live is a world of geographical oneness and we are challenged now to make it spiritually one."[12]

For King, the unity of all persons was at the center of his vision for a world without walls.

Long Walk to Freedom, Nelson Mandela

Few persons in history have been as dedicated and fierce an advocate for overcoming the dividing walls of hostility as Nelson Mandela. His journey, from being a staunch supporter of armed struggle against white Afrikaners who imposed apartheid upon black people and other people of color in South Africa, to the president who sought to bring black and white together, is legendary.

The son of a chief, he left his village home to become a lawyer and defend persecuted black people. In his late twenties, he joined the African National Congress (ANC) and cofounded its Youth League, gradually assuming leadership and calling for armed struggle against the dominant minority of white Afrikaners. In 1960, the ANC was formally outlawed, leading to the arrest of many of its leaders, including Mandela, who were tried and convicted of conspiracy to commit violence against the government. During his twenty-seven-year imprisonment, he found a new voice.

In prison, he discovered common ground with some of his captors with whom he'd cultivated mutual respect. For years, he had sought to make alliances with people regardless of race, but now he found himself genuinely dialoguing with the "enemy," trying to find or create commonality wherever possible. Just two years after the 1976 Soweto uprising in which black school children were killed in protests against using the Afrikaans language, Mandela said with remarkable insight and generosity of spirit, "South Africa has almost three million Afrikaners who will no longer be oppressors after liberation but a powerful minority of ordinary citizens, whose cooperation and goodwill will be required in the reconstruction of the country."[13] Released from prison in 1990 by Afrikaner president F. W. de Klerk, he and de Klerk shared the 1993 Nobel Peace Prize in recognition of their leadership to create a peaceful transition to democracy. In his acceptance speech, Mandela lifted up the moral foundations upon which the struggle against apartheid stood—the recognition that everyone is harmed by injustice, and the vision of a united humanity. "These countless human beings, both inside and outside our country, had the nobility of spirit to stand in the path of tyranny and injustice, without seeking selfish gain. They recognized an injury to one is an injury to all and therefore acted together in defense of justice and a common human decency. Because of their courage and persistence for many years, we can, today, even set the dates when all humanity will join together to celebrate one of the outstanding human victories of our century."[14]

Ubuntu, Desmond Tutu

The moral imperative to embrace has roots in an extraordinary range of societies, cultures, religions, and philosophies. Among the oldest is the indigenous African tradition of *Ubuntu* that was the basic principle for the Truth and Reconciliation Commission (TRC).

Since 1948, South African apartheid laws divided the nation into white people, Indians, colored people, and black people, in a descending order of freedom, economic opportunity, and justice. Almost three and a half million people were removed from their lands and forced into Bantustans, segregated territories characterized by poverty, government surveillance and abuse, and inferior education. With the end of apartheid in 1994, the nation faced the choice to punish or heal. There were conflicting voices within the ANC: some called for punishment of the white Afrikaners while others, influenced by the leadership of Nelson Mandela, believed a new beginning demanded healing and nonviolence. In the end, they chose to seek healing and reconciliation rather than punishment and reprisal. The TRC was established and began holding its meetings in 1996. Its mandate was to provide a venue that would illuminate the human rights abuses under apartheid, help with healing the victims, including reparations, and provide amnesty in rare cases for those who committed heinous crimes (provided they were politically motivated). Many criticized the process as being soft on the offenders and not holding them accountable. Whatever its shortcomings, however, the TRC helped to avoid the violence that might have followed apartheid's end.

Of primary importance for the TRC was Ubuntu, the traditional philosophy of some of the sub-Saharan African tribes: what makes us a person is our relationship to other persons. Relationships are essential to being human. The Zulu phrase, *umuntu ngumuntu ngabantu*, is difficult to translate literally. One translation is "a person is a person through other people." Another way to say this is a person depends upon others just as others depend on them. This definition underscores both our interconnectedness and our concern to meet the needs of others. What makes us human is not our independence from one another but rather our interdependence. Our connectedness is much deeper than simply treating others fairly—it is a sense of being essentially part of one another. This is reflected in the deeply spiritual belief we are still bound to our ancestors.

Ubuntu, or humanness, expresses the moral imperative to embrace all people. It is a deeply ethical philosophy that calls us to mutual responsibility. So, it is both an ontological claim—we are inextricably related—and also an ethical claim—we have a responsibility to care for the other, no matter who they may be.

The culture of Ubuntu was not limited to South Africa. Long before colonialization, many African communities practiced this philosophy in resolving conflicts and preserving unity. They approached divisions and harm as a problem suffered by everyone, not just an individual victim; therefore, the entire community needed to be involved in healing. When one is harmed, the entire community is harmed. Similarly, harming someone was seen as not solely the act of an offender; it impacted the entire community. They considered how all persons, and even the structures of their society itself, might be complicit in the offender's actions. Hence, their approach has been to bring together as many as possible who are involved and to seek mutual understanding, remorse, forgiveness, restitution, and healing. This communal approach to reconciliation has been used historically in Africa to resolve familial controversies, criminal acts (even murder), tribal conflicts, and wars. It is a form of restorative justice.

Archbishop Desmond Tutu, the Anglican priest who chaired the TRC, drew upon both this traditional African philosophy and Christian theology. For him, there was a consonance between the values of Ubuntu and the biblical claim all human beings are created in God's image. There are no disposable people—even those who commit egregious acts—because we are inextricably connected.

It is striking that so many black South Africans, people who were systematically suppressed, tortured, and murdered, were able to move beyond their grief and rage. Archbishop Tutu's words, uttered during the oppressive days of apartheid, carried their truth: "White South Africans would never be truly free until we black people were free as well."[15] It is also striking that many white people who had formerly supported apartheid found freedom from hatred and began a new life. Even in those dark days, there was the recognition that everyone was connected and the way forward would inescapably involve the freedom of all.

For Archbishop Tutu, this understanding grounded his fundamental assertion that forgiveness is a necessary condition for creating a new future. He believed, difficult as it is to forgive an oppressor, it is our inescapable responsibility. Some felt strongly that the living could not forgive on behalf of the dead, that the evil of the past could not be forgiven by those in the present, but he responded, "We cannot go on nursing grudges even vicariously for those who cannot speak for themselves any longer. We have to accept that what we do we do for generations past, present and yet to come. That is what makes a community a community or a people a people. . . ."[16] In this quote, we see the profound impact of Ubuntu. There is no escaping our interconnectedness, even with those who have come before us and those who will come after us. We are one.

The point was driven home to me by a conversation I had with three grandmothers in the township of Gugulethu who had lost their children to the ravages of apartheid and now bore the responsibility of raising their grandchildren. Despite their anger, they spoke of the need to forgive the perpetrators. When I asked how they could possibly find it in their hearts to forgive, they responded it was for their own peace and for the sake of a new future for their grandchildren. They understood the truth of Ubuntu—we are all connected.

Mana, Maori Relationships

The Maori are the indigenous people of New Zealand whose culture, similar to the American Indians, was significantly devastated by colonization. Today, after losses in the 1800s, they are a growing percentage of the population, numbering around 775,000 or about 16.5 percent of the total. Their philosophy and approach to life have shaped many aspects of New Zealand's public life, among other things, the nation's juvenile justice system. Because the Maori approach life as communal, their response to crime and harm involves the entire community rather than only the offender and victim. In addition, their approach seeks healing rather than retribution or punishment. This has led to the formal adoption of restorative justice in dealing with juvenile crimes.

Central to the Maori approach is the concept of *mana*, the interconnectedness of all things, both human and environmental: all of life is related. In fact, everything has *mana* or is *mana*. Therefore, like many of the indigenous African tribes, the Maori have a strong sense of ancestral relationships and a deep connection to nature. Anthropologist Marshall Sahlins refers to the Maori "kinship system," by which he means "a manifold of intersubjective participations, founded on mutualities of being."[17] This sense of kinship is evident in the use of "I" in Maori culture that Sahlins explains at great length. Saying I defeated an enemy (three centuries ago) or I own this land (obviously vaster than any one individual could own), the Maori indicate their essential connection with all others, living or dead.

Those who have been so heavily influenced by both individualism and a binary approach to life may see the Maori understanding of the tribal *mana* as displacement of the individual, succumbing to a group identity and losing one's individual distinctiveness and contribution. But according to John Patterson, philosophy professor at Massey University in New Zealand:

> The misunderstanding stems from seeing the individual and the community as quite distinct entities, and then trying to account for one of them in terms of the other. Transcending both individualism and collectivism in their crudest manifestations, a better way is to see them as so intimately related that there is no possibility that either could be swamped by the 'other' or dismissed as secondary.[18]

There are some limits to the Maori concept of *mana* and its sense of kinship with all. In some cases, the extent of the kinship may stop with the tribe, reflecting less a sense of inextricable relationship to all of existence as advanced by Ubuntu. But it is a clear alternative to the focus on the individual and their particularities that contributes so significantly to our current divisions.

Religious and Philosophical Voices

In the first two chapters, I explained how each of the major religions has been used, or misused, as a basis for division. While there is no denying this fact, it is also true that religion has, at times and for some people, been a source of healing and unity. This positive dimension of religion is what I aim to lift up next. I could have termed this section "spiritual" rather than "religious" since some do not consider Buddhism a religion, some of the biblical prophets were considered marginal to the central religion in their day, and Jesus did not seek to create a new religion of Christianity.

Dependent Origination, Buddhism

At the heart of Buddhism is the experience that we are one. "Just as a mother would protect her only child at the risk of her own life, even so, cultivate a boundless heart towards all beings (Sutta Nipāta 149–150)."[19] "The bodhisattva loves all beings as if each were his only child (Vimalakīrti Nirdeśa Sūtra5)."[20]

Buddhism advances the concept of emptiness as an essential path to understanding and growth, challenging our Western way of thinking to move beyond "our own-being." That is, we must forego dealing with the world and ourselves as if all things, and we ourselves, were independent, self-sufficient objects. According to the Dalai Lama in *The Universe in a Single Atom*, "The philosophy of emptiness reveals that clinging is not only a fundamental error but also the basis of attachment, clinging, and the development of our numerous prejudices."[21]

I draw some parallels between the Dalai Lama's understanding of clinging to self as the basis of our negative behaviors and some of the roots and forms of Othering I detailed in chapters 2 and 3. When we think we are independent of the things and people that shape us, we are deluding ourselves. Because we are essentially relational, we inevitably cling to something that gives us identity, such as a tribe. We substitute an identity based on narrow tribal connections rather than on a more comprehensive understanding of our connectedness to all people and the universe. Our assumption of independence is an illusion.

Clinging is the result of a false understanding of reality. It substitutes loyalty to a person, group, or cause for the basic understanding that I am a part of all that was, is, and shall be. Tribalism is a clinging to a false loyalty in the same way that the notion of independence clings to a false idea of what it is to be human.

When we empty ourselves of uncritical attachments, we realize we are not independent but interacting. As the Dalai Lama says, we change each other: "Things and events are 'empty' in that they do not possess any immutable essence, intrinsic reality, or absolute 'being' that affords independence."[22]

Fundamental for Buddhist ethics is the principle of *dependent origination*: "No thing or event can be construed as capable of coming into, or remaining in, existence by itself. The universe is an organism and each part is dependent upon the whole."[23] Indeed, there would be no whole without the parts, nor the parts without the whole. The Dalai Lama concludes the chapter on dependent origination with the affirmation of the connectedness of all things, including the linking of our interests.

In many ways, this resonates with Ubuntu, as mentioned by the Buddhist South African professor, Michel Clasquin. In searching for the similarities and differences between Buddhism and African thought, he sees a consonance between the basic presuppositions of each in understanding our fundamental interdependence. "From a Buddhist point of view, Ubuntu points towards an understanding of non-duality, of interconnectedness and *anatta* . . . Ubuntu is not merely an expression of social solidarity. It is that, but it also expresses a mystical connection with unseen beings, and, indirectly, a connection with the all-that-is."[24]

The Jesuit scholar Michael Barnes summarizes it well. For Buddhism, "there is '*no thing*,' no inherently existent reality which can be separated from every other 'thing.' Everything is part of one interdependent continuum of being."[25]

Tikkun Olam, Judaism

The Hebrew words *tikkun olam* mean "repairing the world," a phrase first used in the Mishnah, the early compilation of Jewish interpretation. It has come to express a sense of responsibility for social justice, following the assertion that all persons have been made in God's image and, consequently, are worthy of recognition and care. In other words, our relationships are rooted in the divine, which Rabbi Michael Lerner calls the spiritual reality of the universe. These words provide the guiding principle for the Network of Spiritual Progressives of which Lerner is a leading voice.

Lerner has been deeply influenced by his mentor, Rabbi Abraham

Heschel, who consistently drew upon the Jewish prophetic tradition with its insistence on the correlation between holiness and justice. Lerner calls this connection between holiness and justice the politics of meaning, illustrated in the words of the prophets. In the midst of a litany of denunciations against the injustice and corruption of Israel, Hosea points to Yahweh's words of healing, "I desire steadfast love and not sacrifice, the knowledge of God rather than burnt offerings."[26] In the same way, Micah goes to the heart of the response to injustice, reminding the people of Yahweh's command, "He has told you, O mortal, what is good; and what does the Lord require of you but to do justice, and to love kindness and to walk humbly with your God."[27] In both these prophetic utterances, the underpinning of any action to bring about justice and healing is rooted in our relationship with ultimate reality, which is what is meant by holiness. For Heschel and Lerner, overcoming the divisions caused by injustice is rooted in a holiness characterized by a recognition of the profoundly relational nature of reality.

Holiness can mean different things. For the temple priesthood, holiness meant ritual purity, such as abstaining from certain foods, following Torah prescriptions, avoiding contact with "unclean" people and objects, and observing the Sabbath. For Hosea and Micah, ritual observances were secondary to maintaining right relations among people, and thereby with God. Only after the repair of injustice and the healing of relations among people take place—tikkun olam—do ritual observances serve to honor the relation with God. The holiness of which Heschel and Lerner speak is our essential interrelatedness and embrace of all people.

Swords into Plowshares, Biblical Prophets

Many biblical prophets delivered their oracles directly to the king, especially in times of war. Micah described the horrors of impending devastation to Samaria and Jerusalem. Isaiah walked with King Hezekiah while he inspected Jerusalem's water system before a siege by the Assyrians, and Jeremiah sent repeated messages to kings facing the threat of Babylonian invasion.

This observation is noteworthy because their accusations against the elites came at a time of great domestic economic injustices, as well as external pressures. From Micah, for example: "Hear this, you rulers of the house of Jacob and chiefs of the house of Israel, who abhor justice and pervert all equity, who build Zion with blood and Jerusalem with wrong!"[28] "Therefore because of you Zion shall be plowed as a field; Jerusalem shall become a heap of ruins."[29] And Isaiah: "Wash yourselves; make yourselves clean; remove the evil of your doings from before my eyes; cease to do evil, learn to do good; seek justice, rescue the oppressed, defend the orphan, plead for the widow."[30] To the prophets, the threat of enemy attack was the result of God's displeasure with the elites' treatment of those in their own land who were other: the poor, the landless, the tenant farmers.

God still offered hope, if they would change their priorities and repair their societies. With justice would come peace. If not, no amount of armed might and city defenses would protect them. The dire warnings of Micah and Isaiah were fulfilled a hundred years later, but those who transmitted their words also preserved visions of an alternative future. From Micah, "they shall beat their swords into plowshares, and the spears into pruning hooks; nation shall not lift up sword against nation, neither shall they learn war anymore. But they shall all sit under their own vines and under their own fig trees and no one shall make them afraid."[31]

And the words of the prophet Isaiah, made famous in Handel's *Messiah*, describe a time when descendants of those who were taken into exile will return, when divisions of wealth, power, and privilege shall no longer exist. "Every valley shall be lifted up and every mountain and hill made low; the uneven ground shall become level, and the rough places a plain."[32] Isaiah's and Micah's words are a promise that the dividing walls will be torn down.

Jesus must be understood as part of this prophetic tradition. His time in the first century was also characterized by deep divisions—economically, socially, religiously, politically, and physically. The lame, the sick, and the blind were considered untouchable to those observing holiness; women without a male head of household easily became destitute and vulnerable to abuse; the Jews were subjects of Rome; and men dominated politics, religion, and the economy of a small colonial province.

But Jesus refused to abide by the constructed walls. He resisted. He touched the sick when others went out of their way to avoid them. He included women among his closest followers. He spoke to a woman who was alone at a well, had disciples from all social classes, and dined with the outcasts. According to Luke, he inaugurated his ministry by aligning himself with the words of Isaiah announcing good news to the poor, release of the captives, recovery of sight to the blind, and freedom for the oppressed.[33] He challenged the heart of patriarchy by relating to women as full persons. At the core of his approach to life was resistance to the political and religious leaders and a willingness to embrace everyone, which challenged the divisions that benefited those in power.

One of the most visible forms of his all-encompassing embrace was his table fellowship, evidencing his belief in the dignity and worth of all persons, no matter their status.[34] In those days, dining reflected the prevailing social boundaries. To be invited to someone's table was considered an honor limited to persons of note. But Jesus broke with the social conventions and ate with those normally not invited. In keeping with his actions, he told a parable about a man who prepared a banquet and invited certain people to dine with him. One by one, the invited guests claimed pressing affairs and asked to be excused. When the host saw they were not coming, he invited "whosoever will" to come and dine.[35]

The parable reflected Jesus's attitude and behavior as someone challenging the imperial power and religious leaders who were dependent on it. Some of the privileged leaders attempted to repudiate him and his movement by denigrating him for eating with publicans, sinners, and tax collectors. His embrace of the outcasts led to his being treated as an outcast, as Other. But their rejection did not turn him back, for he believed that no one, not even the least, should be discarded. In the end, his resistance to the imperial and religious power structures led to his execution, but even then he embraced his executioners, praying for their forgiveness.

Three in One, Trinity

One of the most perplexing ideas of Christianity is the doctrine of the Trinity. In an attempt to maintain the monotheism of Judaism, while treating Jesus as divine and the Holy Spirit as God's indwelling presence, early Christianity considered numerous, often tortuous proposals, rejections, and counterproposals. Following debates among theologians, philosophers, arguments at councils, and after much political intrigue, the doctrine was finally affirmed in the fourth century as the orthodox position: God is three persons in one essence: Father, Son, and Holy Spirit.

Countless millions of Christians sing or recite, weekly, the doxology that concludes with "God in three persons, blessed Trinity." And many of those countless millions remain perplexed by a speculative notion that defies logic and leaves them feeling somewhat heretical. This is not surprising, as the compromise that resulted from the victory of the Constantinian religious hierarchy never made conventional sense.

But I suggest there is a way to understand this inscrutable doctrine that offers a basis for embrace. The notion God is three in one can be understood as a metaphor to explain that the very foundation of existence is essentially relational. There is nothing deeper, nothing more basic than relationships. And if that is true of the ground of being,[36] it is true each of us is inextricably related. There is no one and no thing that is unrelated.

The Face, Emmanuel Levinas

Emmanuel Levinas, a Jewish philosopher, was deeply impacted by the horrors of World War II. As a French officer, he was captured and imprisoned for most of the war. His entire family was murdered by the Nazis. For him, one's reality is to be found in the Face of the other, and that Face confronts us with the claim, "Thou shall not kill." This responsibility is not reciprocal, that is, dependent upon the other's feeling for me. Rather, it is based completely on the realization that, in the other's Face, I encounter vulnerability and need, and I am, therefore, invited to care. I am responsible for the other.

In response to a questioner about our responsibility to the Other, Levinas refers to the biblical story of Cain and Abel. When Cain is asked by God, "Where is your brother?" Cain responds, "Am I my brother's keeper?"[37] For Levinas, Cain's answer is not an evasion. It is an honest acknowledgment of his feeling they are separate. The problem for Levinas is Cain's answer is predicated "only on ontology. I am I and he is he. We are separate ontological beings."[38] What is lacking is any ethical sense of responsibility.

The Face of the other invites us into a relationship with the infinite. It is more than just a separate being I encounter. In meeting the other, I am face to face with the infinite, more than my reason or categorizations can apprehend. The Face I encounter is filled with complexity no single category can capture: citizen or refugee; male or female; white, black, brown, yellow, or red; straight, gay, or questioning; full or hungry; Republican or Democrat; Christian, Jew, Muslim, Buddhist, Sikh, Hindu, or atheist. The other cannot be prejudged by my stereotypes and classifications, and, as a result, that person is no longer Other, but essentially human, and, hence, one for whom I am responsible.

Contrast Face with *persona*. The Latin word *persona*, meaning mask, is the face one puts on or the face of the other we perceive, but the essential person is hidden by that mask. A society that is essentially commodified relies upon the *persona*. Modern product development is based on the *persona*. To design and sell a product, a person is fabricated based on characteristics such as age, race, gender, class, height, weight, tastes, and social location. But this aggregate of particularities is not the essential person, rather it is a mask, a social construction.

Our political culture is dependent upon the masks that hide us from one another. This reality is created by dominant structures that prevent us from seeing one another's face and that benefit from this failure by remaining in power. We see another's class, race, gender, choice of media, or political candidate and do not see the person behind the mask.

The creation of masks has been common throughout history. As Edward W. Said has pointed out, Western conquest and domination have created the notion of Orientalism, which grants essential status to particular elements and actions that fit Western stereotypes, thereby missing the true essence of what it means to be Arab or Muslim.

Persona can be in the perception of either the one perceived or the perceiver. For years, many LGBTQ+ people hid behind masks that presented themselves to a world that heterosexual persons wanted to see. Many black people similarly have offered a public face the white world expects or even demands. Elijah Anderson speaks of a "tax" on black men—namely, "The need to prove that they are not who others fear they are. While white people are free to be themselves, black people must take special measures to distance themselves from the ghetto image by their dress and demeanor."[39] Both perceiver and perceived live in a world of masks. But when we come face to face, the other person's Face makes a claim upon us based upon their suffering and need: do not kill me, help me, give me bread. To be encountered by another person's Face is to look beyond any specific characteristic, to discover their vulnerability and need—hence, to be responsible for them.

Face, for Levinas, is not something we create but rather what is offered to us in the most intimate encounter. For him, the antidote to treating people as Other lies in being open to their Face, with all its vulnerabilities, and accepting responsibility for their life. In doing so, we discover the depth of our own humanity.

There is an interesting corollary in the neurobehavioral research of Mark R. Dadds from the Child Behavioral Research Clinic of New South Wales. He hypothesizes eye contact, or its lack, between a parent and child is a critical factor in developing a loving relationship. If a child fails to return a parent's gaze, there is a tendency for the parent to withhold their love out of frustration, resulting in further distancing and even aggressive behavior by the child.[40] Truly encountering the other's face is critical.

I and Thou, Martin Buber

In his famous paraphrase of the Gospel of John, "In the beginning was the Word," Martin Buber underscores the reciprocal connection of all that exists: "In the beginning is the relation."[41] The fundamental imperative of life is to relate to other beings as a Thou (in early English, *thou* was a more intimate word for *you*).

An authentic relation is between two beings (I and Thou) rather than between a being and an object (I and It). For Buber, there are always borders between an I and an object, whereas those walls are overcome when the relation is between and I and Thou. What we have seen in previous chapters is how common it is for another person to be cast as an object, to be spoken of and treated as an It.

Buber sees the I–Thou relationship in three arenas of life: nature, persons, and God. When we relate to something in nature (for example, a tree, an animal, or a sunset) we may respond to it as an object for observation, scientific study, or description. But when we relate to nature as Thou, we are enveloped in a reality that goes far beyond language—what he calls the threshold. This also can be observed in Nobel Prize winner Barbara McClintock's reply to the secret of her successful gene research on corn. When asked what led to her discovery, she replied, "To do great science you have to learn, somehow, to lean into the kernel."[42]

Clearly, there is a place for the objectification afforded by science, but in that claim, McClintock went below the surface to the almost mystical relationship she had with corn.

When we relate to another person as Thou, all the specific aspects of the person—whether race, gender, religion, age, size—are still present, but we are encountering the person's essence, which is reciprocal. This is in sharp contrast to the "essentialism" by which, for example, certain characteristics of Arabs have been elevated by Westerners to the level of essence. An I–Thou relationship is not shaped by the specific characteristics of the other, but rather by an unexplainable symbiosis. This is why the language of Thou is often poetic and metaphorical; it is the language of transcendence. To encounter another at this level overcomes the walls that have been built in response to the particularities.

For Buber, our relationship to God is unmediated by doctrines and rituals. It is the foundation of an authentic life. Like love of another, there is no way to speak of this relationship other than with metaphor.

Herein lies the power of Buber's understanding of I and Thou. "The relation to the You is unmediated. Nothing conceptual intervenes between I and You, no prior knowledge and no imagination; and memory itself is changed as it plunges from particularity into wholeness."[43] While this may appear naïvely idealistic, it is precisely what happened for some people during the TRC hearings when the victims encountered their former enemy as a human being rather than simply as a torturer or prison guard. This is what happens between victims and offenders when restorative justice is effective. Neither is an It. Mandela's imprisonment demonstrated this: he treated his captors as fellow human beings, and eventually they, in turn, came to view him as a person of dignity and worth.

For Buber, the world of politics and economics is characterized by I–It relations: instrumentalzing, calculating, profiling, controlling. This is the world in which the dividing walls have been and are being constantly erected, the world in which we are inevitably engaged. Buber understood it is possible (and even necessary) to live in the world of It. In that regard, he was a realist. But at the same time, he was deeply spiritual. The issue for him was whether the world of It is constantly influenced and directed by the Spirit of You. He believed "as soon as we touch a You we are touched by a breath of eternal life."[44] I am reminded of the words from the musical *Les Misérables*, "to see another person is to see the face of God."[45] When we relate to another as Thou, they are no longer Other.

This is fine for a mystic, but what about the rest of us? How do we translate Buber's vision into practice? How do we create I–Thou relationships in an I–It world? The next chapter seeks to address that question.

Women's Voices

As a theologian and ethicist, my thinking has been fundamentally reshaped by the recovery of women's voices. At its most basic, the famous quotation one sees on T-shirts and bumper stickers, attributed to Cheris Kramarae, expresses that the division between male and female is false: "Feminism is the radical notion that women are human beings." They have claimed their space, their rights, and their voices in all arenas of life, including reimagining the theological corpus, with the revival of metaphorical approaches to traditionally rational doctrines. And, for our purposes here, they have given fresh impetus to the moral imperative to embrace by turning the field of ethics on its binary head with an emphasis on relationships.

Empathy

Empathy can be understood in a variety of ways. It differs from sympathy, which can be thought of as merely feeling sorry for another. To empathize with another is to feel with them, not for them; to experience at least some of the emotions of the other. For example, watching or even reading about a family seeking refuge, only to be torn apart, can engender not just sadness for them but a visceral response of being separated from a loved one. As such, it includes both emotion and observation. To empathize is to walk in another's moccasins,[46] to actually feel, at least to a certain degree, what the other is experiencing.

Empathizing with someone's distress or suffering does not necessarily entail feeling all the emotions the other may have. For example, I do not empathize with a person's racist feelings of rage that might eventuate in violence. On the other hand, I can empathize with the other person's feelings of being bypassed, harmed, or afraid—feelings that touch my own vulnerability. But my empathy does not lead me to draw their conclusion.

Cris Beam provides an excellent exploration of the nature, practice, and consequences of empathy, including an overview of the history leading up to its importance. Her book, *I Feel You*, is filled with deeply moving stories that provide evidence of the power of empathy.[47] As someone interested in the workings of our criminal justice system, I found her notion of entangled empathy particularly pertinent. "Entangled empathy, in other words, doesn't just see a defendant and a victim but people with histories who live in families, who live in a neighborhood and a city and a state and a country. . . . Entangled empathy means considering the fabric as well as the thread."[48]

The notion of empathy came into prominence in the twentieth century and was at first primarily related to aesthetics, the feeling generated by music or art. It was, in part, a response to the self-centered idea popularized by Friedrich Nietzsche's "will to power" as the essence of the human being. From the beginning, the question has been whether empathy is "natural" or learned. Beam's tentative conclusion is, while it is an innate characteristic of human nature, it can be enhanced or diminished; therefore, learning to be empathic is critical. "Empathy, as art, can be genius and inborn, as practice, be refined and improved. But it's also moral in that it's a way one chooses to angle herself rightly in the world, interrupting power and remaining vulnerable, both."[49]

There are numerous testimonies to the power of empathy to overcome barriers. It has been used by therapists, behaviorists, and those working in product development and marketing. The movement called Design Thinking that is used in the schoolroom, counseling sessions, and market analysis begins with empathy. This approach utilizes dialogue to uncover the feelings of the other, touching upon our own vulnerability as well.

Beam's own struggle to deal with an abusive marriage affirmed the power of empathy, both for herself and for her abusive spouse. However, empathy for her spouse did not persuade her to remain—she left him—but it did "interrupt" the power of his rage that affected both of them. She ends the book with these words: "When we have empathy for the enemy outside, we can fold it back to the littlest tyrant within us all. This is, after all, my hope."[50] In so doing, we dismantle the walls that separate us.

Ethics of Care

Akin to the growing importance of empathy is what has been labeled the ethics of care. One of its early proponents is Carol Gilligan, who defined an ethics of care as rooted in relationships and a commitment to giving voice to everyone. As she developed in her seminal work, *In a Different Voice*,[51] this ethic challenges the traditional patriarchal binary approach to ethics—mind versus body, emotion versus reason. For Gilligan and others, an ethic based on relationship and equal voice is healthier, more just, and more realistic. While this approach has been labeled "feminist," it is basically a recovery of a holistic and democratic understanding of what it means to be human.

One of the criticisms of an ethic of care is that in emphasizing relationships, autonomy is lost, which is a red flag in a society that emphasizes individualism. But this is an unnecessary either/or. Fiona Macdonald counters with what she terms *relational autonomy* that stresses the fundamentally social nature of autonomy.[52] That is, our individualism, rather than being subsumed or even lost, is always acted out in relation to others. An authentic autonomy is one that is constantly being empowered and transformed through those relationships.

Another criticism is that principles are eliminated or trampled when we rely upon feelings. This is carefully repudiated by Nel Noddings, one of the foremost proponents of an ethics of care. Principles are not ignored, but rather one does not start with an abstract principle, for example in the case of a crime, "an eye for an eye." Rather, one begins with being disposable, that is, available, both to the one harmed and to the one who has created the harm. This entails uncovering the feelings leading up to and following the crime. In her concluding section on moral education, she illustrates how an ethics of care would function in the case of a student who is consistently late. Rather than dispensing punishment because they have broken the rule (a principle), the administrator or teacher could try to understand why they are late. "What we should unceasingly work toward is a thorough examination of laws and rules that will allow us to sort ethically among them."[53] For her, rules, laws, and principles are always at play, but whether we agree to obey, reinterpret, resist, or reject them should ultimately be rooted in an ethic of care that affirms our essential oneness.

The Power of Anger in the Work of Love

Beverly Wildung Harrison was one of the most influential voices in feminist social ethics. She cautioned, though, that in building relationships we must recognize the realities of a world in which the divisions are created and maintained by structures of dominance and privilege. Her ethic is based on the radical mutuality of love, an act that demands enormous courage in the face of the powers of hatred and division. "Radical acts of love—expressing human solidarity and bringing mutual relationship to life—are the central virtues of the Christian moral life."[54] She insisted, however, that acts of love, given an oppressive reality, require anger at the forces that prevent them.

Harrison understood the dynamic connection between building relationships in which persons are treated with dignity and self-respect, and the necessity for anger and resistance to the forces of oppression. She cautioned, though, to not allow that anger to be turned inward "and lead us to portray ourselves and other women as victims. . . . The creative power of anger is shaped by owning this great strength of women and others who have struggled for the full gift of life against structures of oppression."[55]

Her approach acknowledges that creating a world without walls (a utopian vision) requires action at several levels. It is essential we seek to reach out to others in love, as do those who speak of the need for empathy and care. However, she recognized the need for basic structural changes to provide the possibility for building relationships. In other words, it is critical we engage in the struggle against the forces and structures that create and maintain the walls that divide us.

Many other women have affirmed the necessity for anger. One of the most powerful current voices is Emma Gonzalez, a survivor of the 2018 mass shooting at the Marjory Stoneman Douglas High School in Parkland, Florida. Her fury was infectious as she led the crowd in chants of "We say BS" in a speech responding to Trump's claim that the shooting was due to mental illness when he had repealed an Obama regulation that required background checks of persons with apparent mental illness.[56] And she called BS to the politicians who said nothing could be done to stop the shooting, all the while receiving money from the National Rifle Association. Her cry of BS has resonated with young people (and many others) throughout the nation. It is a cry of righteous anger that resists our gun culture.

It is important to recognize caring and empathy must never bury rage and anger, lest relationships be created at the expense of justice.

Scientists' Voices

The voices of scientists are also pointing to the inextricably connected nature of all that is. The increasing interest in and acceptance of quantum physics since the early twentieth century offered an alternative voice to the often mechanistic language of science. Its earliest form was what some refer to as "vitalism." While the mechanistic interpretation is valid in seeking to understand what things are made of, the importance of the vitalist approach comes from its search for the relationships among things. The vitalists, however, assumed there must be a nonphysical force beyond the physical, while an increasing number of scientists accepted an organismic approach that understands meaning not as something additional, but rather intrinsic to the organizing of relations. Relationships and patterns of connection are key.

The Tao of Physics

One contemporary scientist to advance this way of thinking is Austrian physicist Fritjof Capra. He is unusual because he is interested in both physics and its implications for other arenas of life—in particular, ecology and the mystical experience. This expanded interest beyond pure science arises from his realization that most of the world's problems can be traced to fragmentation, the inability to see the relationships that constitute the whole.

In his early work, *The Tao of Physics*, he underscores the similarity between quantum physics and Eastern mysticism, both of which understand reality as fundamentally relational. His study of subatomic particles led him to conclude "the constituents of matter and the basic phenomena involving them are all interconnected, interrelated and interdependent; that they cannot be understood as isolated entities, but only as integrated parts of the whole."[57]

Unlike many religions that seek explanations and meaning by looking to the realm of the supernatural, Capra finds meaning in the very relationships that characterize everything, down to the smallest particle. Our world is not simply a collection of discernible units but is a living, ever-changing system. This dynamic system allows for feedback, the correction of mistakes, and the mutual shaping that constitutes relationships. The study of quantum physics also gave rise to the science of ecology, the study of the *oikos*

(Greek for household), from which the words *ecology* and *ecumenical* come. In a later book, Capra and Pier Luigi Luisi describe in great detail the systems approach to life that emphasizes the whole is greater than the sum of its parts and relationships are fundamental.[58]

An Irreducible Perceptual Pattern

The rejection of a Cartesian mechanistic universe gave voice not only to quantum physics, but also to a way of thinking about human behavior by psychologists. One of the most interesting approaches has been that of Gestalt therapy, founded by Fritz Perls, which denotes "an irreducible perceptual pattern" that cannot be explained simply by adding up all the parts. There is a mystery in the pattern that defies reductionism. In Gestalt's approach to dream analysis, for example, one does not simply deduce the meaning of a dream. Nor is the dream simply about the most obvious presentation of oneself as the actor. Rather, one becomes every character and aspect of the dream, even the inanimate parts. In this way, we become aware of the complexity of ourselves and, consequently, of our connection with others. This search for patterns in dreams is akin to our search for patterns in our world. Each of us is found in the other. There can be no final division between us and them.

The Implicate Order

Another theoretical physicist, David Bohm, who did his doctoral research with J. Robert Oppenheimer (physicist and director of the Los Alamos laboratory that developed the atomic bomb), theorized that underneath everything we can see (including atomic particles), there is what he called the implicate order, or wholeness. This broke with early quantum physics both in its notion of wholeness and in the idea nothing is static but rather in a constant state of motion.

Drawing from this idea of the fluid nature of reality, he concluded human interaction also needed to be fluid, which convinced him that dialogue was critical. For Bohm, dialogue meant much more than simply talking to each other. He acknowledged there are tragic divisions such as those based on race. Given this social structure, the normal response is to judge the other and distinguish ourselves as not like them, or to conclude we are the ones with the truth and the others are not. To counter these divisions, he advocated participatory dialogue, which includes facing how we participate in the very actions or ideas we deplore because we are part of the whole. For him, studying what he calls the distractions is crucial, which I interpret to mean the need for a full encounter with our tendency to treat people as Other. He holds out the possibility that when we are strong enough "to stand firm in a distracting environment, then you are strong enough to look at the infinite . . . the ability to dialogue, the ability to participate in communication."[59]

The voices of Capra and Bohm underscore the fact we cannot escape our interrelatedness. It is not simply an imperative for them, it is an inescapable reality. In philosophical and theological language, it is the inextricable connectedness of all beings, indeed of all that is. There can be no final separation.

Public Intellectuals' Voices

Two persons who have raised their voices in the public square are David Brooks and George Yancy. They represent differing approaches, but both have in common a concern for walls that divide us.

Wired to Cooperate, David Brooks

Some prominent conservatives have affirmed the necessity for relationships and ending our divisions. David Brooks is one of the most eloquent and consistent voices among conservatives in challenging the notion of unbridled autonomy and its consequent divisions. In a 2017 article, he excoriated H. R. McMaster and Gary Cohn, who wrote approvingly of President Trump's rejection of the world as a global community and his sense that everyone and every nation is engaged in a competition to win. Brooks rejects the selfishness and self-interest that undergirds President Trump's view of the world. For him, it is our cooperation that is most essential to our humanity:

> The error is that it misunderstands what drives human action. Of course, people are driven by selfish motivations. . . . But they are also motivated by another set of drives . . . that are equally and sometimes more powerful. People are wired to cooperate. Far from being a flimsy thing, the desire for cooperation is the primary human evolutionary advantage we have over the other animals.[60]

In another article, Brooks criticizes Justice Anthony Kennedy's 1992 pronouncement that we each define our "own concept of existence . . . and the mystery of human life" as a failure to understand we are all part of a social order.[61] Brooks sees Kennedy's statement as part of an extreme individualism that characterizes our society. For him, we are not isolates but are connected by our past and our culture.

Brooks calls for recovering the philosophy of Personalism, a philosophy that motivated Martin Luther King Jr.[62] Personalism affirms the dignity of each person, calls us to treat each other as Thou, and seeks to get inside the other's story—to know them for who they really are rather than accepting the stereotypes that superficially define them.

However, he fails to understand or address the structures of domination that extol autonomy as a virtue, regardless of the cost. For Brooks, the transformation that is called for is strictly personal and interpersonal. While an important start, it is not the whole picture. He does not address the depth of obstacles to embracing, that is to say, the structures and systems that create and maintain the walls and the fear of vulnerability by those who are privileged by the walls.

Dear White America, George Yancy

In contrast, in a courageous attempt to reach across the racial divide, George Yancy wrote a letter to white people inviting us to face our complicity and to recognize the privileges garnered from being white in a racist society.[63] A philosophy professor at Emory University whose many books uncover and analyze the racism of our culture, Yancy, in that 2015 letter, revealed how he had bought into the sexist narrative of our culture that portrays women as inferior, as instruments. Although his sexism was exhibited by his silence and complicity rather than intentional acts, by sharing his own vulnerability, he hoped to invite white people to look at our lives and world in the same way with respect to racism.

While the letter generated many positive responses, it also gave rise to an outpouring of hatred, vitriol, racism, and physical threats (including death). He was even added to the Professor Watchlist, which registers professors who are considered anticonservative and a threat to white supremacy.[64] In his newest book, *Backlash: What Happens When We Talk Honestly about Racism in America*, he shares many of those letters, as well as his reactions. It is a painful reminder of how far we still have yet to travel as a country.

But the intent of his letter was clearly to prepare the foundation for a genuine relationship—one that demands a recognition of the reality of racism in both its personal and structural forms. He understands being white is to be "positioned systemically or structurally within a white supremacist world."[65] "What I am asking is that you first accept the racism within yourself, accept all of the truth about what it means for you to be white in a society that was created for you. I'm asking for you to trace the binds that tie you to forms of domination that you would rather not see."[66] His hope is that such an openness might lead to a chipping away the walls of racism.

He wonders aloud if there is any possibility that the imperative to embrace can be achieved, but concludes with a cautious hope:

Unlike Odysseus, who tied himself to the mast of a ship so that he could not fully respond to the songs of the sirens, I ask that if you are prepared to be wounded, to be haunted by the joy of love, compassion and vulnerability, untie your ropes, leave the contrived masts of your own undoing, step out into the water—join me there. It might feel like Sisyphus rolling that enormous boulder up the hill again, but let my history embolden you. As James Baldwin said, Black history "testifies to nothing less than the perpetual achievement of the impossible."[67]

Collective Voices

It is not just individuals who have understood and given voice to the deep connectedness of all humans and the need to resist the systems and persons that maintain divisions. There have been declarations and principles articulated by many groups and organizations.

Among the more effective collective voices were those of some labor unions. They amassed millions of members to claim the rights of workers from employers. At one point, the American Federation of Labor (AFL) had the great majority of organized workers, but they were notoriously remiss when it came to black people and women. Samuel Gompers, the head of the AFL for many years between the 1880s and 1920s, spoke of the inclusion of black people as interference with the culture, politics, and economy of the South and refused to organize them. For years, the AFL only reluctantly allowed women members. While the union gained better pay and benefits for its skilled workforce, it did nothing for many others.[68]

But the Industrial Workers of the World, significantly influenced by the socialists Bill Haywood, Eugene V. Debs, and Mary G. Harris Jones (Mother Jones), understood the fundamental division between employers and workers could only end when all workers united. They argued divisions of class can only be overcome when male and female, and people of color and white people all work together. Using the language and tactics of the labor union movement, they sought to unite workers against class divisions and structures. "The working class and employing class have nothing in common . . . a struggle must go on."[69] They called upon workers to resist the power of the economic system to exploit and marginalize them. Theirs was a call to tear down the walls of class.

As early as 1848, the declaration for women's suffrage from the convention at Seneca Falls identified obstacles to women's full participation. In the "Sentiments," it noted more than sixteen grievances against male hegemony that disfranchised them. While written by Elizabeth Cady Stanton, it was confirmed overwhelmingly by those in attendance at the conference. Based on their role as citizens of the United States, they called upon the government to grant the same rights and privileges that men had been granted. Their resistance to the male-dominated system is captured in their opening words that "refuse allegiance to it, and to insist upon the institution of a new government."[70]

A number of Protestant denominations also have taken stands against the divisions in our culture. One of the more recent is my own denomination's (Presbyterian Church (USA)) affirmation in support of LGBTQ+ persons, including their rights to full membership and ordination in 2011.[71] The Unitarian Universalist Association affirms a set of basic principles that are intended to guide all persons and congregations. They are bracketed by an opening principle that affirms "the inherent worth and dignity of every person" and a final principle that affirms "respect for the interdependent web of all existence, of which we are a part."[72]

In similar fashion, the World Council of Churches' Faith and Order Commission affirms the integrity of all creation. "The understanding of integrity we offer to the ecumenical community has two dimensions. The first is integrity as wholeness, interconnectedness, and interdependence. The second is accountability and moral responsibility. . . . The connection between human dignity and the integrity of creation is inseparable; the violation of one involves the violation of the other . . . the movement from hostility to hospitality may be the most powerful witness of engaging for life and of bringing back life where death has appeared to reign, and thus of the hope that, one day, all violence will be overcome."[73]

Perhaps the most well-known affirmation of the interconnectedness and interdependence of all people is the United Nations Universal Declaration of Human Rights. Following the horrors of the Holocaust and World War II, member nations gathered, and, in 1948, approved the Declaration that affirmed rights that historically have been denied people based on their race, gender, sexual identity, class, religion, country of origin, or physical or mental ability. The Preamble begins, "Whereas recognition of the inherent dignity and of the equal and inalienable rights of all members of the human family is the foundation of freedom, justice and peace in the world . . ."[74] It then chronicles in its thirty articles the rights to food, shelter, health, security, education, speech, freedom from slavery, equality before the law, and others, all based on the affirmation we are all members of the same family. There should be no walls.

Our list could also include pronouncements of the Stockholm Accords on Ethnic Cleansing, Catholic social teaching, and similar declarations of other religious groups. Even when the emphasis is on human rights, as in the case of the UN Declaration, there is an implicit understanding all people have these rights based on the realization all are essentially one.

These voices, and those of many others, offer us an understanding of the interdependent essence of our humanity and provide a vision of what can be. Beginning with the moral imperative does not minimize the critical role of activism and structural change. This chapter on affirmations and the next on actions must be read together. The imperative to embrace and the call to resist are of one piece. It remains for us to find the path forward.

6

And the Walls Come Tumbling Down

We all have the capacity to make change—within ourselves, the world, and our relationships to the world.

—Jennifer L. Eberhardt, *Biased: Uncovering the Hidden Prejudice That Shapes What We See, Think, and Do*

Given the enormity and destructiveness of the divisions in our lives and society, the question arises, "What can we do?" How can we respond to the moral imperative to embrace and resist? Is there any way to eliminate, or at least mitigate, the dividing walls of hostility?

The story of Joshua's Israelite army facing the walls of Canaanite Jericho is a reminder that even when the walls seem immovable, they can be demolished. According to the narrative, by God's direction, Joshua and his band marched around the city once a day for seven days and, upon command, raised a trumpet blast and shouts. The walls came tumbling down. It was not the rag-tag Israelites' military power, nor the divinely ordered parade around the city that imploded the walls. It was obedience to a seemingly unrealistic divine imperative that brought results.

Throughout history, walls that seemed impenetrable have been penetrated, torn down, or fallen: physical walls such as the Berlin Wall, legal walls such as apartheid and Jim Crow, economic walls such as the Enclosures of England, and cultural walls such as the division between LGBTQ+ persons and cisgender heterosexual people. All these walls, and many others, have fallen or been penetrated.

One of the most important lessons we can draw from these victories is the demise of walls can occur in the most unanticipated ways and at the most unexpected times. In fall 1988, I attended a conference of theologians and pastors in East Germany, part of a divided nation. While the conference was not about Germany's division, it was, nonetheless, a constant theme throughout our discussions and informal conversations. They could not see a way that the divide could be overcome.

On the way home, my wife and I stayed with a family in East Berlin for several days in a fifth-floor walk-up in an old, run-down apartment house. Other buildings on the block were also in partial ruin. As I walked the streets, I was struck by the dullness of the city. Store shelves were only partially filled with necessities, and options were few. Pollution hung in the air. Everything seemed gray and bleak.

Then we traveled to the other side of the wall into West Berlin, crossing through Checkpoint Charlie. The contrast was stark. There were tree-lined streets with magnificent homes, modern apartment buildings, and shops on the Ku'damm (the Kurfürstendamm was the main shopping street) that showcased luxurious items. Opulence was in the air.

We stayed in West Berlin for several days and then departed by train for Frankfurt. Traveling again through East Germany, we saw lookout towers, barbed-wire fences, and old boxcars like the ones in World War II movies. Guard dogs searched the undercarriages of each car for escapees, and armed military entered each cabin, checking papers and searching luggage. Little seemed to have changed from the days of Nazi terror, and I imagined what it must have been like to live in that brutal society.

I returned to my privileged life in the United States, and the next spring we entertained some of the theologians and pastors we had met in East Germany who indicated that religious leaders were granted permission to travel outside of East Germany because they were considered nonessential. When conversation turned to the Berlin Wall, they unanimously agreed the wall would not come down in our lifetime. Just six months later, following massive protests in the East, especially by the young, as well as the protests against environmental degradation, the wall was torn down and Germany began the process of reuniting.

Walls can be demolished, but there is no single formula for what will effectively bring them down. There are numerous paths to healing our divided world. What has worked in one venue may prove fruitless in another. On occasion, the walls have fallen from their own internal weakness. Most of the time, however, it has required human intervention to effect change. Even in the biblical story of Joshua, human courage, tenacity, and hope were portrayed as essential.

Tearing down walls requires both individual and collective actions. While there is no simple outline that can capture the variations and nuances of transformation, there are things we can do to remove or, at least, pierce the walls. Some involve personal and interpersonal changes that can open us to those on the other side of the divide. I begin with some of the steps we can take to at least minimize the divisions and, in some cases, build collective actions that seek to address the structures of oppression that created them. I conclude with tasks we must undertake to counteract the powers that seek to maintain the walls.

When we consider history, there have been numerous actions that have made a difference. The lesson of history is that walls can come down.

Individual Actions

Tearing down walls, overcoming barriers, and confronting our divisions are demanding work. While collective actions are critical, it is important to recognize how each of us is capable of change and how changes in individual attitudes, beliefs, and actions may impact others.

Overcoming Ignorance

Overcoming ignorance is a critical first step. As long as we live with a false narrative, we will remain divided. We must uncover the truth.

Ignorance is one of the fundamental roots of Othering. Ignorance based on the false narrative of Africa as a "dark continent" led to centuries of tragedies that continue to this day. Ignorance about homosexuality has contributed to hatred, discrimination, killings, and suicides. Ignorance about Islam has led to the frequent conflation of Islam and terrorism, blindness to its rich religious and cultural history, and the conclusion all Muslims are our enemies. Ignorance about the painfully long historic struggle of women for equal rights has allowed many men to assume women's resentment and demands are merely emotional outbursts. Ignorance about black experiences and communities has led many white people to fail to recognize the significant intellectual contributions of people like W. E. B. Du Bois and Cornel West, the organizing skills of Fannie Lou Hamer, the literary gifts of James Baldwin and Zora Neale Hurston, or the artistic talent of Aaron Douglas.

The dividing walls will not come down as long as they are buttressed by ignorance. So, the first task is to gain as much knowledge as possible about the person or groups we consider Other.

I assume many who are reading this book consider themselves to be supporters of the historically disenfranchised, to be people who want an end to the divisions. So, let me begin with a challenge to each of us. It is important to overcome our ignorance not only about the historically disenfranchised but also about people who support Donald Trump. Why do they believe him when he utters complete falsehoods? After seeing their factories closed, why do they agree raising trade tariffs will benefit them? Why do they continue to believe climate change is a hoax when their neighborhoods are being polluted? Why do they think failed trickle-down economics will make them wealthier in spite of the ever-widening gap between rich and poor, and the relatively stagnant wages for the poor and middle class?

Overcoming our ignorance about those who have opted to follow false promises, fear-mongering, and outright lies is critical if we are to build bridges and find connections with those who have been misled. Of course, there are some who will never change, but there are many who will, and finding ways to help them move from uncritical supporters of charlatans to those who will resist is an important step. We need to increase the number of those standing with us to be able to create new policies and practices, new social structures, and new political-economic systems. Simply haranguing them will cause them to dig in their heels deeper and remain supporters of the status quo. It is imperative we do all we can to overcome our ignorance of their world.

Understanding their stories, hopes, and fears is important. This can begin with reading articles, books, and blogs we have ignored, and reserving judgment. We must move beyond listening to the media's incessant analysis and shift to hearing from the people themselves. At its best, it should involve face-to-face encounters and careful listening, setting aside our inclination to convince them they are wrong to think and feel as they do. This will take us beyond our comfort zone because we will encounter experiences and truths we have ignored or don't wish to hear or believe.

While altogether different from the Trump supporters, the prisoners at Sing Sing Correctional Facility provided a dramatic opportunity for me to deal with my own ignorance. It required undoing long-held assumptions and ideas. I had assumed I was the expert. I soon realized they wrestled with ethical issues that were only theoretical to me, but life and death to them. I had assumed they were in prison because they were fundamentally immoral. I had little or no knowledge of their lives as I had never encountered their worlds except through television, movies, and novels. As I gradually moved from teacher to co-learner, I began to understand about generational poverty, racism, hopelessness, and incarceration. I grew to see the wisdom, humanity, passion, and hope in those I had dismissed as totally evil.

Listening to the men exposed me to a new world and opened me to several important insights. My youthful mistakes could have resulted in my crossing the line. In particular, my reckless driving could have resulted in someone's death. Even more profoundly, I came to realize the men were only secondarily "prisoners" and, most essentially, human beings like me. They bore the image of God. They were my brothers to whom I was accountable. It was their "faces" that inspired me to seek to transform our justice system.

It is difficult to ferret out the truth in what we read or hear, especially when we rely primarily on the media. When we watch, read, or listen to the media, we must be alert to ad hominem attacks, condescension, or headlines that distort the content of an article. Michael Massing warns about both conservative and liberal media biases. He says labeling Trump's supporters as ignorant has fueled Trump's portrayal of the media as promulgators of fake news, further tribalizing our politics. Even more important for Massing is that preoccupation with Trump has distracted from critical journalism that could provide a bridge between the Right and Left. He writes about the failure of the media to critically challenge the banking industry, hedge funds, and other financial organizations that contributed to the economic crises that led us to our current economic state and huge political divide.[1] Gaining knowledge about the larger systemic reasons why people stand on the other side of the divide is a critical first step.

Part of the media problem is the increasingly smaller number of newspapers in our nation. According to a recent PBS report, "between January 2014 and May 2018, it is estimated that at least 900 communities in the US lost all local newspaper coverage."[2] Most of these closures have been in poorer and rural areas, leaving people with less information about what is going on in their community, state, nation, and world, and forcing them to rely upon talk radio, TV, and social media—many of which are heavily biased.

Rather than relying solely on the media's portrayals of those who have associated themselves with the extreme Right, we can turn to studies that offer insights into their motivations, thinking, and feelings. Arlie Russell Hochschild's *Strangers in Their Own Land* and Katherine J. Cramer's *The Politics of Resentment* about supporters of the Louisiana Tea Party and Scott Walker in rural Wisconsin, respectively, provide insights into what induces (I would add, seduces) and sustains them.[3] Both the right- and left-wing media contribute to our dismissal of one another, rather than helping all of us to discover what moves the other. When we dig beneath the surface, we discover we are all part of the unreflective mass that is manipulated by the systems and persons in power. We have much to learn about those we have considered Other.

In addition to those from whom we are divided politically, it is critical we tune our ears to the voices of the marginalized and oppressed. Those voices are systematically silenced by the corporate media, so we must go elsewhere to hear them. Liberation theology speaks about the "epistemological privilege of the poor," which means if one wants to know the truth, it is important to turn to those who are most impacted by it. If we want to know about childbirth, we can gain some insights from the professionals who attend the event. But for the real source of knowledge, we can ask people who give birth. In the same way, if we want to know what it is like to be racially oppressed, we should turn to the victims of racism. If we want to understand what drives people to take the enormously costly step to migrate, the most accurate and complete account comes from the refugees and immigrants themselves. There is no excuse for ignoring those who are resisting the current systems of oppression.

We need to listen to those who are at the margins and who are often portrayed as hate-filled and seeking to undermine the very heart of democracy and civility. The media characterizes those who resist as troublemakers, unpatriotic, anti-white, and anti-male.

Many have been labeled as such. Paul Robeson was blacklisted and his passport was taken away. Muhammad Ali was stripped of his title for being "anti-American." Young Pakistani Malala Yousafzai was shot in the head during an assassination attempt by the Taliban because of her outspoken affirmation of a girl's right to education.

If you are like me, you may find yourself uncomfortable confronting truths you had long ignored. But we have no excuse. Books like Marc Lamont Hill's *Nobody*, Michael Eric Dyson's *Tears We Cannot Stop*, Michelle Alexander's *The New Jim Crow*, Mumia Abu-Jamal's *Death Blossoms: Reflections from a Prisoner of Conscience*, and Mary Beard's *Women and Power: A Manifesto* offer those among the privileged the opportunity to hear a different reality.

Fiction also provides insight into the lives of persons different from us. In the moving account of Celie in *The Color Purple*, Alice Walker unlocks the pain of a black woman who has suffered abuse. Sherman Alexie's novels of American Indian life reveal a world largely invisible to most of us. Tony Kushner's play, *Angels in America*, discloses the life of gay people and the AIDS epidemic. Carolyn Chute's *The Beans of Egypt, Maine*, provides a chilling portrayal of trailer life in rural Maine. Each of these, and hundreds of other novels, offer us the opportunity to examine a world about which many of us have been largely ignorant.

We live in an age when information is available globally and instantaneously, often leading to information overload. A common response is to shut down and retreat into our bastions of privilege. We dare not. Our lack of knowledge about others is willful ignorance. There is no excuse for not obtaining at least a rudimentary understanding of the experiences and feelings of those who stand on the other side of the dividing walls. Overcoming ignorance will not eliminate the divisions, but it is an essential step.

Engaging in Dialogue

How do we establish a dialogue if the other is unwilling or if we assume our position is indisputable?

While dialogue and negotiation are commonly used interchangeably, there are distinctions that set them apart. Negotiation involves a mutuality of interest and usually entails two parties seeking a common agreement. Both realize some compromise or problem solving is worth striving for and is in the interest of both parties. Negotiation assumes a relationship, however tenuous. Building a relationship through dialogue must precede negotiation. In our world of walls and divisions, I see dialogue as a means to restore relations, to overcome the status of enemy, and to create an I-Thou relationship. Parties divided by a wall do not necessarily trust each other, do not necessarily recognize shared goals, and need not assume there can be mutual self-interest, which is a defining aspect of negotiation. Once having achieved dialogue, negotiation may be the appropriate next step, but there is no assumption that will be the case.

Dialogue needs to happen at three levels to address the divisions within our world: the interpersonal, the systemic, and the intrapersonal.

Most of us enter into dialogue at the interpersonal level. We dialogue with loved ones, friends, colleagues, bosses, teachers, and classmates when we seek both to understand and to make ourselves understood. Many of these interchanges are friendly and involve a level of trust. Sometimes we venture into dialogue with those with whom we fundamentally disagree and often find ourselves in an argument rather than a dialogue.

We can fall into two traps: a desire to convince rather than to build the relationship, and/or a failure to recognize the existence of power imbalances.

We cannot achieve authentic dialogue if we are unwilling to hear and fully consider the other's viewpoint. Doing so does not mean we must abandon our values and succumb to the other's opinion, but it does require taking the perspective and life experiences of others with utmost seriousness. For dialogue to occur, the parent, for example, must seek to understand what is going on in their child's life that leads them to certain attitudes or behaviors. Short of that, they are reduced to demanding or arguing.

If it is difficult to dialogue with those with whom we are amicable, it is even harder when the relationship is adversarial. To attribute stupidity, gullibility, or racism to those who voted for Trump means we have failed to hear their fundamental pain, fears, and hopes. To bridge the divide, engagement is essential. Similarly, Trump supporters need to understand the pain, fears, and hopes of many so-called liberals who are not their enemies but who have been portrayed to them as such. Dialogue is a two-way street.

It is not necessary to accept a racist comment or action to try to understand what lies behind it. Granted, such an openness is exceedingly difficult to achieve, but it is essential we try if a genuine dialogue is to occur. The obverse is equally true. We must be willing to share openly what lies behind our viewpoint and actions. That, of course, demands that we be in touch with the depths of our own thoughts, feelings, and actions. It also necessitates trusting the other person not to use our vulnerability against us and to steel ourselves should that happen. We need to live with the tension between vulnerability and inner strength.

Failure to recognize the differing levels of power between the dialoguers can also derail true dialogue.

For example, the vocabulary, grammar, and syntax in which I was educated and to which I am exposed every day cannot be the benchmark for all dialogue. It is a language that is privileged in our country by much of the media and most educational institutions. The language of immigrants, and of the street, is often demeaned and considered second class. When I came to this realization, I discovered the power of rap. Rap offers another medium of communication that is distinctive and unveils a world that, in many ways, stretches my comfort level and understanding. Being open to a way of articulating that comes out of a different world of experiences is critical to the possibility of dialogue.

It is not only the language itself that is privileged, but also the content or subject matter being communicated. Many men consider stereotypical women's conversation about knitting or cooking to be unworthy of their attention. "Real men" speak of cars, sports, and money. Even when women speak in professional settings, they are often ignored by men while the same idea communicated by a man gets full attention. When a white person seeks to dialogue with a black person, there is a history of privilege that should not be ignored. To be white is to have enjoyed a position of privilege, whether recognized or not. Early childhood training and opportunities, uneven levels of funding for public education, and employment opportunities all factor in the imbalance. To truly enter into dialogue requires an open recognition of these imbalances and a willingness to transgress the limits they create.

In the mid-1970s, I was directing an urban-based consortium program of eastern seminaries designed to link students, faculty, pastors, and members of urban churches. I interviewed a black pastor as a potential co-teacher who knew the reality of the black community and the critical role of black churches in the city. Our goals, however, were different. He was searching for funds to assist black churches and I wanted someone who would mentor our students. As we talked, things quickly deteriorated. Neither of us could really hear the other and after forty-five minutes, we both walked away disappointed and angry with no intention of seeing each other again.

When the person who had introduced us urged us to meet again, we reconvened with a new intent to hear each other's concerns and find ways to create something that would truly honor each of our goals. Our dialogue led to a creative partnership that lasted over eight years and a friendship that continues to this day.

Dialogue at the systemic level often is even more difficult. The history of dialogue between Palestine and Israel is a case in point. There is a fundamental power imbalance, often expressed as occupier and occupied, or oppressor and oppressed. Each side does possess certain powers, but economic and military power lies more heavily on the side of Israel while Palestine has relied primarily on the powers of threat (to delegitimize Israel as a nation), protests, boycotts, and attacks. The dynamics have been further complicated by attacks and several outright wars with Arab countries bordering Israel. As the external threats have diminished through diplomacy (with Jordan and Egypt, for example), there is greater need for authentic dialogue in which differences are not only acknowledged, but redress of power imbalance also is sought. In their analysis of the negotiations' failure, Gallo and Marzano conclude, "According to the structure of the asymmetric conflicts we have been analyzing, low power balance and scarce conflict awareness—i.e., reciprocal awareness of the goals and living conditions of the other side—mean a very slight chance of successful negotiation and henceforth of reaching a sustainable peace."[4] Before a settlement can be negotiated, a true dialogue must occur. The US administration's increasing support for Israeli interests and withdrawal of humanitarian aid to Palestinians contribute to the power imbalance and undermine the legitimacy of peace proposals.

One serious barrier to dialogue after armed conflict is the demand of unconditional surrender, in which the victor treats the loser as totally powerless. The absence of dialogue following World War I was a significant factor in the rise of Hitler and the events leading to World War II. The requirement that Germany accept total guilt and make reparation payments that were far beyond its capacity laid the groundwork for nationalism that led to the rise of the Nazi Party. Had the legitimate needs of Germany following World War I been included in the Treaty of Versailles, and had the treaty resulted from a dialogue rather than a one-sided demand, World War II might have been avoided. The US Marshall Plan for European recovery after World War II was designed to promote a different outcome.

Frequently overlooked, and sometimes the most difficult, is intrapersonal dialogue. As long as we avoid dialoguing with "the Evil within us,"[5] we can pretend others are evil and we are good. The reality is each of us harbors the potential for prejudice, hatred, and even violence. Despite my commitment to forgiveness and healing, when a tenant in our brownstone was raped at knifepoint, my first reaction was to seek vengeance.

If dialogue is to occur, each of us must recognize there is no Manichean division between us (the good guys) and them (the bad guys). We are all struggling with demons. In fact, like people who have overcome addiction and still refer to themselves as recovering addicts, many of us may acknowledge we are recovering racists or sexists, as the feelings and thoughts of the disease are always potentially there. With this recognition, an I–Thou relationship becomes a possibility.

Experiencing Empathy

Dialogue demands empathy; empathy demands discipline and practice. It involves an openness to experiences, languages, and values different from our own. While there are undoubtedly exceptions, such openness is difficult. As sociobiologist David Allen says, "there is practically no such thing in nature as an easy and relaxed acceptance of a stranger, without turmoil, tension and stress."[6]

There is a distinction between sympathy and empathy. To feel sympathy for another involves sadness or pity *for* them. Seeing pictures of a starving, emaciated Yemenite child can evoke feelings of sadness, revulsion, and rage. We feel sympathy for their plight. Empathy involves entering into their feelings, not only understanding their emotional condition, but actually *identifying with* their hunger, fright, and powerlessness by acknowledging our own experiences of hunger, fright, or powerlessness. In doing so, we become one with them. Sympathy allows us to see and walk away. Empathy engages us in their life.

Cris Beam says "empathy is a starting point for something more. Empathy creates a space, an opening for spontaneous, unchoreographed connection; it's a way of listening that fosters the potential for deeper meaning."[7]

Sometimes our empathy is triggered not by pictures or direct experience but through language. The language of empathy often is metaphorical, since some truths can only be captured in metaphor. For example, it is impossible to speak of the deep mysteries of life such as love, God, or death without resorting to metaphor. Entering into an empathic relationship is always a mystery, one that we may try to capture in metaphors.

I have claimed that war is one of the inevitable consequences of Othering. Those of us who have never experienced war firsthand cannot possibly walk in the moccasins of those who have survived the horrors of combat or who have lost their loved ones. But we may be able empathically to feel, however partially, the terror of war, through the metaphorical language of poetry. Poetry's power lies in its use of metaphor, the language of the soul. In *Voices of Wartime*, a young Indian woman, Sampurna Chattarji, offers us a powerful image of death: "Death is easy to pronounce. It's the smell of burning children that's hard."[8] Her words challenge our facile acceptance of declarations of war, gratuitous philanthropy, and cheap religiosity. When we smell the burning children, we can no longer remain casually removed.

Elie Wiesel tells of having to watch the hanging of a Jewish child with other prisoners in the concentration camp. As the child hung there, dying slowly because his body was so light, one of the inmates asked, "Where is God now?" Wiesel heard a voice within him answer, "Where is He? Here he is—He is hanging on these gallows."[9]

Burning children and gallows.

Millions of Christians regularly celebrate the Eucharist, a rite in which partaking of bread and wine is interpreted either as the actual body and blood of Christ or as a memorial of his death. To walk in the moccasins of the millions who are being slaughtered on the gallows of war and starvation is to eat the bread and drink the cup, knowing the crucifixion is not over. When the Eucharist tastes of the death of those being killed by war, displacement, starvation, and drugs, we have crossed the line from memorial to the depths of empathy.

It is an extremely difficult step for us to move from empathy for those suffering from war to having empathy for those we consider to be the enemy. If we are to find a way to end the violence of suicide bombing, for starters, we must understand the underlying causes and reasons that trigger such behavior.

Similarly, while I disagree with those who support Trump or label Muslims, people of color, or transgender people as deviants or dangerous, we must understand what has led them to this position if we are not to allow our differences to divide us. We may not like those with whom we disagree, and we may not trust them, but it is incumbent we use all that is within our power to understand why they do what they do. For example, to dialogue with the Afrikaners, Mandela learned about the oppression and second-class citizenship they endured at the hands of the British. He learned about the fear with which they lived. This did not excuse apartheid, but it made it possible for Mandela to find a meeting place with the oppressors.

Empathy for those from whom we are divided, including our enemies, is essential if we are to begin breaking down the walls of hostility. It does not necessarily eliminate bitterness, nor does it make us forget. But sometimes, it helps us build a bridge across the divide.

Making Contact

In chapter 5, I cited Levinas's belief that encountering another's face discloses their claim to life and justice. To overcome personal prejudice and hatred, there is no substitute for face to face.

Conflict theory suggests increased contact with persons and groups of a different race, religion, or gender identity intensifies prejudice, mistrust, and hatred. On the other hand, intergroup contact theory argues such interaction enhances appreciation for persons and groups who are different—a theory that was confirmed by a large study reported by Pettigrew and Tropp.[10] For example, it is not uncommon for formerly homophobic parents of young people who come out to embrace their child's identity, understand something of the enormous pain and pressure of being different, or even to become ambassadors for gender-identity diversity.

In her carefully researched work on understanding and addressing implicit bias, psychologist Jennifer L. Eberhardt confirms how bias often is overcome by contact:

> Research shows that close attachments between people from different groups can puncture holes in stereotypic beliefs and negative attitudes. Parents and family members can overlook the "otherness" of a caregiver they depend on because of their own needs to push back against the pull of bias. And the openness of that relationship can leave a mark that lasts well beyond the moment and extends past that particular person.[11]

While contact between blood relatives or close friends often thwarts divisiveness, there are similar possibilities in heterogeneous societies. A study by Birte Gundelach concludes "in ethnically more heterogeneous societies, people tend to trust outgroup members more than in homogeneous countries."[12] This is encouraging for those of us living in the United States where 38 percent of the population are racial minorities and approximately 10 percent of the population affirm a different gender identity from cisgender. Our diversity means that we have the opportunity to come in contact with a rich mix of people.

In a chapter analyzing the impact of public spaces in Stockholm, the authors show how certain kinds of street configurations contribute to segregation. They assert there is a relationship between physical segregation and social marginalization, particularly in urban areas that are populated by impoverished immigrants.[13] While their study focuses on suburban and urban areas, there are parallels between rural and urban communities in our country, where the absence of shared public spaces also presents a barrier for contact. Many people who live in rural Maine, for example, often have limited or no contact with the migrant communities that are clustered in several cities. Without direct contact, many are influenced by the media that often portray people of color in a negative manner, further contributing to the divisions. In the absence of contact, it can be a small step from difference to Othering.

If we wish to end the divisions, one approach is to find ways to enhance public contact. As Elijah Anderson points out, contact in public spaces can foster understanding. He suggests certain public areas provide occasions for people to look beyond their differences, if only partially, thus increasing the possibility for civility.[14] This is not easy in large rural areas that tend to be more racially homogeneous, but it should be eminently manageable in many cities where diverse racial communities live side by side and where public spaces are frequently shared. The story of the Lewiston High School soccer team I mention later is a case in point. It can happen.

But even if racial diversity is less prevalent in some areas of our nation, there are other forms of diversity that become fodder for our divisions: rich and poor, straight and queer, and progressive and conservative, as evidenced in our politics. While it is critical we seek contact with those of other races, it is equally critical we make contact with those who think, feel, act, and even vote differently from us.

Seeds of Peace is an inspiring model for developing contact across divisions. Their mission is "to inspire and cultivate new generations of global leaders in communities divided by conflict. [They] equip them with the skills and relationships they need to accelerate social, economic and political changes essential for peace."[15] They bring together fourteen- to sixteen-year-olds from communities in conflict such as Israel and Palestine or India and Pakistan. For two weeks, they live and dialogue with "the enemy" and learn to understand, respect, and care for one another. This is followed by a year-long program in their home country. While some participants relapse into their previous identity upon returning home, many have become adults who actively seek to remove the physical, economic, religious, and political walls that have divided their countries. At present, Seeds of Peace alumni are involved in forty Israeli and Palestinian organizations seeking peace.

Face-to-face communication can lay the foundation for trust and overcoming personal prejudice and hatred. It's not always easy, and it doesn't always work out. There are times when contact leads to conflicts, when tempers flare, and when trust evaporates.

Wanting our young daughter to avoid the kinds of prejudice we had growing up, we moved to a block in Mt. Airy, Philadelphia, that was largely black. Friendships developed, the kids played together, and my daughter and her best friend, a black girl, shared overnights, trips, and school activities. But when Martin Luther King Jr. was assassinated, everything changed. The understandable rage of the black parents was passed on to their children, who began to pick on the few white kids on the block. We were shattered when my daughter came home and said, "I don't like black people." We had intentionally moved into a mixed-race community to foster interracial contact that would facilitate embracing others. Fortunately, years of interracial contact after that led her to celebrate diversity.

There is often a tension between the desire to have contact with a group considered Other and the desire of those who have been Othered to separate and focus on their own identity. There is a lively debate over whether to have integrated schools or ones that foster and affirm black, Latinx, or American Indian identity. Often, that choice is eliminated as schools today are "nearly as segregated as they were before the 1954 Supreme Court decision of *Brown v. Board of Education*."[16] In many respects, this tension is a replay of the difference between Martin Luther King Jr.'s commitment to integration and Malcolm X's early call for black separatism. Both proved necessary. But in both cases, the level and form of contact were to be determined by the excluded community, not by policies and decisions by those in power.

Those who have been historically privileged may make ourselves available for contact, but we should not attempt to determine its terms.

In *One Goal*, Amy Bass recounts the remarkable story of the Lewiston High School boys' soccer team, which highlights the significance of contact. Lewiston, the second-largest city in Maine, is a former mill town that has seen better days. The majority of its population is of French-Canadian descent—a people who helped build a once-prosperous city. They are deservedly proud of their heritage, work hard to get ahead, and experience ongoing struggles to overcome discrimination. It is ironic, although understandable given the way our economy pits people against each other, many of them have objected to receiving immigrants from Somalia. Despite their own struggles, many exhibited prejudice, discrimination, and even hatred. Somalis were told to "go home," called the N word, spit upon, and accused of living on handouts and draining resources from the state and city. The mayor publicly asked the Somalis to stop coming. The city was divided.

When coach Mike McGraw decided to put Somalis on the high school soccer team, there was initial resistance, but he persisted, as did the Somali players, who refused to be baited by the racist remarks and treatment they received from both the town and opponents.

With a mostly Somali team, the victories piled up, and, while they lost the 2014 state championship game, they persevered and won the championship in 2015. Remarkably, many in the city overcame (at least temporarily) their divisions and embraced the Somali players. High school students from different races began doing things and going places together. As Bass said about the response to the championship victory, "They [the players and members of the community] were together, chanting, shouting and drumming. . . . Soccer created space, at least at this moment, for them to come together and rejoice. *We are all Blue Devils*, he [Shobow] thought, one community sharing, celebrating one goal."[17]

As Bass herself recognizes, the contact between Somalis and white people, between players and the larger community, did not totally dispel the hatred, but it did change some people's negative attitudes and behaviors. It was a beginning. And with that beginning, it is possible electoral and legislative changes can follow. This may be the most one can hope for at this time in such a divided culture. Because some attitudes have changed, there is the possibility of even more far-reaching bridges across our divisions.

Mitigating our ignorance and seeking empathically to identify with those who are on the other side of the wall are acts we can, and should, engage in as individuals. Engaging in dialogue brings us into relationship with others. Being in contact has the potential to lead to understanding and acceptance.

Collective Actions

Each of the previous steps can be taken on an intrapersonal and/or interpersonal level. Each is important in changing us and others, and in opening the possibilities of new relationships and building coalitions. But these steps alone are insufficient. It is incumbent we find ways to bring down the walls on a larger scale. The walls are created by systems that benefit a few to the detriment of the many. Oppressive political, economic, and cultural structures must be transformed if the walls are to come down. To approach this level of change demands collective actions. The following approaches offer a variety of ways this can occur.

Truth and Reconciliation, Restorative Justice

Forgiveness is generally thought of as limited to an individual's response. We all know forgiveness is critical to the survival of a marriage or close friendship. There are many times when we must ask forgiveness for a harmful action, a misperception, or a mistake if we wish to maintain personal relationships. But forgiveness also can have a role in larger institutional and social change.

Over the years, forgiveness has played an important role in averting bloodbaths and in leading to significant policy and power changes. It is this institutional level of seeking reconciliation that is crucial.

In his book *No Future without Forgiveness*, Archbishop Desmond Tutu describes the Truth and Reconciliation Commission (TRC) process in South Africa. After forty-six years of apartheid, South Africa elected a black president in 1994, and the formerly illegal African National Congress (ANC), which had long led the fight for racial freedom, now controlled the nation's politics. It was a new day, but the question remained whether to punish those who had wreaked such horror on people of color, to forget and move on, or to find a way to reconcile the formerly warring races.

It was important not to forget, lest the evils of the past be repeated. But it was also clear the adversarial judicial approach used at Nuremberg could result in violence of recrimination and lead to a reactionary response by the Afrikaners, who still controlled military services. An interim Constitution was written that provided the basis for the transition to an all-inclusive political process, and its postscript laid the foundation for the TRC. In the words of the postscript, "There is a need for understanding but not for vengeance, a need for reparation but not for retaliation, a need for *ubuntu* but not for victimization."[18] And so the TRC was formed with the mandate to reveal the truth about apartheid's violence, make reparation for some of the victims, and, in some cases, grant amnesty to the perpetrators who came forward and admitted their crimes—provided they had been committed for political rather than personal reasons.

There were many critics among the Afrikaners, the ANC, and others. Some felt granting amnesty would be selling out and conceding equal moral footing to the offenders and their victims. Many Afrikaners feared this would incite vengeance and recrimination. Neither proved to be the case. Underlying this approach was the fundamental belief forgiveness was possible. And indeed, some victims found it possible to forgive their former adversaries. If there was to be a future that was truly inclusive, it was essential to recognize the humanity of everyone and hold out the possibility of reconciliation.

One of the most difficult questions this approach poses is, when to forgive? Does forgiveness precede or follow acts of contrition and restitution? Does someone have to change their behavior before they can be forgiven or can forgiveness lead to changed behavior?

These questions are fundamental to restorative justice—an international movement that has its roots in American Indian, Canadian First Nations, African, and New Zealand Maori cultures—and was promoted in the United States in the 1970s by the Church of the Brethren.

Restorative justice has been used most commonly in response to crime. When a crime is committed, it is frequently because the perpetrator views the victim as Other—to be used, exploited, robbed, bullied, beaten, raped, or even murdered. The victim, likewise, often views the perpetrator as Other—an agent of harm or violence, not a fellow human with whom they can engage. The law views perpetrators as Other by labeling them "thief, assailant, rapist, murderer," and charges them as such. The general public views the perpetrator as Other: immoral, trash, human waste to be discarded.

Restorative justice provides an approach that engages the victim, offender, and community; it challenges or goes beyond the traditional justice system that, as I have shown, functions to oppress people of color and the poor, and benefit those in power. One has only to consider the privilege of property in our current legal system to realize protection of privilege overrides the needs of the oppressed. In focusing on healing rather than punishment, restorative justice seeks to eliminate the element of social control that is the primary purpose of our current justice system.

One of the most effective methods involves a process whereby the perpetrator is brought face to face with their victim. Sometimes this is accomplished through third-party mediation, but its most common approach has involved circles. Using a trained facilitator and surrounded by supporters, both the one who caused the harm and the one harmed share their experience. During the sharing, sometimes empathy occurs, and sometimes a genuine dialogue between the victim and offender takes place. In bringing the victim and offender together, an opportunity is provided for the two to begin to view and treat each other as a human being with whom they are connected beyond the criminal act.

In the circle, the victim shares how they have been impacted, asks why they have been targeted, and expresses their anger and/ or fear. At this point, the offender is no longer faced with an object they can dismiss as Other, but with a flesh-and-blood person with feelings, hopes, fears, dreams. Similarly, the offender shares the motive behind their actions, what they were thinking or feeling, why they did what they did, and how they feel after having heard the victim. Sometimes, an offender has come to realize the impact on the victim and has been surprised by the consequences of their action, genuinely moved to remorse. Sometimes, a victim has come to understand the dysfunctional background that has shaped the offender's behavior and has reached out empathically to someone they now view as a fellow human being. Restorative justice is a movement that brings adversaries face to face and, in doing so, helps to overcome Othering.

In addition to developing mutual understanding, restorative justice seeks to make things right by correcting, as much as possible, the circumstances of the harm. A common result is an agreement in which reparations are made, steps are agreed upon that can help to rehabilitate the offender. In some cases, changes in the structure of an organization result. An example of the latter is how some schools have changed their policies regarding disciplinary actions.

For many years, I have been involved with the restorative justice movement in Maine and have witnessed individuals being able to forgive another person in advance of any change, freeing them to begin afresh. At other times, it was judicious to see evidence of change before granting forgiveness.

I facilitated a circle that involved a young boy who destroyed some construction equipment. The contractor was willing to forgive the boy, as well as the cost of repair, but insisted he work for him to understand how much work was required to pay for the repair. The boy turned out to be a good worker; and when the circle gathered eight months later, the contractor offered the boy a job when he finished school. This was a case of forgiveness preceding changed behavior. Obviously, it is possible the forgiven one could revert to their old behavior, in which case it is important to enforce account-ability.

There are times, though, when it's appropriate to require changed behavior before forgiving. When one is the victim of bully-ing, for example, one can be expected to forgive only after the bul-lying stops and amends have been made. If someone continues the actions that brought harm, it is important they first show remorse, take steps to reduce or undo the harm by making some form of restitution, and show that they are actively working to not repeat their action. In that case, forgiveness can follow.

While restorative justice was initially used primarily when a crime was committed, the use of healing circles has now spread beyond the criminal justice system to include situations in which no crime has been reported, but where harm has occurred. Victims of bullying, elders who have suffered psychic abuse, persons who have been the victims of power exercised over them, and women who have suffered abuse are drawing upon restorative justice to discover healing. Any circumstance in which harm is done can benefit from a restorative, rather than punitive, approach.

Importantly, restorative justice is increasingly dealing with sys-temic injustice that seeks to address the larger factors such as racism, generational poverty, and gender discrimination that lie behind individual acts. To the extent it helps to heal unjust struc-tures and individuals, it is transforming culture and systems. For example, in Maine, several district attorneys have developed poli-cies to divert many perpetrators from court to restorative justice processes. Such diversion addresses, at least in part, the enormous discrepancy in the number of poor who are convicted and impris-oned. In many cases, diversion is an alternative to debtor's prison in which the poor, who cannot afford bail, are sent to jail until their hearing. Law enforcement is also finding it is more beneficial to refer a person to restorative justice than to arrest them and send them to court. Judges are suspending sentencing in lieu of a restorative justice agreement. Each of these shifts, although limited, represents significant change in the justice system as it has traditionally functioned.

This more encompassing approach is also increasingly occurring in both individual schools and entire school systems that institute restorative practices as central to their disciplinary system, offering an alternative to detention, suspension, and expulsion. In many school systems, people of color historically have been disproportionately suspended or expelled as an automatic response to unruly behavior. Restorative justice offers a way in which all students (regardless of race, class, gender identity, or religion) can be brought face to face with those they have harmed, often leading to transformed dynamics within the classroom. Students, themselves, are frequently calling for a circle when a controversy erupts or when an altercation occurs. When this happens, both individual and organizational policies and practices are transformed.

Restorative justice is not a panacea and does not always lead to understanding, empathy, dialogue, and justice. Victims may feel pressured. Offenders may feign remorse. Agreements may not be carried through, and recidivism may occur. But in a majority of cases, victims have expressed gratitude and satisfaction; most offenders have not recidivated, or at least not as severely as before; communities have experienced healing; and sometimes policies and practices have been changed. Restorative justice is a viable approach to overcoming enormous divisions.

In both the TRC process and the restorative justice movement, there is a fundamental commitment to healing and forgiveness that involves attitudinal changes. But in each of them there is also a collective process that requires collective action, policy changes, and new practices.

Organizing

Many great leaders have made significant contributions to tearing down the dividing walls: Harriet Tubman, Martin Luther King Jr., Mohandas Gandhi, Nelson Mandela, Malcolm X, Mother Teresa, and Elizabeth Cady Stanton, to name a few. Their words have inspired and galvanized people into action. But their leadership would have amounted to little had it not been backed by like-minded organized groups. There is no substitute for people banding together to demand change, to resist, to create alternatives, to overturn the status quo, or to revolt.

Organizing work takes many forms, but whatever the form, it has some common elements. First, it is critically important to know the self-interest both of those who are being organized and of those who are being challenged. That is why overcoming ignorance, developing empathy, engaging in dialogue, and being in contact can provide a basis upon which to build a collective action.

Paulo Freire, a Brazilian educator, helped organize illiterate peasants to change their circumstances.[19] His method was to uncover the peasants' "generative themes" such as adequate housing, potable water, and sufficient food. He developed literacy training programs around those themes to empower the peasants to claim their agency and organize to change the policies and practices of the landowners. Unfortunately, the Brazilian government considered his philosophy and teaching subversive and expelled him from the country.

Nelson Mandela learned Afrikaans, the language of his oppressors, to understand their world, history, and fears, and to communicate with them. Saul Alinsky insisted the first stage in organizing is to fully understand the life of the community—not simply to force one's way into a community and try to organize it.[20] Everyone has self-interest, and good organizing addresses this.

Organizing empowers people to be agents of change. Since it is common for people to assume things must stay the way they are—that there is nothing we can do to change the situation or others—organizing gives people a sense of power and potential.

Over the years, I have heard people say homophobes are hopeless, that the leopard cannot change its spots. As a result, many gay persons remained in their closets, afraid to be known for who they were, afraid to claim their rights. But look what has happened. One of the results of organizing by the LGBTQ+ community and its supporters has been the legalization of gay marriage, which has led many people to a full (or fuller) acceptance of expanded sexual orientations and gender identity. Organizing has helped bring gender-identity issues out of the closet, thereby hampering homophobia, although by no means eliminating it, as evidenced by our current administration's stance against transgender people in the military.

Another important element of organizing is the willingness to achieve partial victories when that is all that is possible at the moment. The world is complicated, and compromise is often necessary when organizing against powerful forces. The systems against which people resist are tenacious, and most of the time it is not possible to effect total transformation, and certainly not in quick fashion.

In the 1980s in Jersey City, I was part of a community organizing group that blocked the mayor's efforts to prevent Section 8 housing. (In our city, Section 8 was an important vehicle to provide affordable housing for persons forced out of their homes by gentrification.) While we judged gentrification to be an elephant stampede that could not be stopped, providing housing for displaced families appeared both necessary and doable. We organized and were successful in winning that battle for hundreds of poor families. It wasn't the whole loaf, but it was an important slice.

One of the limits of organizing is sometimes people can become complacent with a small victory and fail to press for further change. When Paulo Freire went to Chile after being expelled from Brazil, he organized peasants in the Santiago barrios. They were forced to carry water buckets long distances uphill to their homes from a single source at the bottom. Since water was one of their most frequent and significant generative themes, he organized them around the need for accessible, potable water. Eventually, they won the battle, and water was piped to a number of places along the way. It was a significant but small victory. Regrettably, the people became contented with this victory and the organizing ceased, although there were many other injustices that still needed to be addressed.

Freire's approach was a first step in the process of transformation, that is to say, making people aware of the structures of oppression and their potential to change the circumstances. But it stopped too soon.

When organizing, it is always critical to anticipate and work toward the next step or issue. Complacency is the enemy of organizing.

Advocacy

Another approach to healing our divisions involves working for structural changes within organizations, both corporate and governmental, which can have a significant impact. Most of the time, this approach will result in a negotiated compromise. As always, all involved must feel they have something important to gain.

Government provides multiple examples of policies instituted in response to organized pressure by groups or even an individual. The New Deal of the 1930s sought to bring the marginalized poor into the economic mainstream, largely as a result of the efforts of Frances Perkins, the US Secretary of Labor under President Franklin D. Roosevelt. Her priorities included a minimum wage, unemployment compensation, social security, and health insurance, many of which became hallmarks of the New Deal. The Civil Rights Act of 1964 was a step in granting equal rights to historically oppressed and disenfranchised black people and other people of color. It was the result of collective public pressure and advocacy that influenced or arm-twisted the White House and Senate.

The First Step Act of 2018 is federal legislation that received rare bipartisan support and has been signed by President Trump. While it pertains only to federal prisoners, who are less than 10 percent of the total incarcerated population, its passage offers some incentive for changes at the state and local levels, where the majority are imprisoned. The First Step Act allows thousands to be released earlier, loosens the mandatory sentencing requirements that can reduce the amount of time persons must spend in prison for nonviolent crimes, and supports rehabilitative and reentry programming. Each of these steps has been advocated by groups across the political spectrum based on rationales ranging from antiracism to fiscal savings. The wide spectrum of advocates for this legislation is important to note: the ACLU, Jared Kushner, The Sentencing Project, the Koch brothers'–backed Right on Crime, congressional members, prisoners, and religious bodies. Senate Majority Leader Mitch McConnell threatened to hold the bill but finally gave in to the pressure of so many. The bill is the result of sustained advocacy, persuasion, and legislative negotiation over many years. While it is only a small step, it is an example of what can be accomplished by working with institutional levers and personnel, and especially working across political lines, as was the case with this legislation. Unfortunately, sometimes that is not possible.

Changes as a result of advocacy have occurred in the corporate arena also. Sometimes the leadership of a single person—a CEO, chair of the board, or someone else in a position of power—can result in significant changes in response to advocacy by others. IBM has been a leader in addressing the division between women and men, pioneered by Tom Watson, IBM's founder. Under Watson's leadership, IBM instituted an equal pay and equal opportunity policy in 1935 and, for over a decade now, has provided domestic partner benefits to LGBTQ+ persons.

Advocacy is not limited to those in power. Ordinary people reaching out to persons in power through advocacy, persuasion, or personal experience can often result in transforming their organization or the country. Public opinion and pressure can make a difference. As the website for NonProfit PRO points out, there are five important steps to successful advocacy: commitment to the long-term, momentum-building work; prioritization of growth; understanding those whom you are seeking to change; strong leadership; and use of technology.[21] Despite its slow pace, disappointments, and compromises, advocacy is the predominate way people seek change in our nation, as evidenced by the focus and work of a plethora of nonprofit agencies.

Numerous groups are advocating for environmental justice, freedom for political prisoners, early childhood education, and reproductive rights, as well as opposing bullying, the sex slave trade, and poverty. They are seeking to change the policies and practices of the existing systems by educating the public and exerting pressure on those in power.

Working with and through existing structures is subject to cooptation, manipulation, or neglect. There are too many instances when a good policy, law, or practice, such as the Voting Rights Act of 1965, is advanced only to be substantially watered down. Constant vigilance is demanded for real progress to be sustained. Advocacy for change within the current structural arrangements is probably the predominant approach that has been and is being used by millions. In some cases, change has occurred. But it can often leave the dominant power arrangements intact.

Alternatives

There is power in creating new ways of thinking, feeling, and acting to advance a new possibility for oneself and society. When both a personal and societal impact are intended, alternatives are most powerful. Unfortunately, some alternatives are limited in their scope and power as they are designed primarily to benefit only their adherents rather than to change society. The purpose of those alternatives is to seek purity: purity of lifestyle, as the separatism of the Amish; spiritual purity practiced by the Shakers who anticipated the Second Coming of Jesus and believed sexual intercourse was the cause of all suffering; or educational purity where the intent is not to change the public school system per se but to offer a form of education to a select group of children by which they can improve themselves. These approaches tend to be utopian in outlook. One of the unintended consequences of these kinds of religious and educational alternatives is they often isolate or marginalize the alternative and further exacerbate the existing divisions.

On the other hand, there are alternatives that intentionally seek to advance a better way for all by offering a model for how things can be done and structured differently. The feminist movement has promoted gender equality as an alternative to the patriarchal ways of organizing, decision making, and remunerating. Gender equality is not just words. It is an alternative that works and can have systemic impact.

Sweden's minister for foreign affairs, Margot Wallström, developed a foreign policy in 2014 that provides an alternative to sexual violence, lack of representation, and availability of resources: "We have prevented several hundred thousand unsafe abortions in East Africa by providing safe options . . . increased the participation of women in peace processes . . . [and] provided training for female political candidates in Somalia, which has led to real political change."[22] According to Wallström, a number of other countries are following Sweden's lead.

Finally, there are alternatives that may begin as only a stopgap but could lead to reshaping policies and structures. In the 1960s, abortions were illegal in most states, including New York, except for therapeutic reasons (e.g., the life of the mother). Women without money turned to back-alley providers or to self-induced abortions, notoriously with coat hangers. Complications and infections were common, and thousands died. In 1967, the Clergy Consultation Service on Abortion (CCS) was formed by the Rev. Howard Moody, Arlene Carmen, and other clergy to provide counseling and referrals to women seeking abortion. The CSS gathered a list of medical doctors willing to provide abortions illegally and began to refer women to them. They also negotiated lower rates for the women. Eventually, the success of this alternative made an impact on state government, and in 1970, New York State passed a law making abortions legal. But there was still a need for an alternative to the hospital-based, high-cost procedure, so the CCS set up its own clinic that provided non-hospital-based abortions in a user-friendly environment at a cost as low as twenty-five dollars for the truly poor. Once again, the alternative model had an impact on how abortions were provided throughout the nation.

A similar alternative health care system initiated and run by women was being established in Chicago in the early 1970s by the Jane Collective. Originally a referral project, many of the women became trained in the practices of abortion and provided help for thousands of women until 1973 when the *Roe v. Wade* decision by the Supreme Court legalized abortion.

In both these instances, the creation of alternatives helped pave the way for legislative changes at the state and, eventually, national level. It has often been said legislation follows precedent. It was true in this case.

A caution is necessary. Alternatives always run the danger of being co-opted. Rap music, which began as an alternative of the street, has now become mainstream, prevalent in advertising, and embraced by major record labels. Graffiti art, once maligned as the scribblings of malcontents, is now in art galleries. The Declaration of Independence and US Constitution were created as alternative guides to governance that would place power in the hands of the people (then defined as propertied white men). The definition of "person" has been co-opted by the 2010 Supreme Court decision in *Citizens United v. Federal Elections Commission*. Now, corporations have been granted the same power of speech once thought to be only the purview of human beings.

All alternatives must be constantly on guard lest they be co-opted.

Nevertheless, alternatives have challenged and sometimes led to changes that brought down walls that divide.

Resistance

Sometimes, despite our best intentions and efforts, attempts to bridge the divide are unsuccessful. That is why so many who have been oppressed are resisting. Black Lives Matter, #MeToo, Occupy Wall Street, labor union strikes, the Sanctuary Movement, We Call BS are among the notable.

Resistance can come at a high price. I was in Beijing the night of the Tiananmen Square massacre in 1989. Earlier that evening, I asked some of the young people gathered at a resistance rally at a nearby university what their goal was. They were demanding the government loosen its control over the economy. Some of them went to the square to join the protest against governmental control. I wonder how many of them were among the murdered. But we don't have to wonder about the four Kent State students who were killed protesting the Vietnam War in 1970, or the thirty-three prisoners killed at Attica who were demanding better conditions in 1971.

Words matter. It is interesting to note how resistance is often described by the media and the official powers as riots. In fact, much of the literature related to the Stonewall Inn uprising fifty years ago refers to what occurred as a riot. However, the rioting that ensued was preceded by a sustained resistance by the LGBTQ+ community against the harassment, repression, and brutality of the police. Only at the boiling point did physical resistance occur, and then the major factor leading to action was excessive police force. Similarly, the Attica uprising that resulted in so many deaths began as resistance to the inhumane treatment of the prisoners and escalated to a riot when the governor ordered state troopers to attack. Conveniently linked with the term *riot* is the common allegation that those resisting are subversives or radical revolutionaries who collude with outside movements.

Sometimes, people engage in resistance as a preventative measure—to stop something from materializing or being successful. During World War II, the Danish government mounted a systematic campaign to shield Jews from the Nazis' attempts to label, detain, and send them to concentration camps. But the government had dissolved, and in 1943, Nazis moved to deport all the Jews. It is estimated ordinary Danes assisted approximately 90 percent of the Jewish population to hide or escape to the safety of neutral Sweden. While their resistance did not change the Nazis' attitudes or behavior, it saved many lives.

Today, many places of worship are resisting the government's immigration clampdown by providing sanctuary for undocumented persons in danger of deportation. *The Nation* published a series of articles about the role of legal sanctuary offered by churches, mosques, and synagogues. One of the stories related how Amanda Morales and her three children found sanctuary in the Holyrood Church (Iglesia Santa Cruz) in upper Manhattan following a deportation order to send her back to Guatemala from which she had fled. Afraid to return to the violence and wanting to be with her three children who are US citizens, she sought refuge in the church.[23]

The Sanctuary Movement in the United States emerged in the 1980s in resistance to the US government's rejection of many Central American immigrants seeking asylum. Then, over five hundred churches and synagogues provided protection for the asylum seekers; today, more than a thousand faith communities are part of the sanctuary movement.

This movement has roots far back in history. In ancient Israel, persons who unintentionally killed someone could flee to one of six cities of refuge where they remained safe from vengeful actions by the family of the victim or the larger community. In medieval times, persons fleeing the law or vigilante justice could find refuge in certain churches if they confessed and gave up all property and rights. During the era of slavery in the United States, the Underground Railroad was a major form of resistance that provided sanctuary in many places of worship for runaway slaves. Our history is filled with acts of resistance: hunger strikes by prisoners responding to unjust treatment; Elizabeth Cady Stanton's claim that resistance to tyranny is obedience to God; Rosa Parks's refusal to move to the back of the bus; individuals who burned their draft cards; and athletes who kneel during the national anthem.

Among the most well-known acts of resistance was the movement of nonviolent civil disobedience led by Martin Luther King Jr. In refusing to obey Jim Crow laws, many black people experienced severe reprisals—sometimes even death. But they resisted. Their resistance, and that of some white people, exposed the injustice of the existing laws and helped to build a national awareness that would lead to overturning those laws. This resistance was not merely to prevent injustice—it was for the sake of social change. King called the nation to its highest principles as expressed in our founding documents and religious teachings. A result was the Civil Rights Act of 1964 banning discrimination in various forms. Continued vigilance is necessary to support the law. During the Poor People's Campaign in 1968, workers wore signs that said, "I am a Man." Later, Jesse Jackson and others wore signs that said, "I Am Somebody." More than fifty years later, we still need signs that read "Black Lives Matter," a powerful current resistance movement designed to prevent the violence inflicted on black people at the hands of some police.

Even the Voting Rights Act of 1965, intended to guarantee everyone the right to vote, has been severely undermined, as state after state has been enacting or seeking to enact legislation to undo that gain. In June 2019, the US Supreme Court declared gerrymandering the boundaries of electoral districts for political reasons is not something the court can rule on, ignoring the fact gerrymandering makes it more difficult, if not impossible, for people of color and the poor to have their votes counted proportionally in a fair and representative way.

One of the most significant ways the Civil Rights Act failed to alter the situation of black people can be seen in our criminal justice system and the subsequent resistance this has engendered. As Michelle Alexander has pointed out, the mass incarceration of black people has had the effect of criminalizing black people, leading to a new form of Jim Crow.[24] There is developing resistance to the criminal justice system as it operates. Prisoners are striking; lawyers, including Bryan Stevenson mentioned earlier, are challenging death sentences; journalists are unearthing evidence of illegal and biased police actions; prosecutors are diverting offenders from courts and prison; and people of color and white people are demonstrating. Since 1997, the Critical Resistance organization, cofounded by Angela Davis, has worked to challenge and abolish the "prison-industrial complex."

When resistance seeks to redress the harms done and to prevent injustice, it can play a vital role in overcoming divisions. However, when resisters revert to Othering, such as calling police "pigs," it is counterproductive and only deepens the divisions. There is always the potential for those being resisted to increase the violence and double down on the injustice, further aggravating the divisions.

The hallmark of resistance is a willingness to stand against the powers of injustice and division. Authentic resistance is not designed to violently overthrow the existing order as some forms of revolution intend. Rather, resistance can be either a preventative act, such as the Danes' protection of the Jews during World War II, or a confrontational struggle to change the way people and governments think and act, such as the civil rights struggle and the #MeToo movement.

Revolution

This path to tearing down the walls conjures up chaos and violence, and we have been socialized to reject revolution. In the minds of many US citizens, the only revolution that has been legitimate is the American Revolution. But there have been times when the divisions seem intractable, when all other approaches have failed, and revolution remains the only option. From revolution, new nations have emerged, new leaders have risen up, and formerly oppressed groups have claimed justice.

Revolutionary struggle may be either nonviolent or violent. But as John F. Kennedy famously said in 1962, "those who make peaceful revolution impossible will make violent revolution inevitable."[25] While the means may differ, the goal of both nonviolent and violent revolution is the replacement of the established power and structures of control so a radically new possibility can emerge. Revolution involves a fundamental change, a turning, a conversion.

Sometimes, like the American Revolution, armed struggle has seemed necessary and appropriate. On July 4, 1776, the signers of the Declaration of Independence stated they would no longer negotiate with England, which they declared was abusing the colonies, refusing their representation, and tyrannically ruling over them. They spoke of the right of "overthrow" and war with an enemy. Their declaration supported the armed conflict that had begun the year before.

Just war theory, as originally developed by Augustine, states war is a last resort. But it is *a* resort. Violent overthrow should be a last resort too. This was the case with the signers of the Declaration of Independence. Of course, what seemed like a revolution for justice to the signers of the Declaration was viewed as an illegal uprising by the British. One group's liberation can be seen as terrorism by others.

At other times, nonviolent revolution, as advocated by Mahatma Gandhi or Nelson Mandela in his later years, can prove effective. Pacifism has been a successful instrument of revolution. Given the appropriate oppressor, nonviolent disobedience may lead to revolution. Gandhi's nonviolent revolution was successful, in large part, because England, wanting to avoid a bloody war, was ready to leave India. Similarly, apartheid ended in South Africa when President de Klerk recognized more conflict and violence was in no one's interest, and he accepted Mandela's leadership of nonviolent change.

Although revolutions often appear to be spontaneous uprisings, they almost always have a significant gestation period during which organizing, resistance, advocacy, and alternatives are used. In the end, the intransigence of the existing structures and the failure of those in power to recognize the legitimate grievances of those being harmed lead people to revolt.

Those who oppose revolution as a means say revolutions fail, that they substitute the players but do not change the underlying policies and structures. Despite enormous cost, injustice remains. In part, they are correct. Whatever the gains made by revolution, just as with resistance, organizing, and alternatives, the potential for relapse is always close at hand because the powers of oppression are ready to reclaim their privilege.

In the 1980s, the Sandinistas overthrew the Somoza regime in Nicaragua, much to the displeasure of the United States. I was a member of the board when Witness for Peace sought to shine light on the revolution's goals and to stand with the people of Nicaragua. Many of us supported the elected president Daniel Ortega at that time (1984–1990). But the revolution hailed by the masses was eventually perverted. Reelected in 2007, Ortega has turned his back on the goals of the revolution and become a corrupt dictator whom many are now seeking to overthrow. But that reversal is not sufficient reason to condemn the revolution.

It is recognized now that the United States played a role in undermining a genuine revolution that sought to create justice for the people of Nicaragua. Ronald Reagan's clandestine support of the Contras and our government's refusal to tolerate a mixed economy that involved limited nationalization helped destroy the economic goals of the revolution. It is possible Ortega might have turned to dictatorship, no matter what. However, it is certain our government's refusal to allow a mixed economy to develop and thrive in Nicaragua drove a spike into the heart of the revolution. What our government could not accomplish by military means, it did by economic force.

In a similar manner, the Cuban revolution in the mid-1950s was stymied by our government's refusal to support the development of a mixed economy and the nationalization of property and industry. The Cuban revolution overthrew Fulgencio Batista in 1959, a dictator concerned only for the wealthy and United States corporations. But with Fidel Castro's nationalization of much US property and industry, as well as his increasing ties to the Soviet Union, our government's support turned to opposition. What could not be achieved by US backing anti-Castro Cuban exiles invading at the Bay of Pigs in 1961, or by assassination attempts on Fidel Castro, was accomplished through half a century of economic embargo, solidifying Castro's dictatorial rule and dependence on Soviet markets. It is interesting to conjecture what might have been the course of Cuban history had the United States supported Cuba's modified socialist economy, rather than placing an embargo on the island that largely remains to this day.

The revolutionary electoral victory achieved in 1970 by socialist president Salvador Allende in Chile also was overthrown by a military coup in 1973 that had the backing of US corporate money and, allegedly, our CIA.

Might the Nicaraguan, Cuban, and Chilean revolutions have been successful if given a chance? We cannot know. But we do know the powerful economic and political interests of US businesses and government successfully destroyed what might have been a new day for the people of those nations.

Revolution may be understandably an effort of last resort because the costs of both nonviolent and violent revolutions can be enormous for both advocates and opponents of change. The cost in lives is often immense and always tragic.

The Libyan civil war in 2011 was bloody, involving pro- and anti-government forces, the North Atlantic Treaty Organization (NATO), and a UN-mandated no-fly zone. Estimates of casualties vary widely, but it is agreed thousands died. In October 2011, Colonel Muammar Gaddafi was captured and killed, and many considered the revolution a success. The National Transitional Council was recognized by the United Nations, and Libya's liberation was declared. Unfortunately, the revolution was short-lived. There are currently three rival governments, a new civil war has erupted, thousands have been killed, and hundreds of thousands of persons have been displaced.

Despite the forces that work to sabotage revolutionary movements and the constant temptation faced by those newly empowered, revolutions can sometimes result in fundamental changes. South Africa's revolution began with violence (advocated by Mandela and others), and gradually became nonviolent when he later realized nonviolence was the only effective way to create a new society. His leadership led to free elections in which the formerly disenfranchised majority was able to vote. The result was ending apartheid and replacing the Afrikaner National Party control with the African National Congress (ANC). As with any revolution, there is much yet to be done. Several decades after the nonviolent revolution in South Africa, poverty remains the plight of millions, corruption is rife, and the ANC is now under intense criticism. The revolution that began must continue lest the people once again become subject to unjust power.

When the forces of oppression will not yield, revolution may become the only option. But the failure of a revolution to totally fulfill its promise is insufficient reason not to engage. No approach to change is without the possibility of being derailed, distorted, or defeated.

Our own American Revolution is a case in point. Even the ideals of our nation's revolution remain unrealized. We are still wrestling with what it means to say, "all men [sic] are created equal." While the founders, limited by their historical context, may not have explicitly envisioned the equality of women, the poor, and people of color, their principles still provide a way to measure progress toward overcoming those divisions.

What began as a rebellion to overthrow British colonial rule has continued for over two hundred years. Success in a revolution that began in 1775 has needed continual rebellion, as Thomas Jefferson famously indicated would be necessary.[26] Our revolution continued structures and policies that were misogynist and based on class. Later, the practices and policies of slavery became part of our government's structure of exploitation, further countering the goals of the revolution. Our struggles have expanded the understanding of "all men" to include all people, not just privileged white males. But our failure to live up to the promises and claims of our revolution does not deny its fundamental and long-lasting impact.

The examples of partial victories and failed attempts at revolutionary change could go on and on. Those who criticize the use of revolution because of its failures should bear in mind the reversals that can accompany any effort to tear down the dividing walls of injustice and hostility, given the tenacity of the forces of oppression. The criticism of revolutionary changes should be tempered by the history of all changes. Co-optation, regression, and betrayal are always possible. The forces of injustice are powerful and can undo change, whether brought about by revolution or not.

On the other hand, there are examples of structural changes that have made a difference for millions: The revolution of India against British colonialism freed millions to pursue a fuller life. Unfortunately, the caste system Gandhi opposed has yet to be completely overcome. The French Revolution brought feudalism to its knees, supported equality of people based on their worth as humans rather than their status, and influenced many subsequent movements for change that led to democracy in some cases.

The calls for revolution persist. There have been many recent supporters of revolution, both nonviolent and violent, within our own nation and globally. During his time with the Nation of Islam, Malcolm X referred to white people as devils and argued for totally separate nations, as well as self-defense and advancement by any means necessary. After his experience of the worldwide pilgrimage of Muslims to Mecca changed his view of what was possible, he advocated working with whomever was committed to ending racism, made an alliance with the nonviolent approach of King, and urged black people to try to change the structures of racism by voting. In no case did he turn his back on the need for a total revolution or even the possibility of violence. What changed for Malcolm X was the notion of who could be included in the revolutionary task and the means to achieve it. He came to understand advocates of nonviolence, such as King, and white people who were in solidarity with the goal of racial justice were neither enemies nor devils.

In the second wave of feminism are women who identify themselves as feminist Marxists. They insist the only way to a just world is for women, who have been oppressed as both workers and as women, to engage in the dual struggle against both capitalism and patriarchy.[27] They see themselves as revolutionary agents in the same way many Marxist-Leninists viewed themselves as the necessary agents of revolution.

One of the most notable calls for revolution by women has been in the Sudan, where they led the challenge to President Omar al-

Bashir's tyrannical thirty-year rule that included a failed economy, a civil war in Darfur, and oppressive laws curtailing the basic human rights of women. Bashir has resigned and been sent to the International Court of Justice for charges of genocide and other crimes by the Sovereign Council, a transitional government after a military coup, but there is no guarantee the goal of democracy will be reached.

Presidential candidate Bernie Sanders has called for a political revolution in our nation. Underscoring the great economic divide between the top 1 percent and the working class, he says the change we need is from capitalism to democratic socialism. To bring about that change, "we need a political revolution where millions of people stand up and fight and demand a government that works for us—not just the 1 percent."[28]

One of the most compelling voices for revolutionary change comes from a man once on death row. Found guilty in 1982 of the murder of a Philadelphia police officer, Mumia Abu-Jamal's multiple appeals have resulted in reduction of the death sentence to life, but his contested conviction remains. Despite these circumstances, he has consistently offered a vision of nonviolent revolution, significantly shaped by MOVE, the organization founded by John Africa that describes itself as a "powerful family of revolutionaries." Despite the allegations against Abu-Jamal as a murderer, he maintains that while violence is "what the system practices," his fight against the system will not "employ the same tactics and methods the system uses every day. . . . We need a new system, one where people are free of the violence of the system. . . . I reject the tools and weapons of violence."[29] His combination of love and ferocity, of the personal and the political, offers us a model for the way ahead.

The calls for revolution will not cease so long as injustice and oppression prevail, so long as the dividing walls exist.

Each of the collective actions outlined in this chapter offers both possibility and risk, just as each of our individual actions does. There are no guarantees, no matter which approach we take. If the dividing walls and the systems that erect and support them are to be dismantled, we must use every means at our disposal from the personal to the political. Indeed, it is only as we engage in the full range of transforming options available to us that we may see a day in which justice shall reign and the walls will be dismantled.

But how much dare we imagine is possible? Is there a reason for hope? This is the final issue that needs to be addressed.

Epilogue

It's been a long, a long time coming
But I know a change's gon' come, oh, yes, it will

—Sam Cooke

Are our society's divisions so intractable that to hope is to be blinded to the depth of our hostilities? Are the moral imperatives of Buber, King, the Buddha, the Prophets, Jesus, Noddings, and the Dalai Lama just wishful thinking? Are the lyrics of Sam Cooke's "A Change Is Gonna Come" overshadowed by the continuing horror of racism? Are we to be a divided nation forever? We must face these questions squarely, lest we be overcome with cynicism and despair.

Whether we speak of a higher power, God, the universe, Gaia, eternal laws, the moral imperative, or our guts, those of us who live with hope have faith the struggle will prove victorious. Our hope is based on that faith. When Martin Luther King Jr. said "the moral arc of the universe bends toward justice," he was aware of the history of the suppression of black people, and yet he believed, in the end, God's power would be victorious over evil. Gandhi believed the nonviolent struggle to free India from British colonial control was worth his life because he believed nonviolence is an eternal law, similar to gravity.

Perhaps it is sufficient to stake out a more modest claim for hope. To live with hope is not to expect the future to be perfect, and certainly not to last forever, but to expect the walls will be dismantled, at least for a time. The future needs not be as bleak as the present. The dividing walls of hostility need not be the final word.

When I was very young, the word of my parents was authoritative and final. When they told me everything would be all right, I believed them. I counted on them. When they said Santa Claus was real, I believed them. Gradually, I discovered sometimes they were wrong. And when I found out there was no Santa, my uncritical acceptance of their word was shattered. I then had to decide whether to discard everything they said as nonsense, incorrect, or even a lie, or accept my responsibility to discover truth.

Later, the word of the preachers seemed authoritative and final. When they told us everything was in God's hands, I believed them. Little by little, I discovered sometimes, they were wrong. Some things just didn't fit with being part of God's will. How could a good and all-powerful God allow tragedy and evil to exist? How could the Bible include such contradictory claims? Why were so many of these authorities in disagreement with one another? I had to decide whether to accept their fundamentalisms, discard everything and become an atheist, or take responsibility for reimagining and reinterpreting my faith.

Today, we are at a junction in the road. One option is to turn back and uncritically accept the authority of those in power who seek to maintain the status quo. However, if we do not want to revert to the comfort of authoritarianism, then we have two more choices. We can opt for total relativism and anarchy, or we can choose the path that invites us to become critically engaged. That last path demands responsibility to create the future, rather than either passively accepting the status quo or assuming nothing matters.

One of the most pervasive and pernicious conditions of our time is fatalism, the belief that things are inevitable. At a conversation around the table in our home, Paulo Freire, the Brazilian educator, spoke of the fatalism of so many of the peasants whom he had taught to read. When asked why the landlord lived in a mansion while they lived in shacks, he said they often replied, "It is God's will" or "because it has always been that way." He understood that fatalism is the result of systems of control.[1] In the same way, many people in previous times took for granted that the king would be replaced by the king's son, and the peasant's son would follow in his father's path because that was the way things were, or it was God's will. Today, we hear a similar phrase, "You can't fight city hall."

We dare not rely on such easy answers to the burning issues of our day. The dividing walls of hostility remain standing because we allow them to stand, not because it is God's will or the way things are meant to be, or the powers-that-be are too strong. Living with hope, rather than fatalism, is essential if we are to move forward, to tear down the walls, and to discover common ground.

There is a difference between living with hope and with wishes. A wish has to do with specifics—for example, I wish I could play tennis like Roger Federer. Hope is a way of living; it is a stance toward life rather than an optimistic picture of the future. To live by hope is to make a commitment to a way of life. Although the possibilities may be slim and the odds against tearing down the walls seem insurmountable, to live by hope is to persevere. To live by hope is to commit to the long haul, to be a long-distance runner. There will be setbacks, hurdles, and times when all seems lost. Our resolve will be shaken, and we may question whether the struggle is worth fighting. But still, we live with hope. As Freire said, "to be utopian is not to be merely idealistic or impractical, but rather to engage in denunciation and annunciation."[2]

We can be inspired by many examples of hope. Harriet Tubman's hope led to the Underground Railroad, challenging the tenacious and seemingly insurmountable evil of slavery. Susan B. Anthony, Elizabeth Cady Stanton, and others kept the hope alive from the Seneca Falls Convention in 1848 until women's right to vote was ratified in 1920. Nelson Mandela kept hope alive for the twenty-seven years he was imprisoned, and his tenacity helped turn his country around. The peasants of Nicaragua during the 1980s were willing to give their lives in the fight against US-backed Contra troops because they lived with hope for a new day free of dictatorship. The refugees who have overcome incredible odds just to reach our border are motivated by hope for a safer and better future.

There are many signs of hope. For years, I attended worship services in black churches. Their hope, despite the odds and the tenacity of racism, overwhelms me. Their faith stands against all odds. The Paralympics are a testimony to human hope in the face of enormous obstacles.[3] The Othering and Belonging Institute at UC Berkeley is actively proposing an alternative of "belonging and bridging."[4] The Parkland, Florida, high school students whose classmates were murdered are filled with hope for a robust and saner gun policy and safer schools, inspiring them to protest and organize a nationwide youth movement.[5]

None of these persons or communities I have mentioned, along with thousands of others who have chosen to live with hope, has the last word. There is no cause for optimism: exploitation continues; the walls keep being erected; the hatred raises its ugly head again and again. But hope holds out the possibility of a new day, a resurrection, a time when the lion shall lie down with the lamb. We must decide if we are willing to live with tragedy as the final word or if we choose to live with hope and fight for a transformed world.

Can the walls come tumbling down? It is a matter of choice—our choice as to where we stand and who we stand with in the struggle to resist the dominating powers that erect and maintain the walls of systemic containment, exploitation, and death.

Notes

Foreword

1. James Baldwin, "Stranger in the Village," in *Collected Essays*, ed. Toni Morrison (New York: The Library Press of America, 1998), 129.
2. Abraham Joshua Heschel, *Abraham Joshua Heschel: Essential Writings*, ed. Susannah Heschel (Maryknoll, NY: Orbis Books, 2011), 69.
3. Simone de Beauvoir, *The Second Sex* (New York: Vintage Books, 1989), xxiii.
4. James Baldwin, *The Fire Next Time* (New York: The Modern Library, 1995), 94.
5. Cornel West and Kelvin Shawn Sealey, *Restoring Hope: Conversations on the Future of Black America* (Boston: Beacon Press, 1997), xii.
6. Martin Luther King Jr., *A Testament of Hope: The Essential Writings and Speeches of Martin Luther King Jr.*, ed. James M. Washington (New York: HarperCollins, 1991), 293.
7. King, *A Testament of Hope*, 290.

Introduction

1. T. Richard Snyder, *Divided We Fall: Moving from Suspicion to Solidarity* (Louisville, KY: Westminster John Knox, 1992), 15.
2. Richard W. Heinberg, *Memories and Visions of Paradise: Exploring the Universal Myth of a Lost Golden Age* (Los Angeles: Jeremy P. Tarcher, 1989).
3. John A. Powell and Stephen Menendian, "The Problem of Othering: Towards Inclusiveness and Belonging," Othering andBelonging.org, June 29, 2017, https://tinyurl.com/ tm6zd24.

4. Jeffrey C. Alexander, "Citizen and Enemy as Symbolic Classification: On the Polarizing Discourse of Civil Society," in *Cultivating Differences*, ed. Michele Lamont and Marcel Fournier (Chicago: University of Chicago Press, 1992).

5. Alexander, "Citizen and Enemy," 298.

6. Laura Petrecca, "America's Division: We United in the Wake of 9/11, then Partisanship Re-emerged," *USA Today*, September 11, 2017, https://tinyurl.com/txarngl.

7. Katherine J. Cramer, *The Politics of Resentment: Rural Consciousness in Wisconsin and the Rise of Scott Walker* (Chicago: University of Chicago Press, 2016), 211.

8. Peggy Noonan, "Trump and the Rise of the Unprotected," *Wall Street Journal*, February 25, 2016, https://tinyurl.com/s2en79b.

9. Gavin McInnes, "This Is War," *Taki's Magazine*, June 1, 2017, https://tinyurl.com/sz2kmjh.

10. Michael D. Shear, Adam Goldman, and Emily Cochrane, "Congressman Steve Scalise Gravely Wounded in Alexandria Baseball Field Ambush," *New York Times*, June 14, 2017, https://tinyurl.com/w54069e.

Chapter 1: The Dividing Walls of Hostility

1. Lev 19:18.

2. Amos 4:1–3 is just one example.

3. Josh 6:17–19.

4. 2 Kgs 25; Jer 4:13–17.

5. Matt 15:24.

6. Matt 10:5.

7. John 4; Luke 10.

8. Page duBois, *Centaurs and Amazons: Women and the Pre-History of the Great Chain of Being* (Ann Arbor: University of Michigan Press, 1991), 4.

9. R. I. Moore, *The Formation of a Persecuting Society: Authority and Deviance in Western Europe, 950–1250* (Malden, MA: Blackwell, 2007).

10. Moore, *The Formation of a Persecuting Society*, 147.

11. Moore, *The Formation of a Persecuting Society*, 147.

12. Gerardo Martí, *American Blindspot: Race, Class, Religion, and the Trump Presidency* (Lanham, MD: Rowman and Littlefield, 2020), 49–52.

13. Michael P. Jeffries, "Suffering and Citizenship: Racism and Black Life," in *Healing Our Divided Society: Investing in America Fifty Years after the Kerner Report* (Philadelphia: Temple University Press, 2018), 314.

14. Donald Bogle, *Toms, Coons, Mulattoes, Mammies, and Bucks: An Interpretive History of Blacks in American Films* (New York: Continuum, 1993), 8.

15. Ralph Ellison, *Invisible Man* (New York: Vintage International, 1990), 95.

16. Derrick Bell, *Faces at the Bottom of the Well: The Permanence of Racism* (New York: Basic Books, 1992), viii.

17. Bell, *Faces at the Bottom of the Well*, 27. Bell had taught at Harvard for twenty-three years and was a tenured professor of law, holding the Weld Chair. But he took a two-year unpaid leave of absence in protest against the law school's failure to hire any black women professors. The university dismissed him when they upheld the two-year limit on unpaid leaves of absence.

18. Ellis Cose, *The Rage of a Privileged Class* (New York: HarperCollins, 1993).

19. Cornel West, *Race Matters* (New York: Vintage, 1994), xiv and xv.

20. Marc Lamont Hill, *Nobody: Casualties of America's War on the Vulnerable, from Ferguson to Flint and Beyond* (New York: Atria Books, 2016).

21. "Trends in U.S. Corrections: U.S. and Federal Prison Population, 1925–2017," The Sentencing Project, https:// tinyurl.com/yx73ocwf.

22. "Shadow Report to the United Nations on Racial Disparities in the United States Criminal Justice System," The Sentencing Project, August 31, 2013, https://tinyurl.com/rvvxzns.

23. The Sentencing Project, "Shadow Report to the United Nations."

24. The Sentencing Project, "Shadow Report to the United Nations."

25. Michelle Alexander, *The New Jim Crow: Mass Incarceration in the Age of Colorblindness* (New York: The New Press, 2012).

26. Chris Hayes, *A Colony in a Nation* (New York: W. W. Norton, 2017).

27. Catherine Allgor, "Coverture: The Word You Probably Don't Know but Should," National Women's History Museum, September 4, 2012, https://tinyurl.com/srbjc9k.

28. Cheryl C. Smith, "Out of Her Place: Anne Hutchinson and the Dislocation of Power in New World Politics," *The Journal of American Culture* 29, no. 4 (2006): 442, https://tinyurl.com/wzldxwa.

29. Kathleen Elkins, "Here's How Much Men and Women Earn at Every Age," CNBC, April 2, 2019, https://tinyurl.com/rrjep4a.

30. Gerald Michael Greenfield and Carlos E. Cortés, "Harmony and Conflict of Intercultural Images: The Treatment of Mexico in US Feature Films and K–12 Textbooks," *Mexican Studies/Estudios Mexicanos* 7, no. 2 (Summer 1991): 285, https://www.jstor.org/stable/1052067.

31. Antonio Flores, Gustavo López, and Jynnah Radford, "2015, Hispanic Population in the United States Statistical Portrait," Pew Research Center, September 18, 2017, https://tinyurl.com/suaph2e; "Characteristics of the US Hispanic Population: 2015," Pew Research Center, September 2017, https://tinyurl.com/vjkyvbd.

32. Krystal D'Costa, "What Are the Jobs That Immigrants Do?" *Scientific American*, August 9, 2018, https://tinyurl.com/yaz5taz7.

33. Lauren Kaori Gurley, "What We Don't Talk about When We Talk about Rural Poverty," *In These Times*, March 27, 2017, https://tinyurl.com/wv3mtho.

34. Sarah Jones, "J. D. Vance, the False Prophet of Blue America," *New Republic*, November 17, 2016, https://tinyurl.com/hzdnya9.

35. Thomas C. Leonard, *Illiberal Reformers: Race, Eugenics, and American Economics in the Progressive Era* (Princeton, NJ: Princeton University Press, 2016), 127.

36. Colin Calloway, "George Washington's 'Tortuous' Relationship with Native Americans," Zócalo, August 2, 2018, https://tinyurl.com/qndwcvl.

37. James P. Gregory Jr., "Better Dead Than Red: The Treatment of Native Americans in the Southwest during the Cold War," *Armstrong Undergraduate Journal of History* 7, no. 2 (November 2017): 96, https://doi.org/10.20429/aujh.2017.070207.

38. "'Kill the Indian, and Save the Man': Capt. Richard H. Pratt on the Education of Native Americans," History Matters, last saved March 7, 2020, https://tinyurl.com/w66af4l.

39. Robert A. Williams Jr., *The American Indian in Western Legal Thought: The Discourses of Conquest* (New York: Oxford University Press, 1992).

40. History.com Editors, "Japanese Internment Camps," History.com, last updated February 21, 2020, https://tinyurl.com/ydbgw6av.

41. History.com Staff, "Chinese Exclusion Act," History.com, last updated September 13, 2019, https://tinyurl.com/u3sa5qo.

42. Quentin Fottrell, "No Chinese Allowed: Racism and Fear Are Now Spreading along with the Coronavirus," MarketWatch.com, February 3, 2020, https://tinyurl.com/rnrd53s.

43. Edward W. Said, *Orientalism* (New York: Vintage, 1979), 286 and 287.

44. "Muslim-American Demographics Reveal a Diverse Group That Rejects Categorization," HuffPost, December 6, 2017, https://tinyurl.com/ybxl6bd2.

45. Ted Genoways, "The Only Good Muslim Is a Dead Muslim," *New Republic*, May 15, 2017, https://tinyurl.com/k4k8hl5.

46. Genoways, "Only Good Muslim."

47. Katayoun Kishi, "Assaults against Muslims in US Surpass 2001 Level," Pew Research Center, Nov. 15, 2017, https://tinyurl.com/w789r29.

48. Tucker Higgins, "Supreme Court Rules That Trump's Travel Ban Is Constitutional," CNBC, June 26, 2018, https:// tinyurl.com/y9wrtrxn.

49. Stephanie Ebbert, "In Maine, Trump Takes Aim at Somali Refugees," *Boston Globe*, August 4, 2016, https://tinyurl.com/sb8x4fs.

50. Scott Thistle, "Trump's Statements about Somali Immigrants in Maine Draw Rebuke," *Portland Press Herald*, August 5, 2016, https://tinyurl.com/wkvb5ah.

51. Daily Mail Reporter, "Evangelist Franklin Graham Praises Putin's Crackdown on Homosexuals, Calls Obama's Support of Gay Rights 'Shameful,'" DailyMail.com, March 19, 2014, https://tinyurl.com/vxnf4ba.

52. Lily Wakefield, "There Are 16 states in the US That Still Have Sodomy Laws against "Perverted Sexual Practice.' It's 2020," Pink News, January 24, 2020, https://tinyurl.com/yda7fwyz.

53. The following are several resources related to trans persons: https://tinyurl.com/wrav3pm; https://tinyurl.com/yx6nn dsx; https://tinyurl.com/t6skkqt.

54. Judith Bradford et al., "Experiences of Transgender-Related Discrimination and Implications for Health: Results from the Virginia Transgender Health Initiative Study," American Journal of Public Health 103, no. 10 (October 1 2013): 1820–29, https://doi.org/10.2105/AJPH.2012.300796.

55. David Welna and Bill Chappell, "Supreme Court Revives Trump's Ban on Transgender Military Personnel, For Now," NPR, January 22, 2019, https://tinyurl.com/v4vjr2c.

56. Adam Liptak, "In Narrow Decision, Supreme Court Sides with Baker Who Turned Away Gay Couple," New York Times, June 4, 2018, https://tinyurl.com/y8tdme3q.

57. Pat Moore with Charles Paul Conn, Disguised: A True Story (Waco, TX: Word Books, 1985).

58. T. Richard Snyder, The Protestant Ethic and the Spirit of Punishment (Grand Rapids, MI: Eerdmans, 2001).

59. Michael Schwirtz, Michael Winerip, and Robert Gebeloff, "The Scourge of Racial Bias in New York State's Prisons," New York Times, December 3, 2016, https://tinyurl.com/uaqqo9y.

60. Isabel Fonseca, Bury Me Standing: The Gypsies and Their Journey (New York: Vintage Departures, 1996), 7.

61. Fonseca, Bury Me Standing, 161.

62. Fonseca, Bury Me Standing, 164.

63. Alexander Nazaryan, "Fox News: 'Gypsies' Are Threatening America, Defecating Everywhere, and Beheading Chickens, Tucker Carlson Warns," Newsweek, July 21, 2017, https://tinyurl.com/quq5bm6.

64. Nazaryan, "'Gypsies' Are Threatening America."

65. Kayla Webley, "Hounded in Europe, Roma in the US Keep a Low Profile," Time, October 13, 2010, https://tinyurl.com/qoghvft.

66. Patrick McKenna, "When the Irish Became White: Immigrants in Mid-19th Century US," Irish Times, February 12, 2013, https://tinyurl.com/ycsq9so4.

67. Ibid.

68. Corey Dade, "Blacks, Gays and the Church: A Complex Relationship," NPR, May 22, 2012, https://tinyurl.com/t7bspo2.

69. Hill, *Nobody*, xviii.

70. Hill, *Nobody*, xix and xx.

Chapter 2: The Roots of Othering

1. Michelle Bachelet, "International Women's Day—Day 7," The Interfaith Project, March 7, 2017, https://tinyurl.com/trwffkk.

2. Michael Schwalbe, "The Elements of Inequality," *Contemporary Sociology* 29, no. 6 (November 2002): 775–81, http:// www.jstor.org/stable/ 2654084.

3. Chelsea Hale and Meghan Matt, "The Intersection of Race and Rape Viewed through the Prism of a Modern-Day Emmett Till," American Bar Association, July 16, 2019, https://tinyurl.com/ya6jjwaw.

4. Moore, *The Formation of a Persecuting Society*.

5. Erdman B. Palmore, *Ageism: Negative and Positive* (New York: Springer, 1999), 66.

6. "Concept of the Dark Continent Created through European-Erased Maps of Interior Africa," *The Journal of Blacks in Higher Education*, no. 11 (Spring 1996): 53, https://www.jstor.org/stable/2963313.

7. "The True True Size of Africa," *The Economist*, November 19, 2010, https://tinyurl.com/yc8e7cpt.

8. For the difference between the two, see Frederick Copleston, S.J., *A History of Modern Philosophy*, vol. 7, part II (Garden City, NY: Image Books, 1965), 77.

9. Kayleigh Garthwaite, "Stigma, Shame and 'People Like Us': An Ethnographic Study of Foodbank Use in the UK," *Journal of Poverty and Social Justice* 24, no. 3 (October 2016): 277–89, https://doi.org/10.1332/ 175982716X14721954314922.

10. Terrence McCoy, "In Former Coal Country, the Working Poor Show Open Contempt for Neighbors Who Seek Handouts," *Chicago Tribune*, July 21, 2017, https://tinyurl.com/w3n5a8d.

11. William Ryan, *Blaming the Victim* (New York: Vintage, 1976).

12. Amin Maalouf, *In the Name of Identity: Violence and the Need to Belong*, trans. Barbara Bray (New York: Arcade, 2001), 58.

13. Snyder, *Protestant Ethic*.

14. Maalouf, *In the Name of Identity*.

15. Maalouf, *In the Name of Identity*, 82.

16. Hans G. Kippenger, "'Consider That It Is a Raid on the Path of God': The Spiritual Manual of the Attackers of 9/11," *Religion and Violence* 52, no. 1 (2005): 42, https://doi.org/10.1163/1568527053083485.

17. "Genetics vs. Genomics Fact Sheet," National Human Genome Research Institute, last saved March 1, 2020, https://tinyurl.com/sbajp3u.

18. "Interview with Richard Lewontin," Race, the Power of an Illusion, PBS.org, last saved on December 12, 2019, https://tinyurl.com/vkds39m.

19. Vivian Chou, "How Science and Genetics Are Reshaping the Race Debate of the 21st Century," Harvard University Graduate School of Arts and Sciences, April 17, 2017, https://tinyurl.com/v8v5kvw.

20. Sharon Begley, "Three Is Not Enough," *Newsweek*, February 12, 1995, https://tinyurl.com/sr7pmzv, 67 and 68. Also see: "What Color Is Black?" in the same issue, https:// tinyurl.com/vpu8620, 63–65.

21. Cornel West, *Prophesy Deliverance!: An Afro-American Revolutionary Christianity* (Philadelphia: Westminster, 1982), 50.

22. West, *Prophesy Deliverance!*, 48–59.

23. Alexander, *The New Jim Crow*, 162.

24. Alexander, *The New Jim Crow*, 162.

25. Ana Patricia Muñoz et al., "The Color of Wealth in Boston," Federal Reserve Bank of Boston, last saved December 16, 2019, https:// tinyurl.com/stjua28, 20.

26. Muñoz et al., "The Color of Wealth," 22. See for example, Blau and Graham 1990, Menchik and Jianakoplos 1997, Conley 1999, Chietji and Hamilton 2002, Charles and Hurst 2003, Gittleman and Wolff 2007.

27. "Justice Department Announces Findings of Two Civil Rights Investigations in Ferguson, Missouri," The United States Department of Justice, March 4, 2015, https://tinyurl.com/t4ubutp.

28. William Wan and Sarah Kaplan, "Why Are People Still Racist? What Science Says about America's Race Problem," *Washington Post*, August 14, 2017, https://tinyurl.com/u65tsvt.

29. Arlie Russell Hochschild, *Strangers in Their Own Land: Anger and Mourning on the American Right* (New York: The New Press, 2016).

30. Hochschild, *Strangers*, 218.

31. Hochschild, *Strangers*, 221, 222.

32. Bobbi J. Carothers and Harry T. Reis, "Men and Women Are from Earth: Examining the Latent Structure of Gender," *Journal of Personality and Social Psychology* 104, no. 2 (February 2013): 385, https://doi.org/10.1037/a0030437.

33. Mary Beard, *Women and Power: A Manifesto* (New York: Liveright, 2017), 3.

34. Charles Darwin, *The Descent of Man, and Selection in Relation to Sex* (London: John Murray, 1871), https://tinyurl.com/w2ytyfe.

35. John Gray, *Men Are from Mars, Women Are from Venus: The Classic Guide to Understanding the Opposite Sex* (New York: Harper Paperbacks, 2012).

36. Gen 3:16.

37. Eph 5:24.

38. Q Nisa 4:34.

39. "Saudi Police 'Stopped' Fire Rescue," BBC News, March 15, 2002, https://tinyurl.com/vkjopgn.

40. Jordain Carney, "Sanders, Dems Read Coretta Scott King's Letter after Warren Silenced," The Hill, February 8, 2017, https://tinyurl.com/se5y2dv.

41. "Henry Morgenthau Jr. and War Refugee Board," Franklin D. Roosevelt Presidential Library and Museum, accessed March 10, 2020, https://tinyurl.com/tuyxbnw.

42. "US Policy during the Holocaust: The Tragedy of the SS St. Louis," Jewish Virtual Library, accessed March 10, 2020, https://tinyurl.com/rxrynmq.

43. A fuller description of the US response to the Holocaust is available on the PBS documentary, America and the Holocaust (2014).

44. Frantz Fanon, The Wretched of the Earth, trans. Richard Philcox (New York: Grove Press, 1963).

45. Albert Memmi, The Colonizer and the Colonized (London: Earthscan, 2003).

46. Pablo Neruda, Five Decades: A Selection (Poems: 1925–1970), trans. and ed. Ben Belitt (New York: Grove Press, 1974), 79.

47. Encyclopaedia Britannica Online, s.v. "Jacobo Arbenz," last updated, January 23, 2020, https://tinyurl.com/scmlfsx.

48. Federico Ferro Gay, "Cultural Colonialism," The Southwestern Journal of Philosophy 5, no. 1 (Spring 1974): 153, www.jstor.org/stable/43154975.

49. Uri Friedman, "Anthropology of an Idea: American Exceptionalism," Foreign Policy, no. 194 (July/August 2012): 22–23, http://www.jstor.org/stable/23242774.

50. Robert Farley, "Obama and 'American Exceptionalism,'" FactCheck.org, February 12, 2015, https://tinyurl.com/t7fxxay.

51. Charles W. Freeman Jr., "This Too Shall Pass: Remarks to the Camden Conference on The New World Disorder and America's Future," Chasfreeman.net, February 18, 2018, https://tinyurl.com/r3kc3bz.

52. Said, Orientalism.

Chapter 3: The Forms of Othering

1. Deut 6:14; 7.

2. Elaine Pagels, The Origin of Satan: How Christians Demonized Jews, Pagans, and Heretics (New York: Vintage, 1996), 180.

3. For a comprehensive catalog see Randall Bytwerk, "German Propaganda Archive," Calvin College, Grand Rapids, MI, https://bhecinfo.org/links/german-propaganda-archive-calvin-college and https://www.bytwerk.com/gpa/.

4. Karen Robertson, "When Art Meets Army: The Dangerous Propaganda of World War II," June 8, 2017, https:// tinyurl.com/tnps24f.

5. Maggie Griffith Williams and Jenny Korn, "Othering and Fear: Cultural Values and Hiro's Race in Thomas and Friends' *Hero of the Rails*," *Journal of Communication Inquiry* 41, no. 1 (January 2017): 22–41, http://doi.org/ 10.1177/0196 859916656836.

6. Williams and Korn, "Othering and Fear," 31.

7. Josiah Clark Nott et al., *Types of Mankind* (Philadelphia: Lippincott, Grambo, 1854), https://tinyurl.com/yx4m8ldp.

8. "Americans Still Linking Blacks to Apes," Science Blog, February 8, 2008, https://tinyurl.com/sghpa6o.

9. Phillip Atiba Goff et al., "Not Yet Human: Implicit Knowledge, Historical Dehumanization, and Contemporary Consequences," *Journal of Personality and Social Psychology* 94, no. 2 (February 2008): 292–306, https://doi.org/10.1037/0022 -3514.94.2.292.

10. Rebecca Ruiz, "A New Book Argues against the SAT," New York Times Choice Blog, November 9, 2011, https:// tinyurl.com/rzcvgnv.

11. Robert Farley, "Fact Check: Trump's Comments on Women," *USA Today*, August 12, 2015, https://tinyurl.com/ux5p7wr.

12. Lori Baker-Sperry and Liz Grauerholz, "The Pervasiveness and Persistence of the Feminine Beauty Ideal in Children's Fairy Tales," *Gender and Society* 17, no. 5 (October 2003): 723, http://www.jstor.org/stable/ 3594706.

13. Baker-Sperry and Grauerholz, "Feminine Beauty," 724.

14. Sally Satel, "I Am a Racially Profiling Doctor," *New York Times Magazine*, May 5, 2002, https://tinyurl.com/yav5dcxp.

15. "Genetics vs. Genomics Fact Sheet," National Human Genome Research Institute, last updated September 7, 2018, https://tinyurl.com/sbajp3u.

16. Satel, "I Am a Racially Profiling Doctor."

17. Renate G. Justin, "Medical Errors Due to Patient Profiling." *The Permanente Journal* 5, no. 4 (Fall 2001): 63–65, https://tinyurl.com/wv6yz7v.

18. Michael Eric Dyson, *Tears We Cannot Stop: A Sermon to White America* (New York: St. Martin's Press, 2017), 31.

19. Matt Taibbi, *The Divide: American Injustice in the Age of the Wealth Gap* (New York: Spiegel and Grau, 2014), 57.

20. "Human Trafficking by the Numbers," Human Rights First, January 7, 2017, https://tinyurl.com/u3cgpcs.

21. Erdman B. Palmore, *Ageism: Negative and Positive* (New York: Springer, 1999).

22. George Dohrmann, *Superfans: Into the Heart of Obsessive Sports Fandom* (New York: Ballantine, 2018), 48.

23. Grace Guarnieri, "Trump Tells Rich Mar-a-Lago Friends, 'You All Just Got a Lot Richer' after Tax Bill," *Newsweek*, December 24, 2017, https://tinyurl.com/yx3vjeqw.

24. Arlie Russell Hochschild, *Strangers in Their Own Land: Anger and Mourning on the American Right* (New York: The New Press, 2016), 158, 159.

25. Amy Chua, *Political Tribes: Group Instinct and the Fate of Nations* (New York: Penguin, 2018), 5, 187, 188.

26. A. S. King and C. J. Bott, "A. S. King and C. J. Bott Talk about Bullying," *The English Journal* 101, no. 6 (July 2012): 51, https://www.jstor.org/stable/23269407.

27. Dyson, *Tears We Cannot Stop*, 126.

28. Sarah Johnson, "NHS Staff Lay Bare a Bullying Culture," *The Guardian*, October 26, 2016, https://tinyurl.com/yx6xzh6e.

29. Paola Chavez, Veronica Stracqualursi, and Meghan Keneally, "A History of the Donald Trump–Megyn Kelly Feud," ABC News, October 26, 2016, https://tinyurl.com/thsl9sq.

30. David Von Drehle, "Trump's Continued Attacks on Clinton Tell Us Why the Democrats Lost," *The Washington Post*, August 4, 2017, https://tinyurl.com/v9r4mmb.

31. Stephen Marche, "The Left Has a Post-Truth Problem Too. It's Called Comedy," *Los Angeles Times*, January 6, 2017, https://tinyurl.com/sp90oxg.

32. *In Stitches*, produced by Bowdoin College graduates Hannah Raskin and Meg Robbins, is a documentary film shown at Bowdoin College in 2019.

33. Alan Blinder and Jonathan Martin, "Governor Admits He Was in Racist Yearbook Photo," *New York Times*, February 1, 2019, https://tinyurl.com/scufna8.

34. Roger Ebert, "Danson's Racist 'Humor' Appalls Crowd at Roast," Roger Ebert's Journal, October 10, 1993, https://tinyurl.com/vpk6uc2.

35. Eric Pfeffinger, *Human Error* (a play first produced by the Denver Center Theatre, Denver, CO). Unpublished, 59. A review of the play's world premiere can be found here, Juliet Wittman, "Review: *Human Error* Births Hope for Understanding (and Laughs)," May 30, 2018, https://tinyurl.com/w6mod9k.

36. Neta C. Crawford, "Costs of War: Human Cost of the Post-9/11 Wars: Lethality and the Need for Transparency," Brown University's Watson Institute for International and Public Affairs, November 2018, https://tinyurl.com/upskzx5.

37. David Brooks, "Donald Trump Poisons the World," *New York Times*, June 2, 2017, https://tinyurl.com/twxenry.

38. Edward O. Wilson, *The Social Conquest of Earth* (New York: Liveright, 2012), 195.

39. Jared Diamond, *Guns, Germs, and Steel: The Fates of Human Societies* (New York: W. W. Norton, 1999), 267–73.

40. aalokpatil18, "Genocides in the 20th Century and 21st Century," Time-toast, accessed March 10, 2020, https://tinyurl.com/whm6kq3.

41. David Brooks, interview by Hari Sreenivasan, *PBS NewsHour*, PBS, December 29, 2017.

42. Katie Glueck, "'Extreme Tribalism' Clawing at the GOP as 2018 Opens," *The Olympian*, December 31, 2017, https://tinyurl.com/sutr2ph.

43. Amy Chua, "The Destructive Dynamics of Political Tribalism," *New York Times*, February 20, 2018, https://tinyurl.com/ut6pync.

44. Scott Horsley, "After Two Years, Trump Tax Cuts Have Failed to Deliver on GOP's Promises," National Public Radio, December 20, 2019, https://tinyurl.com/umj3rk5.

45. Bradley Eli, "Freemasonary—Catholics' Deadly Foe," ChurchMilitant.com, February 23, 2017, https://tinyurl.com/wgadzu7.

46. "The Stockholm Accords on Ethnic Cleansing," *Journal of Church and State* 42, no. 4 (Autumn 2000): 703, http://www.jstor.org/stable/23920191.

47. Derek H. Davis, "Editorial: Confronting Ethnic Cleansing in the Twenty-First Century," *Journal of Church and State* 42, no. 4 (Autumn 2000): 697 and 698, www.jstor.org/stable/23920190.

Chapter 4: The Violent Consequences of Othering

1. Etienne G. Krug et al., eds., *World Report on Violence and Health* (Geneva: World Health Organization, 2002), 5, https://tinyurl.com/ub6kf57.

2. For an extensive analysis of the role of executions in the United States, see Mark Lewis Taylor, *The Executed God: The Way of the Cross in Lockdown America* (Minneapolis: Fortress Press, 2015).

3. Jenn Rolnick Borchetta and Alice Fontier, "Commentary: When Race Tips the Scales in Plea Bargaining," The Marshall Project, October 23, 2017, https://tinyurl.com/sqhrrbm.

4. Borchetta and Fontier, "Commentary."

5. Hélder Câmara, *Spiral of Violence* (London: Sheed and Ward, 1971).

6. Kurt Vonnegut, *Slaughterhouse 5* (New York: Random House, 2007).

7. Dr. Seuss, *The Butter Battle Book* (New York: Random House, 1984).

8. Jonathan Hewitt, "His Name Was Steven: A 13-Year-Old Victim of Bullycide," HuffPost, October 16, 2012, https://tinyurl.com/vousg2r.

9. Jenna Russell, "A World of Misery Left by Bullying," *Boston Globe*, November 28, 2010, https://tinyurl.com/tork9wh.

10. Taylor Swaak, "How We Talk About Bullying after School Shootings Can Be Dangerous: Experts," *Newsweek*, February 25, 2018, https://tinyurl.com/sjyza7b.

11. Michael Eric Dyson, *Tears We Cannot Stop: A Sermon to White America* (New York: St. Martin's, 2017), 126, 127.

12. "Ten Days After: Harassment and Intimidation in the Aftermath of the Election," Southern Poverty Law Center, November 29, 2016, https://tinyurl.com/whmnnw9.

13. Debra Pepler et al., "Developmental Trajectories of Bullying and Associated Factors," *Child Development* 79, no. 2 (March/April 2008): 333, http://www.jstor.org/stable/27563486.

14. Eleonora Gullone, "An Evaluative Review of Theories Related to Animal Cruelty," *Journal of Animal Ethics* 4, no. 1 (Spring 2014): 37–57, https://doi.org/10.5406/janimaleth ics.4.1.0037.

15. "Global Estimates of Modern Slavery," International Labour Organization and Walk Free Foundation, 2017, https://tinyurl.com/vfsuwh5.

16. Claudia Lauer and Meghan Hoyer, "Almost 1,700 Priests and Clergy Accused of Sex Abuse Are Unsupervised," NBC News, October 4, 2019, https://tinyurl.com/ve2dume.

17. Maren Machles et al., "1 in 3 American Indian and Alaska Native Women Will Be Raped, but Survivors Rarely Find Justice on Tribal Lands," *USA Today*, October 18, 2019, https://tinyurl.com/s5oqpxz.

18. Machles et al., "Survivors Rarely Find Justice."

19. Will Storr, "The Rape of Men: The Darkest Secret of War," *The Guardian*, July 16, 2011, https://tinyurl.com/t2h4nc7.

20. Joe Ward, Josh Williams, and Sam Manchester, "110 NFL Brains," *New York Times*, July 25, 2017, https://tinyurl.com/us8v4ru.

21. Matt Snyder, "Yankees–Tigers Get into Massive Brawl after Miguel Cabrera Throws Some Punches," CBS Sports, August 24, 2017, https://tinyurl.com/wknbogx.

22. William Wan and Amy Ellis Nutt, "Why Do Fans Riot after a Win? The Science behind Philadelphia's Super Bowl Chaos," *The Washington Post*, February 5, 2018, https://tinyurl.com/taqjyub.

23. George Orwell, *Nineteen Eighty-Four* (Cutchogue, NY: Buccaneer Books, 1949), 5.

24. Sophie Arie, "Historians Say Inquisition Wasn't That Bad," *The Guardian*, June 15, 2004, https://tinyurl.com/qu3eusr.

25. Christine Caldwell Ames, "Does Inquisition Belong to Religious History?" *The American Historical Review* 110, no. 1 (February 2005): 24, https://doi.org/10.1086/531119.

26. Brian J. Foley, "Guantanamo and Beyond: Dangers of Rigging the Rules," *The Journal of Criminal Law and Criminology* 97, no. 4 (Summer 2007): 1044, 1045, http://www.jstor.org/stable/40042859.

27. Wendy Sawyer and Peter Wagner, "Mass Incarceration: The Whole Pie 2019," Prison Policy Initiative, March 19, 2019, https://tinyurl.com/vozfhnu.

28. Christopher Hartney and Linh Vuong, "Created Equal: Racial and Ethnic Disparities in the US Criminal Justice System," National Council on Crime and Delinquency, March 2009, https://tinyurl.com/w46z7cf.

29. "Solitary Confinement: Inhumane, Ineffective, and Wasteful," Southern Poverty Law Center, April 4, 2019, https://tinyurl.com/vu7fnpr.

30. Rick Raemisch, "Why I Ended the Horror of Long-Term Solitary in Colorado's Prisons," ACLU, December 5, 2018, https://tinyurl.com/ubsg5co.

31. Marc Levin, "Make Prison Safer—for Staff and Inmates Alike," The Hill, December 31, 2019, https://tinyurl.com/t26glnt.

32. "Fact Sheet: Incarcerated Women and Girls," The Sentencing Project, June 6, 2019, https://tinyurl.com/vbf9q5t.

33. Joseph Murray and David P. Farrington, "The Effects of Parental Imprisonment on Children," *Crime and Justice* 37, no. 1 (2008): 135, https://doi.org/10.1086/520070.

34. E. Mosley, "Incarcerated—Children of Parents Imprisoned Impacted," Texas Department of Criminal Justice, July 6–12, 2008, https://tinyurl.com/s47gb40.

35. Bryan Stevenson, *Just Mercy: A Story of Justice and Redemption* (New York: Spiegel and Grau, 2014), 258.

36. Bryce Covert, "America Is Waking Up to the Injustice of Cash Bail," *The Nation*, November 6, 2017, https:// tinyurl.com/vbpmlxg.

37. Elizabeth King, "Inside the Fight to End Cash Bail," Pacific Standard, January 8, 2018, https://tinyurl.com/rx9sh67.

38. Bruce Western, *Punishment and Inequality in America* (New York: Russell Sage Foundation, 2006), 129.

39. Schnittker et al., "The Institutional Effects of Incarceration: Spillovers from Criminal Justice to Health Care," *The Millbank Quarterly* 93, no. 3 (September 2015): 516–60, http:// www.jstor.org/stable/24616405.

40. Daniel A. Cohen, "In Defense of the Gallows: Justifications of Capital Punishment in New England Execution Sermons, 1674–1825," *American Quarterly* 40, no. 2 (June 1988): 147–64, https://www.jstor.org/stable/2713065.

41. Cohen, "Gallows," 160.

42. *Facts about the Death Penalty* (Washington, DC: Death Penalty Information Center, 2020), 1.

43. Mona Lynch and Craig Haney, "Mapping the Racial Bias of the White Male Capital Juror: Jury Composition and the 'Empathic Divide,'" *Law and Society Review* 45, no. 1 (March 2011): 70, http://www.jstor.org/stable/23011959.

44. Jeffrey L. Johnson and Colleen F. Johnson, "Poverty and the Death Penalty," *Journal of Economic Issues* 35, no. 2 (June 2001): 517–23, https://doi.org/10.1080/00213624.2001.1150 6386.

45. "Illinois Gov. George H. Ryan Commutes Death Sentences," Northwestern Pritzker School of Law, January 11, 2003, https://tinyurl.com/rpbh9hk.

46. Samuel R. Gross et al., "Rate of False Conviction of Criminal Defendants Who Are Sentenced to Death," *PNAS* 111, no. 20: 7230–35, https://doi.org/10.1073/pnas.1306417111.

47. Gross et al., "False Convictions."

48. Gross et al., "False Convictions."

49. Gabriella Robles, "Condemned to Death—and Solitary Confinement," The Marshall Project, July 23, 2017, https://tinyurl.com/ybl9dkda.

50. "The Case against the Death Penalty," ACLU, accessed March 11, 2020, https://tinyurl.com/jky6rsm.

51. See Kelly Phillips Erb, "Death and Taxes: The Real Cost of the Death Penalty," *Forbes*, September 22, 2011, https://tinyurl.com/qtlx7zp; and Richard Dieter, "Millions Misspent: What Politicians Don't Say about the High Costs of the Death Penalty," Death Penalty Information Center, November 1, 1994, https://tinyurl.com/w7fyd6k.

52. Kimberly Amadeo, "What Criminal Sentence Costs More: Death or Life in Prison?" The Balance, updated November 29, 2019, https://tinyurl.com/y6sxjhdz.

53. Susan A. Bandes, "Victims, 'Closure,' and the Sociology of Emotion," *Law and Contemporary Problems* 72, no. 2 (Spring 2009): 26, http://www.jstor.org/stable/40647733.

54. For a fuller exploration of failure of closure, see Robert Jay Lifton and Greg Mitchel, *Who Owns Death?: Capital Punishment, the American Conscience, and the End of Executions* (New York: HarperCollins, 2002), 204–10. They describe some cases in which survivors who began by supporting a death sentence came to oppose or regret the execution of the condemned man for a variety of complex reasons. See also Jeff Goodell, "Letting Go of McVeigh," *New York Times Magazine*, May 13, 2001, https://tinyurl.com/s88dh9b. This article recounts the change of heart of Patrick Reeder, who lost his wife and mother-in-law in the Oklahoma City bombing.

55. The Criminal Justice Project of the NAACP Legal Defense and Educational Fund, Inc., "*Death Row USA: Fall 2018*," Death Penalty Information Center, October 1, 2018, https://tinyurl.com/vf558ak.

56. These figures are deduced from a comparison of the states' incarcerated population with inmates on death row as reported by the NAACP and the black population of each state as reported by index mundi, which is based upon the 2010 Census and current estimates. See "Death Row USA," 36, as well as "Louisiana Facts," indexmundi.com, accessed March 11, 2020, https://tinyurl.com/rwgnsyv.

57. Frank Baumgartner et al., "Studies: Death Penalty Overwhelmingly Used for White-Victim Cases," Death Penalty Information Center, January 28, 2015, https://tinyurl.com/wmj5r2j.

58. "DPIC 2019 Year-End Report: Death Penalty Erodes Further as New Hampshire Abolishes and California Imposes Moratorium," Death Penalty Information Center, December 17, 2019, https://tinyurl.com/r3lm8b2.

59. Alan Bullock and Stephen Trombley, eds., *The New Fontana Dictionary of Modern Thought* (London: HarperCollins, 1999), 862.

60. Edward W. Said, *Orientalism* (New York: Vintage, 1979).

61. Maalouf, *In the Name of Identity*, 64 and 65.

62. Peter O'Brien, *The Muslim Question in Europe: Political Controversies and Public Philosophies* (Philadelphia: Temple University Press, 2016).

63. O'Brien, *The Muslim Question*, 214.

64. PTSD: National Center for PTSD, "How Common Is PTSD?" US Department of Veterans Affairs, accessed March 11, 2020, https://tinyurl.com/ubxxdtb.

65. Matthew Wolfe, "From PTSD to Prison: Why Veterans Become Criminals," Daily Beast, last updated July 11, 2017, https://tinyurl.com/uydqjy4.

66. Toni Morrison, *Beloved* (New York: Alfred A. Knopf, 1998), 86.

67. Alan Bennett et al., *Beyond the Fringe* (New York: Random House, 1963), 45.

68. Christine Dell'Amore, "Why Animals 'Adopt' Others, Including Different Species," *National Geographic*, May 12, 2013, https://tinyurl.com/v3886lh.

69. Michelle Chen, "How US 'Free Trade' Policies Created the Central American Migration Crisis," *The Nation*, February 6, 2015, https://tinyurl.com/qnhotbs.

70. Ervin Staub, *The Roots of Evil: The Origins of Genocide and Other Group Violence* (Cambridge: Cambridge University Press, 1997), 156.

71. Jennifer Llewellyn, Jim Southey, and Steve Thompson, "The Costs of the Vietnam War," Alpha History, July 3, 2019, https://tinyurl.com/rqn9eah.

72. Josh Wood, "'We Knew This Would Happen': Kurds in Nashville Say Trump Betrayed Them," *The Guardian*, October 13, 2019, https://tinyurl.com/y2rmvsg7.

73. David Ignatius, "How ISIS Spread in the Middle East: And How to Stop It," *The Atlantic*, October 2015, https://tinyurl.com/y7s9kmnk.

74. Brian L. Villa, "The US Army, Unconditional Surrender, and the Potsdam Proclamation," *The Journal of American History* 63, no. 1 (June 1976): 69, https://doi.org/10.2307/1908990.

75. Villa, "Unconditional Surrender," 70.

76. For the full text, see "Convention on the Prevention and Punishment of the Crime of Genocide," UN.org, December 9, 1948, https://tinyurl.com/yyanyy3u.

77. "The Stockholm Accords," 703.

78. Gregory H. Stanton, "The Ten Stages of Genocide," Genocide Watch, 1996, https://tinyurl.com/vmmbpey.

Chapter 5: Voices of the Moral Imperative

1. Thomas Wolfe, *You Can't Go Home Again* (New York: Scribner, 1940).

2. Langston Hughes, *The Collected Poems of Langston Hughes*, ed. Arnold Rampersad and David Roessel (New York: Alfred A. Knopf, 1994), 191.

3. John 3:1–7.

4. Andrew R. Murphy, "Longing, Nostalgia, and Golden Age Politics: The American Jeremiad and the Power of the Past," *Perspectives on Politics* 7, no. 1 (March 2009): 133, http://www.jstor.org/stable/40407220.

5. Murphy, "Longing," 135.

6. Emily Kaplan, "US Women's Soccer Equal Pay Fight: What's the Latest, and What's Next?" ESPN Online, November 9, 2019, https://tinyurl.com/vv496lo.

7. James Melvin Washington, ed., *A Testament of Hope: The Essential Writings of Martin Luther King Jr.* (San Francisco: Harper and Row, 1986), 124.

8. Malcolm X's separatist views in the Nation of Islam were changed by his experience of the hajj (pilgrimage) to Mecca in 1964 when he saw the unity of Muslims from all over the world.

9. Washington, *Hope*, 118.

10. Washington, *Hope*, 290.

11. Martin Luther King Jr., *Strength to Love* (New York: Pocket, 1954), 46.

12. Washington, *Hope*, 209.

13. Anthony Sampson, *Mandela: The Authorized Biography* (New York: Alfred A. Knopf, 1999), 293.

14. Nelson Mandela, "Nelson Mandela—Nobel Lecture," Nobelprize.org, accessed July 11, 2018, https://tinyurl.com/qsrbsjj.

15. Desmond Mpilo Tutu, *No Future without Forgiveness* (New York: Doubleday, 1999), 8.

16. Tutu, *Forgiveness*, 279.

17. Marshall Sahlins, "What Kinship Is (Part One)," *The Journal of the Royal Anthropological Institute* 17, no. 1 (March 2011): 10, http://www.jstor.org/stable/23011568.

18. John Patterson, "*Mana*: Yin and Yang," *Philosophy East and West* 50, no. 2 (April 2000): 234, http://www.jstor.org/stable/1400143.

19. Marcus Borg, ed., *Jesus and Buddha: The Parallel Sayings* (Berkeley, CA: Ulysses Press, 1999), 25.

20. Borg, *Jesus and Buddha*, 29.

21. Dalai Lama, *The Universe in a Single Atom: The Convergence of Science and Spirituality* (New York: Morgan Road Books, 2005), 46.

22. Dalai Lama, *Universe*, 47.

23. Dalai Lama, *Ethics for a New Millennium* (New York: Riverhead Books, 1999), 37.

24. Michel Clasquin, "UBUNTU DHARMA: Buddhism and African Thought," *Journal for the Study of Religion* 10, no. 2 (September 1997): 67, http://www.jstor.org/stable/24764060.

25. Michael Barnes, "Expanding Catholicity—the Dialogue with Buddhism," *New Blackfriars* 88, no. 1016 (July 2007): 403, http://www.jstor.org/stable/43251150.

26. Hos 6:6.

27. Mic 6:8.

28. Mic 3:9.

29. Mic 3:12.

30. Isa 1:16–17.

31. Mic 4:3; also Isa 2:4.

32. Isa 40:4.

33. Luke 4:16–19.

34. For more on his table fellowship see: Marcus J. Borg, *Meeting Jesus Again for the First Time: The Historical Jesus and the Heart of Contemporary Faith* (San Francisco: Harper, 1995), 55, 56; and John Dominic Crossan, *Jesus: A Revolutionary Biography* (San Francisco: Harper, 1995), 66–70.

35. Matt 22 and Luke 14.

36. Paul Tillich, *The Ground of Being: Neglected Essays of Paul Tillich*, ed. Robert M. Price (London: Mindvendor, 2015).

37. Genesis 4.

38. Emmanuel Levinas, *Entre Nous: On Thinking of the Other* (New York: Columbia University Press, 1998), 110.

39. Elijah Anderson, *The Cosmopolitan Canopy: Race and Civility in Everyday Life* (New York: W. W. Norton, 2011), 280.

40. Cris Beam, *I Feel You: The Surprising Power of Extreme Empathy* (Boston: Houghton Mifflin Harcourt, 2018), 61.

41. Martin Buber, *I and Thou*, trans. Walter Kaufmann (New York: Charles Scribner's Sons, 1970), 69.

42. sschwister, "Leaning into the Kernel: Relational Trust in PLNs," Higher Edison Blog, December 31, 2008, https://tinyurl.com/whx3v65.

43. Buber, *I and Thou*, 62.

44. Buber, *I and Thou*, 113.

45. From the finale of the musical *Les Misérables*.

46. Mary T. Lathrap, "Judge Softly," AAA Native Arts, accessed March 21, 2020, https://tinyurl.com/va3x9tc.

47. Beam, *I Feel You*.

48. Beam, *I Feel You*, 100 and 101.

49. Beam, *I Feel You*, 220.

50. Beam, *I Feel You*, 220.

51. Carol Gilligan, *In a Different Voice: Psychological Theory and Women's Development* (Cambridge, MA: Harvard University Press, 1982).

52. Fiona MacDonald, "Relational Group Autonomy: Ethics of Care and the Multiculturalism Paradigm," *Hypatia* 25, no. 1 (Winter 2010): 196–212, https://www.jstor.org/stable/40602647.

53. Nel Noddings, *Caring: A Feminine Approach to Ethics and Moral Education* (Berkeley and Los Angeles: University of California Press, 1984), 201.

54. Beverly Wildung Harrison, *Making the Connections: Essays in Feminist Social Ethics* (Boston: Beacon Press, 1985), 18.

55. Wildung Harrison, *Connection*, 7.

56. Michele Gorman, "Trump Overturns a Mental Health Regulation on Gun Purchases," *Newsweek*, February 15, 2017, https://tinyurl.com/rvb6h4u.

57. Fritjof Capra, *The Tao of Physics: An Exploration of the Parallels between Modern Physics and Eastern Mysticism* (Boston: Shambhala, 1991), 131.

58. Fritjof Capra and Pier Luigi Luisi, *The Systems View of Life: A Unifying Vision* (Cambridge: Cambridge University Press, 2014).

59. David Bohm, *On Dialogue* (London and New York: Routledge Classics, 2004), 108, 109.

60. David Brooks, "Donald Trump Poisons the World," *New York Times*, June 2, 2017, https://tinyurl.com/twxenry.

61. David Brooks, "Anthony Kennedy and the Privatization of Meaning," *New York Times*, June 28, 2018, https:// tinyurl.com/rp4yek3.

62. David Brooks, "Personalism: The Philosophy We Need," *New York Times*, June 14, 2018, https://tinyurl.com/tos3w28.

63. George Yancy, "Dear White America," in *Modern Ethics in 77 Arguments: A Stone Reader*, ed. Peter Catapano and Simon Critchley (New York: Liveright, 2017).

64. "George Yancy," Professor Watchlist, accessed March 12, 2020, https://tinyurl.com/qm6c8c8.

65. George Yancy, *Backlash: What Happens When We Talk Honestly about Racism in America* (Lanham, MD: Rowman and Littlefield, 2018), 78.

66. Yancy, *Backlash*, 23.

67. George Yancy, "Should I Give Up on White People?," *New York Times*, April 16, 2018, https://tinyurl.com/tmwcwxv.

68. "Impact of Gompers and the AFL," Samuel Gompers, accessed March 12, 2020, https://tinyurl.com/tc9g7lw.

69. Howard Zinn, *A People's History of the United States* (New York: Harper-Perennial, 2003), 330.

70. Elizabeth Cady Stanton, "Declaration of Sentiments," in Susan Archer Mann and Ashly Suzanne Patterson, eds., *Reading Feminist Theory: From Modernity to Postmodernity* (New York: Oxford University Press, 2016), 58.

71. Ordination is decided at the congregational and presbytery level. These bodies have permission from the General Assembly but are not required to marry or ordain, relying on local discernment. See "Sexuality and Same-Gender Relationships," Presbyterian Church (USA), accessed March 12, 2020, https://tinyurl.com/t6nol7g.

72. "The Seven Principles," Unitarian Universalist Association, accessed March 12, 2020, https://tinyurl.com/vmnbs47.

73. "Affirming Human Dignity, Rights of Peoples and the Integrity of Creation—Rwanda, 2004," World Council of Churches, accessed March 12, 2020, https://tinyurl.com/spfqelt.

74. United Nations, *Universal Declaration of Human Rights* (Paris: The United Nations, 2015), 1, https://tinyurl.com/t6jpb8s.

Chapter 6: And the Walls Come Tumbling Down

1. Michael Massing, "Journalism in the Age of Trump: What's Missing and What Matters," *The Nation*, August 13–20, 2018, 13–18, https://tinyurl.com/wgrj9pu.

2. "How the Decline of Local Newspapers Exacerbates Polarization, *PBS NewsHour*, aired January 31, 2019, https:// tinyurl.com/utxqj8e.

3. Arlie Russell Hochschild, *Strangers in Their Own Land* and Cramer, *The Politics of Resentment*.

4. Giorgio Gallo and Arturo Marzano, "The Dynamics of Asymmetric Conflicts: The Israeli-Palestinian Case," *The Journal of Conflict Studies* 29 (April 2009): 33–49, https://tinyurl.com/y82e4l3c.

5. Alexander Sidorkin, "Dialogue with Evil," *Journal of Thought* 34, no. 3 (Fall 1999): 9–19, http://www.jstor.org/stable/4258 9582.

6. David Allen, *Fear of Strangers and Its Consequences* (Garnerville, NY: Bennington Books, 1993), 83.

7. Beam, *I Feel You*, 176.

8. Sampurna Chattarji, "Easy," *Voices in Wartime* documentary film by Rick King, 2005, YouTube video, 1:09, https:// youtu.be/1nc_WMm5fbc.

9. Elie Wiesel, *Night* (New York: Bantam Books, 1982), 62.

10. T. F. Pettigrew and L. R. Tropp, "A Meta-Analytic Test of Intergroup Contact Theory," *Journal of Personality and Social Psychology* 90, no. 5 (2006): 751–83, http://dx.doi.org/10.1037/0022-3514.90.5.751.

11. Jennifer L. Eberhardt, *Biased: Uncovering the Hidden Prejudice That Shapes What We See, Think, and Do* (New York: Penguin, 2019), 287–88.

12. Birte Gundelach, "In Diversity We Trust: The Positive Effect of Ethnic Diversity on Outgroup Trust," *Political Behavior* 36, no. 1 (March 2014): 136, https://www.jstor.org/stable/43653395.

13. Ann Legeby, Meta Berghauser Pont, and Lars Marcus, "Street Interaction and Social Inclusion," in *Suburban Urbanities: Suburbs and the Life of the High Street*, ed. Laura Vaughn (London: UCL Press, 2015), 239–62.

14. Anderson, *The Cosmopolitan Canopy*.

15. See https://www.seedsofpeace.org for more information.

16. Alexander Nazaryan, "School Segregation in America Is as Bad Today as It Was in the 1960s," *Newsweek*, March 22, 2018, https://tinyurl.com/t523bko.

17. Amy Bass, *One Goal: A Coach, a Team, and the Game That Brought a Divided Town Together* (New York: Hachette, 2018), 283.

18. Tutu, *Forgiveness*, 45.

19. Paulo Freire, *Education for Critical Consciousness* (New York: Continuum, 2002); and *Pedagogy of the Oppressed*, 30th anniversary ed. (New York: Continuum, 2003).

20. Saul D. Alinsky, *Reveille for Radicals* (New York: Vintage, 1989), 76.

21. Jennifer Gmerek, "The 5 Building Blocks of Successful Advocacy," Non-ProfitPro, June 30, 2015, https://tinyurl.com/tzkxvbh.

22. Margot Wallström, "What a Feminist Foreign Policy Looks Like," *New York Times*, July 29, 2018, https://tinyurl.com/r8u6k5u.

23. Cinthya Santos Briones, Laura Gottesdiener, and Malav Kanuga, "It Has Been 210 Days since Amanda Morales Last Saw the Sun," *The Nation*, April 9, 2018, https://tinyurl.com/wzvzo5u.

24. Alexander, *The New Jim Crow*.

25. John F. Kennedy, "Address on the First Anniversary of the Alliance for Progress," March 13, 1962, https://tinyurl.com/tvok6gx and https://tinyurl.com/tg5tmcd.

26. "A Little Rebellion . . . (Quotation)," The Jefferson Monticello, accessed March 12, 2020, https://tinyurl.com/r2zaek3.

27. C. H. Thompson, "Marxist Feminists," Sociologytwynham.com, July 1, 2013, https://tinyurl.com/vptv4gm; and "Margaret Benston," Feminist Theory, accessed March 12, 2020 https://tinyurl.com/upvnuzy.

28. Shane Croucher, "Bernie Sanders Calls for 'Political Revolution' in America, Lays Out His Democratic Socialist Vision: 'This Is Not Utopian,'" *Newsweek*, June 19, 2019, https://tinyurl.com/rclp8kd.

29. Mumia Abu-Jamal, *Death Blossoms: Reflections from a Prisoner of Conscience* (Farmington, PA: The Plough Publishing House, 1997), 100.

Epilogue

1. Paulo Freire, *Pedagogy of the Oppressed*, 30th anniversary ed. (New York: Continuum, 2003), 61.

2. Paulo Freire, *Cultural Action for Freedom*, rev. ed., Monograph Series No. 1 (Boston: Harvard Educational Review, 2000), 29.

3. Karen Price, "Paralympians Chuck Aoki, Mallory Weggemann On Why 'We All Deserve to Be Seen Rather Than Dismissed by a One-Liner in the Grocery Store,'" U.S. Paralympics, February 12, 2020, https://tinyurl.com/roh37d3.

4. See the Othering and Belonging Institute, UC Berkeley, https://belonging.berkeley.edu/.

5. Matthew Dessem, "Florida Shooting Survivor Emma Gonzalez to Trump: 'We Call BS','" Slate, February 17, 2018, https://tinyurl.com/sdq9ssq.

Bibliography

Abu-Jamal, Mumia. *Death Blossoms: Reflections from a Prisoner of Conscience.* Farmington, PA: The Plough Publishing House, 1997.

Allen, David. *Fear of Strangers and Its Consequences.* Garnerville, NY: Bennington Books, 1993.

Allgor, Catherine. "Coverture: The Word You Probably Don't Know but Should." National Women's History Museum, September 4, 2012. https://tinyurl.com/srbjc9k.

Alexander, Jeffrey C. "Citizen and Enemy as Symbolic Classification: On the Polarizing Discourse of Civil Society." In *Cultivating Differences*, edited by Michele Lamont and Marcel Fournier, Chapter 12. Chicago: University of Chicago Press, 1992.

Alexander, Michelle. *The New Jim Crow: Mass Incarceration in the Age of Colorblindness.* New York: The New Press, 2012.

American Civil Liberties Union. "The Case against the Death Penalty." ACLU. Accessed April 8, 2020. https://tinyurl.com/u7t8ht6.

Ames, Christine Caldwell. "Does Inquisition Belong to Religious History?" *The American Historical Review* 110, no. 1 (February 2005): 11–37. https://www.jstor.org/stable/10.1086/586875.

Anderson, Elijah. *The Cosmopolitan Canopy: Race and Civility in Everyday Life.* New York: W. W. Norton, 2011.

Baker-Sperry, Lori, and Liz Grauerholz. "The Pervasiveness and Persistence of the Feminine Beauty Ideal in Children's Fairy Tales." *Gender and Society* 17, no. 5 (2003): 711–26. https://www.jstor.org/stable/3594706.

Bandes, Susan A. "Victims, 'Closure,' and the Sociology of Emotion." *Law and Contemporary Problems* 72, no. 2 (2009): 1–26. https://www.jstor.org/stable/40647733.

Barnes, Michael. "Expanding Catholicity—the Dialogue with Buddhism." *New Blackfriars* 88, no. 1016 (2007): 399–409. https://www.jstor.org/stable/43251150.

Bass, Amy. *One Goal: A Coach, a Team, and the Game That Brought a Divided Town Together.* New York: Hachette Books, 2018.

Beam, Cris. *I Feel You: The Surprising Power of Extreme Empathy.* Boston: Houghton Mifflin Harcourt, 2018.

Beard, Mary. *Women and Power: A Manifesto.* New York: Liveright Publishing Corporation, 2017.

Begley, Sharon. "Three Is Not Enough." *Newsweek,* February 13, 1995. https://tinyurl.com/sr7pmzv.

Bell, Derrick. *Faces at the Bottom of the Well: The Permanence of Racism.* New York: Basic Books, 1992.

Bennett, Alan, Peter Cook, Dudley Moore, and Jonathan Miller. *Beyond the Fringe.* New York: Random House, 1963.

Bogle, Donald. *Toms, Coons, Mulattoes, Mammies and Bucks: Interpretive History of Blacks in American Films.* New York: Continuum, 1993.

Bohm, David. *On Dialogue.* London: Routledge Classics, 2004.

Borchetta, Jenn Rolnick, and Alice Fontier. "Commentary: When Race Tips the Scales in Plea Bargaining." The Marshall Project, October 23, 2017. https://tinyurl.com/sqhrrbm.

Borg, Marcus, ed. *Jesus and Buddha: The Parallel Sayings.* Berkeley, CA: Seastone, 1999.

Borg, Marcus. *Meeting Jesus Again for the First Time.* San Francisco: Harper, 1995.

Boulding, Elise. *Cultures of Peace: The Hidden Side of History.* Syracuse, NY: Syracuse University Press, 2000.

Bradford, J., Sari L. Reisner, Julie A. Honnold, and Jessica Xavier. "Experiences of Transgender-Related Discrimination and Implications for Health: Results from the Virginia Transgender Health Initiative Study." *American Journal of Public Health* 103, no. 10 (October 1, 2013): 1820–29. https://doi.org/10.2105/AJPH.2012.300796.

Briones, Cinthya Santos, Laura Gottesdiener, and Malav Kanuga. "It Has Been 210 Days Since Amanda Morales Last Saw the Sun." *The Nation*, April 9, 2018. https://tinyurl.com/wzvzo5u.

Brooks, David. "Anthony Kennedy and the Privatization of Meaning." *New York Times*, June 28, 2018. https://tinyurl.com/rp4yek3.

———. "Donald Trump Poisons the World." *New York Times*, June 2, 2017. https://tinyurl.com/twxenry.

———. "Personalism: The Philosophy We Need." *New York Times*, June 14, 2018. https://tinyurl.com/tos3w28.

Brustein, William I. *The Roots of Hate: Anti-Semitism in Europe Before the Holocaust*. Cambridge: Cambridge University Press, 2003.

Buber, Martin. *I and Thou*. Translated by Walter Kaufmann. New York: Charles Scribner's Sons, 1970.

Bullock, Alan, and Stephen Trombley, eds. *The New Fontana Dictionary of Modern Thought*. London: HarperCollins, 1999.

Bytwerk, Randall. "German Propaganda Archive." Calvin College. Accessed April 8, 2020. https://bhecinfo.org/links/german-propaganda-archive-calvin-college.

Calloway, Colin. "George Washington's 'Tortuous' Relationship with Native Americans." Zócalo, August 2, 2018. https://tinyurl.com/u6n4sgj.

Câmara, Hêlder. *Spiral of Violence*. London: Sheed and Ward, 1971.

Capra, Fritjof. *The Tao of Physics*. Boston: Shambhala, 1991.

Carothers, Bobbi J., and Harry T. Reis. "Men and Women Are from Earth: Examining the Latent Structure of Gender." *Journal of Personality & Social Psychology* 104, no. 2 (February 2013): 385–407. https://doi.org/10.1037/a0030437.

Chua, Amy. "The Destructive Dynamics of Political Tribalism." *New York Times*, February 20, 2018. https://tinyurl.com/ut6pync.

———. *Political Tribes: Group Instinct and the Fate of Nations*. New York: Penguin, 2018.

Clasquin, Michel. "Ubuntu Dharma: Buddhism and African Thought." *Journal for the Study of Religion* 10, no. 2 (1997): 57–74. https://www.jstor.org/stable/24764060.

Cohen, Daniel A. "In Defense of the Gallows: Justifications of Capital Punishment in New England Execution Sermons, 1674–1825." *American Quarterly* 40, no. 2 (1988): 147–64. https://www.jstor.org/stable/i327488.

"Concept of the Dark Continent Created through European-Erased Maps of Interior Africa." *The Journal of Blacks in Higher Education*, no. 11 (Spring 1996): 53. https://www.jstor.org/stable/2963313.

Cose, Ellis. *The Rage of a Privileged Class*. New York: HarperCollins, 1993.

Covert, Bryce. "America Is Waking Up to the Injustice of Cash Bail." *The Nation*, November 6, 2017. https://tinyurl.com/vbpmlxg.

Cramer, Katherine. *The Politics of Resentment: Rural Consciousness in Wisconsin and the Rise of Scott Walker*. Chicago: Chicago University Press, 2016.

Crossan, John Dominic. *Jesus: A Revolutionary Biography*. San Francisco: Harper, 1994.

Croucher, Shane. "Bernie Sanders Calls for 'Political Revolution' in America, Lays Out His Democratic Socialist Vision: 'This Is not Utopian.'" *Newsweek*, June 19, 2019. https://tinyurl.com/rclp8kd.

Dade, Corey. "Blacks, Gays, and the Church." NPR, May 27, 2012. https://tinyurl.com/u8doeen.

Davis, Derek H. "Editorial: Confronting Ethnic Cleansing in the Twenty-First Century." *Journal of Church and State* 42, no. 4 (Autumn 2000): 693–701. https://www.jstor.org/stable/23920190.

D'Costa, Krystal. "What Are the Jobs That Immigrants Do?" *Scientific American*, August 9, 2018. https://tinyurl.com/sx5txgg.

Dell'Amore, Christine. "Why Animals 'Adopt' Others, Including Different Species." *National Geographic*, May 12, 2013. https://tinyurl.com/v3886lh.

Dr. Seuss. *The Butter Battle Book*. New York: Random House, 1984.

Dohrmann, George. *Superfans: Into the Heart of Obsessive Sports Fandom*. New York: Ballantine Books, 2018.

duBois, Page. *Centaurs and Amazons: Women and the Pre-History of the Great Chain of Being*. Ann Arbor: University of Michigan Press, 1991.

Dyson, Michael Eric. *Tears We Cannot Stop: A Sermon to White America*. New York: St. Martin's, 2017.

Ebbert, Stephanie. "In Maine, Trump Takes Aim at Somali Refugees." *Boston Globe*, August 4, 2016. https://tinyurl.com/sb8x4fs.

Eberhardt, Jennifer L. *Biased: Uncovering the Hidden Prejudice That Shapes What We See, Think, and Do.* New York: Penguin, 2019.

Ebert, Roger. "Danson's Racist 'Humor' Appalls Crowd at Roast." Roger Ebert's Journal, October 10, 1993. https://tinyurl.com/vpk6uc2.

Ellison, Ralph. *Invisible Man.* New York: Vintage International, 1990.

Facts about the Death Penalty. Washington, DC: Death Penalty Information Center, Updated May 31, 2019. https://files.deathpenaltyinfo.org/legacy/documents/FactSheet.pdf.

Fanon, Frantz. *The Wretched of the Earth.* Translated by Richard Philcox. New York: Grove Press, 1963.

Foley, Brian J. "Guantanamo and Beyond: Dangers of Rigging the Rules." *The Journal of Criminal Law and Criminology* 97, no. 4 (Summer 2007): 1044–45. https://www.jstor.org/stable/40042859.

Fonseca, Isabel. *Bury Me Standing: The Gypsies and Their Journey.* New York: Vintage Departures, 1996.

Freeman, Chas. W., Jr. "This Too Shall Pass: Remarks to the Camden Conference on The New World Disorder and America's Future." Chasfreeman.net, February 18, 2018. https://tinyurl.com/r3kc3bz.

Freire, Paulo. "Reprint: Cultural Action for Freedom." *Harvard Educational Review* 68, no. 4 (December 1998): 476–522. https://doi.org/10.17763/haer.68.4.656ku47213445042.

———. *Education for Critical Consciousness.* New York: Continuum, 2002.

———. *Pedagogy of the Oppressed.* New York: Continuum, 2003.

Friedman, Uri. "Anthropology of an Idea: American Exceptionalism." *Foreign Policy*, no. 194 (July/August 2012): 22–23. https://www.jstor.org/stable/23242774.

Gallo, Giorgio, and Arturo Marzano. "The Dynamics of Asymmetric Conflicts: The Israeli-Palestinian Case." *Journal of Conflict Studies* 29 (April 2009): 63–65. https://tinyurl.com/y82e4l3c.

Garthwaite, Kayleigh. "Stigma, Shame, and 'People Like Us': An Ethnographic Study of Foodbank Use in the UK." *Journal of Poverty and Social Justice* 24, no. 3 (2016): 277–89. https://doi.org/10.1332/175982716X14721954314922.

Gay, Federico Ferro. "Cultural Colonialism." *The Southwestern Journal of Phi-*

losophy 5, no. 1 (Spring 1974): 153–59. https://www.jstor.org/stable/43154975.

Genoways, Ted. "The Only Good Muslim Is a Dead Muslim." *New Republic*, May 15, 2017. https://tinyurl.com/k4k8hl5.

Gilligan, Carol. *In a Different Voice: Psychological Theory and Women's Development*. Cambridge, MA: Harvard University Press, 1982.

Glueck, Katie. "Extreme Tribalism Clawing at the GOP as 2018 Opens." *The Olympian*, December 31, 2017. https://tinyurl.com/sutr2ph.

Goff, Phillip Atiba, Jennifer L. Eberhard, and Mathew Christian Jackson. "Not Yet Human: Implicit Knowledge, Historical Dehumanization, and Contemporary Consequences." *Journal of Personality and Social Psychology* 94, no. 2 (February 2008): 292–306. https://doi.org/10.1037/0022-3514.94.2.292.

Gottwald, Norman K. *The Tribes of Yahweh: A Sociology of the Religion of Liberated Israel, 1250–1050 B.C.E.* Maryknoll, NY: Orbis Books, 1979.

Gray, John. *Men Are from Mars, Women Are from Venus: The Classic Guide to Understanding the Opposite Sex*. New York: Harper Paperbacks, 2012.

Gregory, James P., Jr. "Better Dead than Red: The Treatment of Native Americans in the Southwest During the Cold War." *Armstrong Undergraduate Journal of History* 7, no. 2 (November 2017): 91–102. https://doi.org/10.20429/aujh.2017.070207.

Gullone, Eleonora. "An Evaluative Review of Theories Related to Animal Cruelty." *Journal of Animal Ethics* 4, no. 1 (Spring 2014): https://doi.org/10.5406/janimalethics.4.1.0037.

Gundelach, Birte. "In Diversity We Trust: The Positive Effect of Ethnic Diversity on Outgroup Trust." *Political Behavior* 36, no. 1 (March 2014): 125–42. https://www.jstor.org/stable/43653395.

Gurley, Lauren Kaori. "What We Don't Talk About When We Talk About Rural Poverty." *In These Times*, March 27, 2017. https://tinyurl.com/wv3mtho.

Hale, Chelsea, and Meghan Matt. "The Intersection of Race and Rape Viewed through the Prism of a Modern-Day Emmett Till." American Bar Association, July 16, 2019. https://tinyurl.com/ya6jjwaw.

Harrison, Beverly Wildung. *Making the Connections: Essays in Feminist Social Ethics*. Boston: Beacon Press, 1985.

Hartney, Christopher, and Linh Vuong. "Created Equal: Racial and Ethnic Disparities in the US Criminal Justice System." Oakland: National Council on Crime and Delinquency, March 2009. https://www.nccd-global.org/sites/default/files/publication_pdf/created-equal.pdf.

Hayes, Chris. *A Colony in a Nation*. New York: W. W. Norton, 2017.

Heinberg, Richard. *Memories and Visions of Paradise: Exploring the Universal Myth of a Lost Golden Age*. Los Angeles: Jeremy P. Tarcher, 1989.

Higgins, Tucker. "Supreme Court Rules That Trump's Travel Ban Is Constitutional." CNBC, June 26, 2018. https://tinyurl.com/s5hxaao.

Hill, Marc Lamont. *Nobody: Casualties of America's War on the Vulnerable, from Ferguson to Flint and Beyond*. New York: Atria Books, 2016.

Hochschild, Arlie Russell. *Strangers in Their Own Land: Anger and Mourning on the American Right*. New York: The New Press, 2016.

Eli, Bradley. "Freemasonary—Catholics' Deadly Foe." ChurchMilitant.com, February 23, 2017. https://tinyurl.com/wgadzu7.

Hughes, Langston. *The Collected Poems of Langston Hughes*. Edited by Arnold Rampersad and David Roessel. New York: Alfred A. Knopf, Inc., 1994.

Ignatius, David. "How ISIS Spread in the Middle East." *The Atlantic*, October 29, 2015. https://tinyurl.com/y7s9kmnk.

Jeffries, Michael P. "Suffering and Citizenship: Racism and Black Life." In *Healing Our Divided Society: Investing in America Fifty Years after the Kerner Report*, edited by Fred Harris and Alan Curtis, 313–21. Philadelphia: Temple University Press, 2018.

Johnson, Jeffery L., and Colleen F. Johnson. "Poverty and the Death Penalty." *Journal of Economic Issues* 35, no. 2 (2001): 517–23. www.jstor.org/stable/4227684.

Jones, Sarah. "J. D. Vance, the False Prophet of Blue America." *The New Republic*. November 17, 2016. https://tinyurl.com/hzdnya9.

Justin, Renate G. "Medical Errors Due to Patient Profiling." *The Permanente Journal* 5, no. 4 (Fall 2001): 63–65. https://tinyurl.com/wv6yz7v.

King, A. S., and C. J. Bott. "A. S. King and C. J. Bott Talk about Bullying." *The English Journal* 101, no. 6 (July 2012): 50–54. https://www.jstor.org/stable/23269407.

King, Elizabeth. "Inside the Fight to End Cash Bail." Pacific Standard, January 8, 2018. https://tinyurl.com/rx9sh67.

King, Martin Luther, Jr. *Strength to Love*. New York: Pocket Books, 1954.

Kippenger, Hans G. "Consider That It Is a Raid on the Path of God: The Spiritual Manual of the Attackers of 911." *Religion and Violence* 52, no. 1 (2005): 29–58. https://doi.org/10.1163/1568527053083485.

Kishi, Katayoun. "Assaults against Muslims in US Surpass 2001 Level." Pew Research Center, November 15, 2017. https://tinyurl.com/w789r29.

Krug, Etienne G., Linda L. Dahlberg, James A. Mercy, Anthony B. Zwi, and Rafael Lozano, eds. *World Report on Violence and Health*. Geneva: World Health Organization, 2002. https://tinyurl.com/ub6kf57.

Lama, Dalai. *Ethics for a New Millennium*. New York: Riverhead Books, 1999.

———. *The Universe in a Single Atom: The Convergence of Science and Spirituality*. New York: Morgan Road Books, 2005.

Lathrap, Mary T. "Judge Softly." AAANativeArts.com. Accessed April 9, 2020. https://tinyurl.com/sc8b8ed.

Legeby, Ann, Meta Berghauser Pont, and Lars Marcus. "Street Interaction and Social Inclusion." In *Suburban Urbanites: Suburbs and the Life of the High Street*, edited by Laura Vaughn, 239–62. London: UCL Press, 2015.

Leonard, Thomas C. *Illiberal Reformers: Race, Eugenics and American Economics in the Progressive Era*. Princeton, NJ: Princeton University Press, 2016.

Levinas, Emmanuel. *Entre Nous: Thinking of the Other*. New York: Columbia University Press, 1998.

Liptak, Adam. "In Narrow Decision, Supreme Court Sides with Baker Who Turned Away Gay Couple." *New York Times*, June 4, 2018. https://tinyurl.com/v2ykydq.

Lynch, Mona, and Craig Haney. "Mapping the Racial Bias of the White Male Capital Juror: Jury Composition and the 'Empathic Divide.'" *Law and Society Review* 45, no. 1 (March 2011): 69–101. http://www.jstor.org/stable/23011959.

Maalouf, Amin. *In the Name of Identity: Violence and the Need to Belong*. Translated by Barbara Bray. New York: Arcade, 2001.

MacDonald, Fiona. "Relational Group Autonomy: Ethics of Care and the Multiculturalism Paradigm." *Hypatia* 25, no. 1 (2010): 196–212. https://www.jstor.org/stable/40602647.

Mandela, Nelson. "Nelson Mandela—Nobel Lecture." Nobelprize.org. Accessed July 11, 2018. https://tinyurl.com/qsrbsjj.

Marche, Stephen. "The Left Has a Post-Truth Problem Too. It's Called Comedy." *Los Angeles Times*, January 6, 2017. https://tinyurl.com/sp9ooxg.

Massing, Michael. "Journalism in the Age of Trump: What's Missing and What Matters." *The Nation*, August 13–20, 2018. https://tinyurl.com/wgrj9pu.

McInnes, Gavin. "This Is War." *Taki's Magazine*, June 1, 2017. https://tinyurl.com/sz2kmjh.

McKenna, Patrick. "When the Irish Became White: Immigrants in Mid-19th Century U.S." *Irish Times*, February 12, 2013. https://tinyurl.com/vzflbge.

McCoy, Terrence. "In Former Coal Country, the Working Poor Show Open Contempt for Neighbors Who Seek Handouts." *Chicago Tribune*, July 21, 2017. https://tinyurl.com/w3n5a8d.

Memmi, Albert. *The Colonizer and the Colonized*. London: Earthscan, 2003.

Moore, Pat, with Charles Paul Conn. *Disguised*. Waco, TX: Word Books, 1985.

Moore, R. I. *The Formation of a Persecuting Society*. Malden, MA: Blackwell, 2007.

Morrison, Toni. *Beloved*. New York: Alfred A. Knopf, 1998.

Mosley, E. "Incarcerated—Children of Parents Imprisoned Impacted." Texas Department of Criminal Justice, July 6–12, 2008. https://tinyurl.com/s47gb40.

Muñoz, Ana Patricia, Marlene Kim, Mariko Chang, Regine Jackson, Darrick Hamilton, and William A. Darity. "The Color of Wealth in Boston." Boston: Federal Reserve Bank of Boston, March 25, 2015. https://tinyurl.com/stjua28.

Murphy, Andrew R. "Longing, Nostalgia, and Golden Age Politics: The American Jeremiad and the Power of the Past." *Perspectives on Politics* 7, no. 1 (2009): 125–41. https://www.jstor.org/stable/40407220.

Murray, Joseph, and David P. Farrington. "The Effects of Parental Imprisonment on Children." *Crime and Justice* 37, no. 1 (2008): 133–206. https://doi.org/10.1086/520070.

Mandela, Nelson. "Nelson Mandela—Nobel Lecture." Nobelprize.org. Accessed July 11, 2018. https://tinyurl.com/qsrbsjj.

Neruda, Pablo. *Five Decades: A Selection (Poems: 1925–1970).* Translated and edited by Ben Bellit. New York: Grove Press, 1974.

Noddings, Nell. *Caring: A Feminine Approach to Ethics and Moral Education.* Berkeley: University of California Press, 1984.

Noonan, Peggy. "Trump and the Rise of the Unprotected." *Wall Street Journal,* February 25, 2016. https://tinyurl.com/s2en79b.

Nott, Josiah Clark, and George Robins Gliddon. *Types of Mankind.* Philadelphia: Lippincott, Grambo & Co., 1854. https://tinyurl.com/yx4m8ldp.

O'Brien, Peter, and Helge Blakkisrud. *The Muslim Question in Europe: Political Controversies and Public Philosophies.* Philadelphia: Temple University Press, 2016.

Orwell, George. *Nineteen Eighty-Four.* Cutchogue, NY: Buccaneer Books, 1949.

Pagels, Elaine. *The Origin of Satan: How Christians Demonized Jews, Pagans, and Heretics.* New York: Vintage Books, 1996.

Palmore, Erdman B. *Ageism: Negative and Positive.* New York: Springer, 1999.

Patterson, John. "Mana: Yin and Yang." *Philosophy East and West* 50, no. 2 (2000): 229–41. https://www.jstor.org/stable/1400143.

Pepler, Debra, Depeng Jiang, Wendy Craig, and Jennifer Connolly. "Developmental Trajectories of Bullying and Associated Factors." *Child Development* 79, no. 2 (2008): 325–38. https://www.jstor.org/stable/27563486.

Petrecca, Laura. "Harmony Gives Way to a Great Divide." *USA Today,* September 11, 2017. https://tinyurl.com/txarngl.

Pettigrew, Thomas F., and Linda R. Tropp. "A Meta-Analytic Test of Intergroup Contact Theory." *Journal of Personality and Social Psychology* 90, no. 5 (2006): 751–83. http://dx.doi.org/10.1037/0022-3514.90.5.751.

Pratt, Richard H. "'Kill the Indian, and Save the Man': Capt. Richard H. Pratt on the Education of Native Americans." History Matters. Accessed March 7, 2020. https://tinyurl.com/w66af4l.

Ruiz, Rebecca. "A New Book Argues against the SAT." *The Choice* (blog), New York Times Choice Blog. November 9, 2011. https://tinyurl.com/rzcvgnv.

Russell, Jenna. "A World of Misery Left by Bullying." *Boston Globe,* November 28, 2010. https://tinyurl.com/tork9wh.

Sahlins, Marshall. "What Kinship Is (Part One)." *The Journal of the Royal*

Anthropological Institute 17, no. 1 (2011): 2–19. https://www.jstor.org/stable/23011568.

Said, Edward W. *Orientalism*. New York: Vintage Books, 1979.

Sampson, Anthony. *Mandela: The Authorized Biography*. New York: Alfred A. Knopf, 1999.

Satel, Sally. "I Am a Racially Profiling Doctor." *New York Times Magazine*. May 5, 2002. https://tinyurl.com/r622hzm.

"Saudi police 'stopped' fire rescue." *BBC News*, March 15, 2002. https://tinyurl.com/vkjopgn.

Schnittker, Jason, Christopher Uggen, Sarah K. S. Shannon, and Suzy Maves McElrath. "The Institutional Effects of Incarceration: Spillovers from Criminal Justice to Health Care." *The Millbank Quarterly* 93, no. 3 (September 2015): 516–60. http://www.jstor.org/stable/24616405.

Schwalbe, Michael. "The Elements of Inequality." *Contemporary Sociology* 29, no. 6 (2000): 775–81. https://www.jstor.org/stable/2654084.

Schwirtz, Michael, Michael Winerip, and Robert Gebeloff. "The Scourge of Racial Bias in New York State's Prisons." *New York Times*, December 3, 2016. https://tinyurl.com/uaqqo9y.

Sidorkin, Alexander. "Dialogue with Evil." *Journal of Thought* 34, no. 3 (1999): 9–19. https://www.jstor.org/stable/42589582.

Smith, Cheryl C. "Out of Her Place: Anne Hutchinson and the Dislocation of Power in New World Politics." *The Journal of American Culture* 29, no. 4 (2006): 437–53. https://tinyurl.com/wzldxwa.

Snyder, T. Richard. *The Protestant Ethic and the Spirit of Punishment*. Grand Rapids, MI: Eerdmans, 2001.

Stanton, Elizabeth Cady. "Declaration of Sentiments." In *Reading Feminist Theory: From Modernity to Postmodernity*, edited by Susan Archer Mann and Ashly Suzanne Patterson, 58. New York: Oxford University Press, 2015.

Staub, Ervin. *The Roots of Evil: The Origins of Genocide and Other Group Violence*. Cambridge: Cambridge University Press, 1997.

Stevenson, Bryan. *Just Mercy: A Story of Justice and Redemption*. New York: Spiegel and Grau, 2014.

Swaak, Taylor. "How We Talk about Bullying after School Shootings Can

Be Dangerous: Experts." *Newsweek*, February 25, 2018. https://tinyurl.com/wf2p4d3.

"The Stockholm Accords on Ethnic Cleansing." *Journal of Church and State* 42, no. 4 (2000): 703–7. https://www.jstor.org/stable/23920191.

Taibbi, Matt. *The Divide: American Injustice in the Age of the Wealth Gap*. New York: Spiegel and Grau, 2014.

Taylor, Mark Lewis. *The Executed God: The Way of the Cross in Lockdown America*. Minneapolis: Fortress Press, 2015.

Thistle, Scott. "Trump's Statements about Somali Immigrants in Maine Draw Rebuke." *Portland Press Herald*, August 5, 2016. https://tinyurl.com/wkvb5ah.

Tutu, Desmond Mpilo. *No Future without Forgiveness*. New York: Doubleday, 1999.

United Nations. *Universal Declaration of Human Rights*. Paris: The United Nations, 2015. https://tinyurl.com/t6jpb8s.

United States Department of Justice. "Justice Department Announces Findings of Two Civil Rights Investigations in Ferguson, Missouri." Justice News. March 4, 2015. https://tinyurl.com/t4ubutp.

Villa, Brian L. "The US Army, Unconditional Surrender, and the Potsdam Proclamation." *The Journal of American History* 63, no. 1 (1976): 66–92. https://doi.org/10.2307/1908990.

Wakefield, Lily. "There Are 16 States in the US That Still Have Sodomy Laws against 'Perverted Sexual Practice.' It's 2020." Pink News, January 24, 2020. https://tinyurl.com/yda7fwyz.

Wallström, Margot. "What a Feminist Foreign Policy Looks Like." *New York Times*, July 29, 2018. https://tinyurl.com/r8u6k5u.

Wan, William, and Amy Ellis Nutt. "Why Do Fans Riot after a Win? The Science Behind Philadelphia's Super Bowl Chaos." *Washington Post*, February 5, 2017. https://tinyurl.com/taqjyub.

Wan, William, and Sarah Kaplan. "Why Are People Still Racist? What Science Says about America's Race Problem." *Washington Post*, August 14, 2017. https://tinyurl.com/u65tsvt.

Ward, Joe, Josh Williams, and Sam Manchester. "110 NFL Brains," *New York Times*, July 25, 2017. https://tinyurl.com/us8v4ru.

Washington, James Melvin, ed. *A Testament of Hope: The Essential Writings of Martin Luther King Jr.* San Francisco: Harper and Row, 1986.

Welna, David, and Bill Chappell. "Supreme Court Revives Trump's Ban on Transgender Military Personnel, For Now." NPR, January 22, 2019. https://tinyurl.com/yx4ekg52.

West, Cornel. *Prophecy Deliverance: An Afro-American Revolutionary Christianity.* Philadelphia: Westminster, 1982.

———. *Race Matters.* New York: Vintage Books. 1994.

Western, Bruce. *Punishment and Inequality in America.* New York: Russell Sage Foundation, 2006.

Wiesel, Elie. *Night.* New York: Bantam Books, 1982.

Williams, Maggie Griffith, and Jenny Korn. "Othering and Fear: Cultural Values and Hiro's Race in Thomas and Friends' *Hero of the Rails.*" *Journal of Communication Inquiry* 41, no. 1 (January 2017): 22–41. http://doi.org/10.1177/0196859916656836.

Williams, Robert A., Jr. *The American Indian in Western Legal Thought: The Discourses of Conquest.* New York: Oxford University Press, 1992.

Wilson, Edward O. *The Social Conquest of Earth.* New York: Liveright, 2012.

Wolfe, Matthew. "From PTSD to Prison: Why Veterans Become Criminals." *Daily Beast,* last modified July 11, 2017. https://tinyurl.com/uydqjy4.

Wood, Josh. "'We knew this would happen': Kurds in Nashville say Trump betrayed them." *The Guardian,* October 13, 2019. https://tinyurl.com/y2rmvsg7.

World Council of Churches. "Affirming Human Dignity, Rights of Peoples and the Integrity of Creation—Rwanda, 2004." Accessed March 12, 2020. https://tinyurl.com/spfqelt.

Yancy, George. *Backlash: What Happens When We Talk Honestly about Racism in America.* Lanham, MD: Rowman and Littlefield, 2018.

———. "Dear White America." In *Modern Ethics in 77 Arguments,* edited by Peter Catapano and Simon Critchley, 300–305. New York: Liveright, 2017.

———. "Should I Give Up on White People?" *New York Times,* April 16, 2018. https://tinyurl.com/tmwcwxv.

Zinn, Howard. *A People's History of the United States.* New York: Harper, 2003.

Index